RECLAMATION

RECLAMATION

SALLY HEMINGS,
THOMAS JEFFERSON,
and a DESCENDANT'S
SEARCH *for* HER
FAMILY'S LASTING
LEGACY

GAYLE JESSUP WHITE

AMISTAD
— *35* —

An Imprint of HarperCollins*Publishers*

"Ties to Thomas Jefferson Unravel Family Mystery" (January 26, 2014) and "DNA Does Not Lie and Neither Did Aunt Peachy" (April 4, 2014) appeared in *The Root*. Permission granted by publisher.

All photographs courtesy of the author unless otherwise noted.

HarperCollins books may be purchased for educational, business, or sales promotional use. For information, please email the Special Markets Department at SPsales@harpercollins.com.

FIRST EDITION

Designed by Nancy Singer

Library of Congress Cataloging-in-Publication Data has been applied for.

ISBN 978-0-06-302865-4

21 22 23 24 25   LSC   10 9 8 7 6 5 4 3 2 1

To Mom, Dad, Janice,
and Aunt Peachie

The Christian parents have long ago gone
to their Heavenly home,
leaving the religiously trained descendants happy
in Earthly homes of their own.

A. C. Nelson
1992

CONTENTS

PART THREE

THE HEMINGS LINE

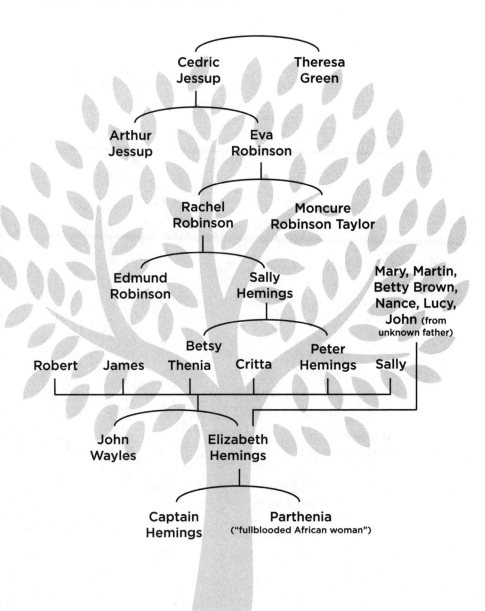

Courtesy of the Thomas Jefferson Foundation

THE HUBBARD LINE

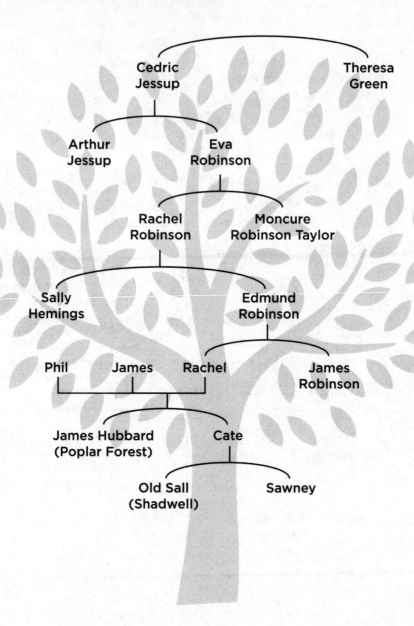

THE JESSUP LINE

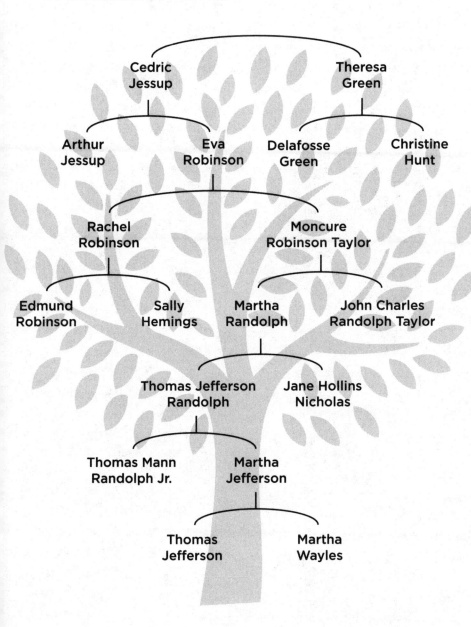

Cedric Jessup — Theresa Green

Arthur Jessup — Eva Robinson

Delafosse Green — Christine Hunt

Rachel Robinson — Moncure Robinson Taylor

Edmund Robinson — Sally Hemings

Martha Randolph — John Charles Randolph Taylor

Thomas Jefferson Randolph — Jane Hollins Nicholas

Thomas Mann Randolph Jr. — Martha Jefferson

Thomas Jefferson — Martha Wayles

Courtesy of the Thomas Jefferson Foundation

PROLOGUE

There are at least two known burial grounds at Monticello, the estate that was Thomas Jefferson's home. One is near the main house and surrounded by an imposing wrought iron fence. It is populated with tombstones marked "Jefferson," "Randolph," "Taylor," and the surnames of other kin. Jefferson's grave is marked by an obelisk adorned with an inscription of how he wished to be remembered:

HERE WAS BURIED

THOMAS JEFFERSON

AUTHOR OF THE DECLARATION OF AMERICAN INDEPENDENCE

OF THE STATUTE OF VIRGINIA FOR RELIGIOUS FREEDOM

& FATHER OF THE UNIVERSITY OF VIRGINIA

The graveyard is still in use. It is the only property on the former plantation not owned by the Thomas Jefferson Foundation, the nonprofit that owns and manages Monticello, but by a group called the Monticello Association, whose members are direct descendants of Thomas Jefferson and his wife, Martha Wayles Skelton. From time to time, members of the association gather for a burial or a wreath-laying ceremony to commemorate their legendary ancestor. Only Jefferson, his white family, and their descendants and spouses are buried there. Only they are welcome. That was made painfully clear a few years after a white descendant invited dozens of his Black cousins to an association reunion. They were guests because they too can trace their origins to the third president.

They were descendants of a liaison between Jefferson and a woman he enslaved, Sally Hemings. In 1999, as the cousins, white and Black, mingled cordially at Monticello and at lunches and cocktail parties, the media followed. The news reports that followed made reconciliation seem possible, even imminent. But three years later when the same white cousin who had orchestrated the reunion sought membership for his Black kin, they were shut out. According to witnesses in 2002 when a vote was taken at the association's annual meeting, a near-riot erupted as white members, fueled by two centuries of denial about who fathered Hemings's children, furiously objected. The episode made the national press. "There was my family being racist on the front page of the *New York Times*," lamented a white descendant twenty years later.

A short walk down the mountain along a gravel path and near the entrance of Monticello's Visitor Center is another gravesite. Bordered by a parking lot, a few trees, and wooden rail fencing is a burial ground for those who were enslaved on Jefferson's plantation. Here are no obelisks or tombstones, only large rocks marking where people—my people—are buried. No one knows the names of those interred there, only that they were enslaved at Monticello.

The burial ground, like much of African American history, was almost lost forever.

What saved it was an oral tradition, which for centuries was how America's Blacks remembered their past. The story goes that when old-timers who had spent their lives living in the shadows of Jefferson's mountain heard that the graveyard was to become a parking lot, they spoke up. They knew bodies were buried there because their mothers and fathers, who had heard it from their mothers and fathers, said it was so.

We can only speculate about who might be buried there. Perhaps Ursula Granger, whose reputation as a great cook induced Jefferson to purchase her at his wife's request in 1773. It was Ursula's breast milk that saved the life of the couple's sickly six-month-old daughter, named Martha after her mother, when her ailing mother was unable to nurse her. Were it not for Ursula I would not be here, because the child she saved would become my great-grandmother four times over. Or skilled worker Cate Hubbard, my four-times-great-grandmother. Two of her sons were among Monticello's few "runaways." Or Elizabeth Hemings, who came to Monticello with her ten children when Jefferson's father-in-law, John Wayles, died in 1773. Elizabeth's remains might rest near her cabin or the burial ground, but we will never know. Though they were human beings, they were treated like property, passed down to Wayles's daughter Martha as part of her inheritance, just like money, land, and livestock. However, the Hemings clan was linked to Martha by an unacknowledged kinship. Wayles was the father of six of Elizabeth Hemings's children, including the infant girl Sally. They were Martha's half-siblings, and in a different world they would have been considered Jefferson's in-laws.

Hundreds of Black people spent their entire lives held captive on a five-thousand-acre plot of mountainous land laboring, as Jefferson put it, for his "happiness" while trying to carve out some happiness of their own.

Aside from an inconspicuous panel describing whose remains may be inside the fencing of the enslaved graveyard, there is little to indicate that this space is hallowed ground. There have been reports that some visitors, assuming the site is a dog park, have allowed their pets to urinate on the trees next to the graves, oblivious to the history they were desecrating. Yet I am not oblivious to it. I can't be.

The Jeffersons, Randolphs, and Taylors at the top of the mountain are as much my kin as the Hemingses and Hubbards whose remains might be at the bottom. But my heart rests with the souls in the graveyard of the enslaved. It is at their final resting place that I find solace and inspiration. It is their spirit that spurs me forward, even when I am feeling weary and battle-scarred after another day spent fighting for equal recognition of Black history that for many is merely an afterthought.

The gravel path from the enslaved at the bottom of the mountain to the enslavers at the top is less than a mile long. But the chasm this distance symbolizes is as deep and dark as the ship hulls that carried human cargo across the Atlantic during the Middle Passage. It began more than four hundred years ago when the first captured Africans were brought to the British colony of Jamestown, Virginia, in 1619. A complex entanglement between Blacks and whites also emerged, one that has left virtually all African Americans with European DNA.

There are few places where those woven relationships are as well chronicled as those that existed at Monticello. At least four generations of Hemingses had close relations with Jefferson family members, from his father-in-law to his great-great-grandson, the man who became my great-grandfather.

I did not grow up knowing this history. In fact, like many Americans I was not taught that the principal author of the Declaration of Independence—the man who declared that all men are created equal—owned human beings. However, from the moment I learned the family lore that we are Jefferson descendants, I was intrigued by the mystery of our family's origins and set out to try to uncover the truth. Sometimes intentional, sometimes not, I have made choices throughout my life that brought me to where I am today—to Monticello, the epicenter of the American paradox—and of my family's story.

While some might have been repelled by a place where their

ancestors were enslaved, I was drawn to it. From my very first visit to the plantation, I knew I wanted to work there. I was in my early forties—no youngster—when I finally took the time for the two-hour drive from my home in Washington, DC, to Charlottesville, Virginia. It was the spring in 2004, and until then I had always been too busy with school, then college and career, followed by marriage and family. But once I carved from my schedule two days to spend in Charlottesville, I was captivated by Monticello's hypnotic beauty. The sun-kissed flower gardens and the winding paths beneath a cloudless blue canopy made it seem like I was strolling through a Monet or Renoir painting.

During that first visit, as I explored the home that Jefferson designed, I waited in vain for the guide to talk about the enslaved people who built the house. Their stories, I believed, reflected my own family's and those of millions of people descended from the enslaved. That day in 2004 the questions sparked when I was an inquisitive child began to grow into something more compelling, something deeper, what activists might describe as a cause, and what the spiritual might define as a calling. That calling was the voice of my ancestors demanding to be heard and imploring me to be their spokesperson. That calling was my ancestors guiding me to confirm the family lore and reclaim our place in American history. That calling was my destiny.

What started for me as a sheltered thirteen-year-old's curiosity about my family's unproven ties to Thomas Jefferson became a passionate cause, and finally an unlikely late-life career.

My fifty-year-long journey began in a cloistered community in Washington, DC, called Eastland Gardens. The neighborhood was distinct, for it was one of few in the nation designed, built, and owned by Blacks.

PART ONE

PART ONE

1

EASTLAND GARDENS

July 26, 1957

I grew up "Negro rich." It meant that my family was well-off for Black people. I attended parochial school for which my parents paid hefty tuition, went to an exclusive summer camp where I learned to swim, and spent vacations in California. My family spent leisure time at Highland Beach, Maryland, the Black resort founded by Frederick Douglass's grandson and where my mom's family once owned a house and a hotel. When I was sixteen, my dad gave me a brand-new car, a red Mustang. He paid cash for it.

Although our family was comfortable, thanks to Dad's employment in what folks in Washington, DC, call "a good government job," we were not part of the city's Black elite. That status was reserved for the families of doctors, dentists, and perhaps a few successful lawyers and businessmen. We were always right on the periphery, invited to the parties but not members of the club. But we were a close family, proud to be Jessups, and for us that was special enough.

Born in Washington, DC, on July 26, 1957, the same year the city became majority Black, I was the youngest of Cedric and Theresa Jessup's five children, my mother's so-called menopause baby. She was almost forty years old when she had me. Dad was forty-three.

Their oldest, Janice, was nineteen, Cedric Jr. was seventeen, Pat was fourteen, and Bruce was nine. The family, especially my sisters, doted on me. They dressed me in pastel-tinted crinoline-lined dresses and tied ribbons in my fuzzy sandy brown hair. Mom made sure I had color-coordinated patent leather shoes, lace-trimmed socks, and white gloves. Properly attired, I accompanied my big sisters downtown for tea at Woodward & Lothrop, one of Washington's high-end department stores and a place where just a few years earlier, people who looked like us would not have been welcome.

The nation's capital and its suburbs were segregated until the Supreme Court ruled in 1954 that racial segregation violated the Constitution. While I never knew of "whites-only" facilities, my parents and older siblings were all too aware of the distinction. Even as an adult, many decades later my brother Bruce still pined over being locked out of Glen Echo, an amusement park in Maryland only a few miles from our house in Northeast Washington that ran seductive commercials on TV featuring a massive roller coaster and an Olympic-size pool accompanied by a catchy jingle:

> *Glen Echo Amusement Park,*
> *a place to have fun,*
> *boy it's a date!*

The youngsters splashing in the pool or laughing on the carousel were all white. Black people like my brother were not invited. For Bruce, the snub has never stopped stinging.

As the youngest of the Jessup children and a privileged member of what some people derisively called the "bougie" Black middle class, I was oblivious to my brother's discomfort or to anyone else's. My parents knew all about segregation and how humiliating it could be, but they did their best to protect their children. They were like many other Black parents of their generation. So protected was I that my earliest memories were feelings of confidence and security. Almost six decades later, I still remember an afternoon standing on our sunlit back porch and feeling like the luckiest little girl in the best family, the best city, and the best country in the whole world.

And why not? My family treated me like a princess. Sometimes Mom placed on my head the rhinestone-studded tiara she wore to her fancy parties. At my first ballet performance, I was the only little girl whose pink tutu included a crown.

Like my parents and older siblings, I was always perfectly turned out. When Washington's once-segregated doors finally opened, my family walked into department stores, boutiques, restaurants—and even Glen Echo—as if they owned the place. I, "Little Gayle," was right there with them, never knowing that we had been anything but welcomed.

Because I was born into a family of adults and older teens, I always felt protected and spoiled. My sisters brought me gifts, little things like plastic dolls, Bazooka bubble gum, and tiny pet turtles. "Where's my 'kaprize'?" I chirped, unable to pronounce "surprise," when Janice and Pat returned home from work or school. I treated their gifts like treasures, hiding them from Bruce, who took perverse pleasure in destroying what I loved. He was jealous that I had stolen his "youngest-in-the-family" status. Still, I adored him as only a younger sister who looks up to an older brother can.

Race was never discussed in our house, at least not within my hearing. I occasionally heard someone say "Negro," "Colored," or "white," but those words held no significance to me, as they came without context. No one, for example, explained to six-year-old me that the 1963 March on Washington was about "jobs and freedom" for Black people. In fact, no one explained to me that I was Black. At 1120 Forty-Second Street Northeast, in the heart of Eastland

Gardens, we were simply American. Like most American households of the era, my father was king.

Daddy was very much like "Jim," the patriarch of my favorite childhood TV show *Father Knows Best*. Played by Robert Young, the show's main character seemed so much like my own dad, right down to the suits, hats, ties, and sweaters. It never registered that the characters didn't look like me or my family. In fact, what I saw was *my* family.

That's how things were in the 1960s. Dads like mine went to work as doctors, lawyers, engineers, postal clerks, school principals, educators, and government employees. The moms stayed home, prepared meals, kept house, and reared the children. If they were really lucky, they had a housekeeper. Much of the time, we were really lucky.

Of course, there was a big difference between our family and the ones I saw on TV, and it wasn't our race. It was our religion. We were Catholic. That's what mattered most in our household, Catholicism, character, and tradition. "John Kennedy is Catholic," I'd hear my parents boast about the first Catholic president. One of the few times I saw my mother cry was when Lee Harvey Oswald assassinated President Kennedy right before Thanksgiving in 1963. I cried too because she was crying. I adored my mother. Aside from the little girl who lived next door, she was my best friend.

Our family was so devout that we not only attended Mass every Sunday but prayed together every evening after dinner. One of my most vivid memories is of Mom bringing me into the living room where Dad and my siblings were already assembled. The room was stuffed—floor-length gold drapes; a baby grand piano, which we all learned to play with various skill; a rose-colored sectional sofa; a cocktail table; end tables; and accent chairs. I was only three years old, and by this time, my siblings were adult size. They looked like giants—the kindly type—to me.

I tip-toed into the room, squeezing between my two sisters, Janice and Pat, and tried to make out what was going on. My father stood looking solemn in front of the brick fireplace. On the mantel facing him was a foot-tall ceramic statue of Jesus looking down at us with sad, forgiving eyes.

There was a mirror on one wall and family photos on the piano, but Jesus's figure dominated the space. Amidst my mother's meticulously decorated room, it seemed out of place, even to me. The statue of Jesus, dark hair touching his shoulders, displayed bloody holes in his hands. One hand was held up as if in absolution, while the other pulled back a red, ceramic robe to expose a bleeding heart. As a little girl, I should have been frightened by the goriness of the thing, but I wasn't. I had seen the statue so many times that Jesus and his bleeding heart seemed normal to me.

Everyone was quiet as Dad said, "Please bow your heads. Let us pray." Following his instructions and everyone's example, I did as I was told. However, those were the only words I understood. What followed was unintelligible to me. Dad somberly spoke first, followed by the family's response that sounded like a chorus of bumble bees. It wasn't long before I lost interest and was on the floor playing with the feet of my all-in-one pajamas and nodding off into sleep. The evening ended with Dad carrying me upstairs to bed and Mom kissing me goodnight.

It was not until first or second grade when I was a student at St. Francis de Sales Elementary School that I got a clearer picture of what all that praying was about. Religion was part of the curriculum, as was reading, math, art, and music. It was a respectable education that laid the foundation for future success. Even now, I occasionally play in my mind a tune I learned in elementary school, "There's a Hole in the Bucket": "There's a hole in the bucket, dear Liza . . . Well, fix it dear Henry . . . With what shall I fix it, dear Liza? . . . With an

ax, dear Henry . . ." And so on. It was an early lesson in problem solv-
ing and logical thinking. We also learned "Kumbaya"; however, Sister
James Lucille didn't explain to our class of mostly Black students the
song's African American origins. We probably wouldn't have understood if she had, as my classmates were as oblivious to race as I.

The nuns were from the Order of St. Joseph and were armored
in full habit: black, ankle-length skirts, stiff white bibs, snug head
coverings, and veils that students assumed hid the sisters' bald heads,
as not a single strand of hair was visible. To me, they looked like the
nun in one of the books Mom read to me, *Madeline*, about a little
French girl at a Catholic boarding school in Paris.

I liked my teachers, even when they tried to explain incomprehensible things, like transubstantiation (wafers and wine turning into
the body and blood of Christ) or transfiguration (Jesus ascending
into heaven). I trusted the sisters and believed what they told us, even
what sounded magical and superstitious.

St. Francis was in Woodridge, a neighborhood about a fifteen-
minute drive from our house in Eastland Gardens. Mom chose the
school because she had taken a job teaching kindergarten at a nearby
daycare where she would briefly work with a woman whom she had
long admired from one of Washington's elite Black families.

Every morning, Mom would drop me off near the schoolyard
parking lot where kids lined up and said the Pledge of Allegiance
before marching, like little soldiers, to class. Until I was old enough,
about ten, to walk to her job, Mom picked me up from school or
from a friend's house. Driving home was our chance to review the
day's activities. I usually wanted to talk about playground cliques.
Mom, always instructing, had her own agenda: "What was the most
interesting thing you learned today? Let's recite your times tables.
Remember, read silently to yourself, not out loud with your lips."

My mother was a very good teacher. I learned to spell "Mississippi" sitting at our yellow Formica kitchen table long before Sister James taught us how to read "see Spot run" in *Fun with Dick and Jane.* I wasn't a showoff in class, but I liked being smart.

By first grade, the long-practiced ritual of the family praying together had ended because the house was emptying. Jan had graduated from college, was teaching elementary school, and had her own apartment. Pat, ever the free spirit, had bolted to Los Angeles and gotten married. And last, Bruce was about to be shipped off to St. Emma Military Academy, a boarding school for Black boys in Powhatan, Virginia, almost a two-hour drive from DC. The campus had a history. It was built on a plantation called Belmead where 150 people had been enslaved.

My other brother, Cedric Jr., Dickie we called him, did not live with us, and had not since he was a child. He was sent away long before I was born. Pictures of him show a cute little boy with large eyes, a turned-up nose, and a head full of big curls. His hair clippings that Mom saved in a small manila envelope were gingerbread brown. The family thought he resembled a 1930s child star named Dickie Moore, thus the nickname he carried the rest of his life.

By all accounts, he was an adorable child. However, early on there were troubling signs. Dickie was not reaching the milestones that parents look forward to—not rolling over or cooing or responding to familiar voices. My parents, young and hopeful, sought help.

It was the early 1940s, and the doctor who assessed his case was not nearly as polite as medical professionals would have been had Dickie been born and diagnosed decades later. "Cognitively challenged" is what my parents would have been told in the twenty-first century, but in the mid-twentieth, the diagnosis was "mentally retarded," a social stigma in those days.

My grief-stricken parents took their baby home and tried to raise him with Jan, who was not quite two years old. But it was too much.

As Dickie grew older and became mobile, he would run away from Mom or scream or throw and break things. Eventually, he became a threat to himself, to Jan, and to the family's new baby, Patricia.

My parents decided that their only choice, the only one that would help him and save their other children, was to make Dickie a ward of the state. When he was eight years old he was sent to live at a place called the District Training School for the Mentally Retarded, a sprawling developmental center in Laurel, Maryland, about thirty miles from their home. In the 1960s, the name was changed to Forest Haven. Dickie was cared for at a facility at the complex called Children's Center.

Mom and Dad never talked about what it felt like to have their child institutionalized and raised by strangers. But years later, my mother's older sister described to me what it was like the day Dickie was "sent away." It was a weekday, so Janice was at school. Mom's family——her mother, a brother, and her three sisters—were at the house. Everyone was crying. Dad, usually unemotional, broke down as well. My aunt said Mom was inconsolable. It was as if someone had died.

In some ways, the family never recovered. According to Jan, in the early years our house was an entertainment hub. Dad's friends would come over to shoot pool, Mom would host parties, kids would play ball in the backyard. All that changed after Dickie's departure. The house, Jan said, went from glee to gloom.

However, by the 1960s when I was growing up, aside from the solemnity of those evening prayers, the household seemed like a cheery place—as I said, like the family-friendly sitcom *Father Knows Best*.

That's when big, gas-guzzling cars and leisurely Sunday drives were wholesome. For our middle-class family, it was another activity that made us typically American, like visiting the Washington Monument or eating TV dinners or watching *Bonanza.* "We're going for a ride after church," Mom announced most Sundays, as if it were a fresh idea.

Often the three of us, my parents and I, would jump in the family's silver Pontiac Catalina with the black vinyl top and make the thirty-minute drive to Children's Center in Laurel that housed Dickie. It was no coincidence that my mother's two unmarried sisters also lived in Laurel. One of them had taken a job as an administrator at Children's Center. She was always on hand to make sure my brother was well cared for.

My aunts lived together with their two Chihuahuas, Geronimo and Pocahontas, in an unpretentious one-level house with screen doors that slammed closed with a loud thud. They were always unlocked, and neighbors would drop by unannounced. The informality reminded me of being at the beach. My parents would leave me with my aunts while they visited my brother. "We're going to Children's Center to see Dickie," Mom would say. I was uninvited. As always, my parents were trying to shield me from what they thought would be a stressful experience, and I didn't question their judgment.

I can remember only one visit with Dickie during a Sunday outing when I was around ten years old. We were in the car for a short ride, just long enough to create a memory. I sat beside Dad, who was driving, while Mom was in the backseat with my brother. Mom had a loaf of Wonder Bread, which she used as a tool to connect with her son. As she broke off pieces of the spongy, white bread, he kept asking for more. "Bread," he said over and over. Dickie knew what he wanted and was able to communicate it, although in the most rudimentary way. Mom looked joyful as she watched him chew, her face never betraying disappointment or hurt. Later that day, I heard her tell Dad that Dickie could take apart a toy clock and put it back together. She was hopeful, always hopeful.

Dad, ever stoic, had little to say about my brother that day or on any other. However, years later when I was in my thirties with a son of my own, he opened up. I was visiting one afternoon when I found him in bed fully dressed and staring at the ceiling. Dickie was now living in a group home, and Dad had just come from a consultation with his caregivers. "It's very depressing, you know. He's my namesake," he told me. My father was more sensitive than he liked to reveal.

That was one of the few times we talked about the family's second born. He was treated like a secret. In spite of the stigma then associated with intellectual disabilities, I don't think my parents were ashamed of him, but rather they preferred to bury the pain. Whatever the case, I would learn that Dickie was not the only family secret.

Indeed, covering up painful or embarrassing matters was almost as much a family tradition as saying the rosary every evening had been. It began with the circumstances of my parent's marriage.

2

DEANWOOD

February 1938

Cedric Jessup and Theresa Green were teenage sweethearts. They grew up in the same neighborhood of Deanwood. Remote and isolated on the far outskirts in Northeast Washington, it was a place unto its own where Blacks of all economic classes blended into a close-knit community. Homes designed by notable Black architects—including J. Alonzo Plater, my mother's brother-in-law and the architect of our house on Forty-Second Street—dotted a landscape of farmland, family grocers, and local shops. There was even a movie theater. It was also home to famous people like R&B singer Marvin Gaye and civil rights activist and educator Nannie Helen Burroughs, as well as a cadre of Black middle-class and working-class homeowners.

Yet in spite of Deanwood's small-town feel, Theresa and Cedric did not meet until she was sixteen and he was nineteen. They were in a church play, *Romeo and Juliet,* where they both had bit parts. She was pretty, vivacious, and smart. Everyone called her "Billye," which seemed to suit her. Enrolled at Dunbar, Washington's legendary Black college-prep high school, she planned to be a teacher. Being a Dunbar student meant something special. One of the nation's first high schools for academically inclined Black youth, Dunbar was well known around the country for educating the city's best and brightest students and sending them off to elite colleges and universities, including the Ivy League. Among its many celebrated alumni were Negro History Week founder Carter G. Woodson, US Senator Edward Brooke, and blood bank innovator Dr. Charles Drew. Noted suffragist Mary Church Terrell taught there. It was the same school Billye's mother, Christine Hunt, attended when it was called M Street High School, and the same one from which her oldest daughter would one day graduate.

When Theresa met Cedric, he was already a Dunbar graduate and a sophomore at Howard University, where he played football and took pre-med classes. He was going to be a doctor. His ambitions matched well with her dreams for the future and with her socially connected family. Billye's father, Delafosse Green, had been a celebrated chef for two US presidents. No one knew who taught him his culinary skills, but it could have been his father, Shelton Green. Shelton was enslaved in Virginia, and his military records indicate that he was a Civil War cook and, after that, a coachman at the French Embassy in Washington, DC. That was where he heard the name "Delafosse," whose French roots translate as "from a ditch." Whatever its meaning, Shelton apparently thought it exalted when he named his youngest son.

One can only guess these things, because Billye did not seem to know the details of her father's background, only that he had been a chef on the president's train and a bit of a bon vivant who liked to gamble. The family swore that one of his gambling successes inspired her first word. "Money," she squealed when her father came home with so much that he tossed it into the air like a handful of rose petals. Her love for affluence—or the appearance of it—never ended.

During Reconstruction, the years that followed the Civil War, freed Black men and women flooded the nation's capital. Many found decent jobs working for the federal government. Even after Reconstruction ended and during the Jim Crow years, when systemic racism was institutionalized, some Black people could find a modicum of success in DC working for the federal government. Most jobs, however, were limited to skilled labor.

Delafosse, who was born in Washington in 1882, was among the lucky few to find gainful employment. He started out as a cook for the famous Pullman Company and ultimately made his way onto the government's payroll. He was on President William Howard Taft's domestic staff but found a slice of fame working for President Woodrow Wilson, who took office in 1913. Wilson was a fervent racist who screened *The Birth of a Nation* at the White House. But my grandfather must have had a gift for getting along with anyone. He was probably also a culinary genius.

He was often mentioned in not only the Negro press but in white-owned papers as well, including the *Washington Star*. At first, he was merely a supporting cast member, as in a 1915 Wilmington, Delaware, newspaper article about the dietary preferences of Wilson and his wife-to-be. He reportedly prepared chicken consommé, fried chicken à la Maryland (Southern style), sweet breads on toast, and charlotte russe. Getting the name wrong, the writer quoted Delafosse: "Adolphus Green, negro cook on the presidential specials for years extended himself to serve his new mistress. 'Ah suttenly will serve some luncheon today,' he confided."

Since the reporter got the name wrong, he probably misrepresented his manner of speaking as well, imposing an obnoxious stereotype on the high school–educated, Washington, DC–born cook. I hate to imagine him bowing and scraping to his "new mistress." But if he did, he would have been like millions of other Black men and women forced to condescend, appease, and appeal to the prejudices of white people in order to curry their favor. For Blacks, their very survival depended upon subservient behavior. It wasn't slavery, but it was not equality either.

A few years later in 1919, Delafosse reached the height of his celebrity when he was featured in a story in the *Washington Times*. The headline read "The King of Cooks." The story was a fairly detailed account, describing how he looked ("a stoutish neat, bustling colored man"), what he earned ("a modest sum of $110 a month"), and how he got his name ("his father was a coachman to the ambassador" of France). It also described his approach to cooking:

> "Food should be cooked and served plainly," said Green. "There should be few mixtures and few sauces. The manner of cooking followed by the early huntsman was the right method. Such food retains its flavor and is good for the stomach. Dr. [Cary] Grayson [Wilson's personal aide and confidante] and I realized that we were associates as guardians of the President's health. I always feel that the health of those for whom I cook is in my hands. It is a responsibility, and I try to live up to it."

That does not sound like the same man who "suttenly will serve some luncheon."

Not only did Delafosse cook for two presidents but also for royalty and world leaders, wealthy industrialists and businessmen, congressmen and cabinet members. One of those officials, Treasury Secretary William Gibbs McAdoo, who also happened to be Wilson's son-in-law, apparently considered raising funds for one of Delafosse's business proposals, a one-thousand-seat "moving picture theatre for colored people." A letter survives to Delafosse from McAdoo outlining how he might lend his support. His one caveat was "that all this work must be done quietly." Evidence abounds that Delafosse was not a man who kept his connections and business dealings private. Perhaps that's why the theater never happened. But he did open a restaurant and catering business when he left government employment.

A wealthy Californian, McAdoo ran for president in 1924 with the support of the Ku Klux Klan. I can scarcely imagine the mental hoops Delafosse, like so many Black people maneuvering through a white supremacist society, must have jumped through as he bargained with a bigot like McAdoo. It must have been like shaking hands with Jefferson Davis. But that was the price many Black folk had to pay to provide for their families. Today we call it code switching. Perhaps the stress of constantly guarding his dignity contributed to Delafosse's death at the age of only forty-one, leaving his wife and six surviving children destitute.

As for the Greens, their diminished circumstances didn't stop them from striving. Four attended college while another was a gifted pianist and composer who, according to family lore, played with Duke Ellington's band. The family's matriarch, Christine, always wore pearls.

Sticking with her plan, Billye graduated from Dunbar High School and enrolled in Miner Teachers College, a segregated normal school that later became part of the University of the District of Columbia. But above all, she wanted to be a doctor's wife. Like the rest of her family, she was ambitious and determined to push her way into Washington's Black social elite.

Cedric's family was not as accomplished, but just as hardworking. His father Arthur Jessup operated the massive machines that printed money at the US Bureau of Engraving, a good job for a Black man in the early twentieth century. Good enough to afford him a mortgage, a luxurious Packard automobile, and the latest contraption, a radio. Good enough to send his youngest boy to college to study medicine.

Billye and Cedric were an attractive couple. He was handsome, tall, broad-shouldered, and athletic. His skin was the color of buttermilk—a complexion that many Black people had been conditioned to believe superior to brown skin. A saying that persists to this day illustrates the colorism that began on plantations and became part of Black social hierarchy: "If you're white, you're all right, if you're yellow, you're mellow, if you're brown, stick around, if you're black, get back."

There was no indication that Cedric felt his skin color made him better than anyone else. Billye probably recognized that his light skin and his plans to become a doctor would give her the entrée to the Black society to which she aspired. One can only speculate, because colorism was not a topic she ever discussed.

Billye had an oval-shaped face with high cheekbones, big brown eyes, and a smooth, walnut-brown complexion. Years later when Cedric reminisced about their romance, he described how beguiling she was. Laughing out loud—a rarity for him—he recounted one of their first dates. It was at a neighborhood ice cream parlor. Seated across from Cedric at a small table, Billye took the straw from her shake and put it into his so they could sip from the same frosted glass. Watching her "bat her big brown eyes," he was completely undone. She was a "pistol," even then, he frequently said years later.

While batting her big browns, Billye was probably imagining her life as a doctor's wife—the fine house, the social clubs, the fancy clothes. She no doubt saw herself at the top of the social heap, the queen of Deanwood, or better than that—the prestigious LeDroit Park where her family had lived before Delafosse's death. The envy of all her friends. But it was not to be.

An unplanned pregnancy, which the young couple kept to themselves and their immediate family, derailed her grand ambitions and their expectations. In those days, anything but a quick marriage was out of the question. Billye and Cedric took their vows on February 6, 1938, at a small civil service. She wore a white business suit. He wore a dark one. There are no pictures of the event. It was not clear if any were taken or if at some point, in a fit of rage, she destroyed them.

To support his family, Cedric quit college, gave up on medical school, and found what was then a good job especially for a Black man, delivering mail for the US Postal Service. The Post Office was a haven for smart Black men during that time period, including ones with college educations, for there were few opportunities available anywhere else.

Even though the job was stable and relatively well-paying, Billye was deeply disappointed. She had dreamed of being married to a doctor, not a mailman. But in the beginning of their marriage, she suppressed her resentment, especially when after just one year the young couple saved enough for a house of their own. They bought a lot in Eastland Gardens not far from their Deanwood roots and built a three-bedroom brick home with white shutters, a screened front porch, and a big backyard. The house was one of the first architectural achievements by Billye's brother-in-law, Alonzo.

Janice was one year old when the young family moved into their new home, and Billye was once again expecting a baby. Always very fashionable, even during pregnancy, the soon-to-be mother of two made her own clothes. She made her new home just as pretty, designing and sewing her own furniture slipcovers and curtains. She also canned fruits and vegetables, baked cakes and pies, and made the best smothered fried chicken her husband ever had.

Cedric dutifully provided for his growing family, never missing a day's work, sometimes picking up part-time jobs for extra cash. He also coached a neighborhood softball team. "Everyone looked up to Uncle Cedric," a nephew he coached said years later. "He was a neighborhood hero. I was so proud to be his nephew."

Billye had a son, Cedric Jr., on November 19, 1940, and another girl, Patricia, on July 26, 1943. As the family continued to grow, so did the pressure on Cedric. Not only did he need more money to support his family, but he needed to satisfy Billye's aspirations. She was not going to settle for being a postman's wife. That was never going to be good enough for her. So she pushed him to move up, helping him prepare for tests that would be a first step toward better government opportunities.

He had his own ambitions as well. He became one of the first Blacks to provide customer service inside a Washington, DC, post office and to be a supervisor. In the late 1950s and 1960s, as the federal government became less segregated, he kept moving up, shedding the uniform and becoming a suit-wearing, white-collar professional. After twenty years with the Post Office, he became a manager and human resources specialist with the power to hire and fire. "When I speak," he would tell his staff, "it is as if the Postmaster General were speaking."

By the 1960s after their youngest was born, Cedric had the position and some of the status his wife had craved her entire life. They hosted parties, bought expensive cars—often convertibles to please her—and always American ones, in keeping with the period when few people bought imported cars. They dined out, played golf, and traveled, mostly to LA to see their daughter Pat.

But that success came too late for Billye. No matter how high Cedric climbed, she remained unsatisfied and disenchanted. She never stopped blaming him for depriving her of the life she had dreamed of as the wife of a doctor. Eventually, her disenchantment turned into bitterness. There was nothing more important in the status-conscious Black community of Washington, DC, than being a physician—or a physician's wife. No matter what Cedric's accomplishments, financial stability, or professional respect, it was never going to be good enough for Billye. He would never be a doctor, which left her in a state of perpetual disappointment.

3

LAS VEGAS:
A TURNING POINT

1967–1970

As a child, I was blissfully unaware of my mother's grievances or of any fractures in my parents' marriage. If they were unhappy, they kept it to themselves. Dad was there with his broad shoulders to lean on and Mom, a consummate baker, with cake-battered spoons for me to lick. My biggest concerns were school, friendships, and having fun.

One of the most impressive days of my young life happened when I was ten. It was the summer of 1967 and my best friend and I were on a ferry headed to Marshall Hall, an amusement park on the Maryland side of the Potomac River. Sheltered from the outside world, we did not know what was happening beyond our cloistered community. We had no idea that earlier that summer, there were riots in cities across the country from Newark to Detroit to Milwaukee that left eighty-three people dead and hundreds injured. We did not know about the smoldering cities or about the racial inequality that ignited the unrest. Nor did we know that Marshall Hall was until recently for whites only. All we knew or cared about that warm, summer day in 1967 was the good time we were about to have at the region's premier amusement park.

BUT WE NEVER GOT TO MARSHALL HALL THAT DAY. NATURE CALLED, and my friend just could not wait until after we disembarked for a bathroom. By the time we made it to the gangway, the boat was pulling away. With tears rolling down my cheeks, I watched the famed Mad Mouse roller coaster fade into the distance.

Never mind, Mom said, we'll take the ferry to Mount Vernon instead. George Washington's home was almost directly across the river from Marshall Hall, and while visiting the first president's estate was not my idea of fun, I accepted my fate.

But once we crossed Mount Vernon's threshold, I was enthralled. I studied as much as a ten-year-old could the dining room where the first president took his meals and the bedroom where he slept and was fascinated by the eighteenth-century china and silverware, the colonial clothing, and the decorative art. The day inaugurated my fascination with presidential history.

That was three years before I learned I was related to Thomas Jefferson, three years before I learned about my parents' troubled marriage, three years before I learned that my skin color made me different from other Americans. Three years before it all came crashing down at once.

• • •

When I was nine, I started spending summers in Los Angeles with my sister Pat and her husband. She and I were born on the same date, July 26, and even though we were fourteen years apart, we were pals. A gifted artist who wanted to be a nurse but ended up as an art education professor at California State University–Los Angeles, Pat was light-hearted and fun. She was also amazingly good-looking— tall, about five feet nine, with closely cropped curls that reminded me of Mom's black lambswool jacket. She had a curvy figure that made hugs feel like squeezing a soft pillow. Her home sparkled with creativity: mobiles, masks, paintings, and all sorts of random shiny objects. Every wall was covered with her art or someone else's. We spent hours making jewelry, ceramic dishes (I still have two), and paper flowers. There were trips to the beach where I swam in the Pacific and was buried in sand, as well as the LA County Museum, Grauman's Chinese Theatre, Watts Towers, and the La Brea Tar Pits. Of course we went to Disneyland, where for the second time in my life I was treated to my all-time favorite ride, "It's a Small World." The first time was at the 1964 New York World's Fair. The third time would come thirty years later with my four-year-old son at Disney World in Orlando. Indeed, summers with Pat were always a treat, but the year I turned thirteen was going to be exceptional because we were going to meet Mom and Dad in Las Vegas.

I was excited about the five-hour drive that would take us through the Mojave Desert. Along the way, Pat and her husband talked endlessly about Las Vegas's restaurants, casinos, and shows. The Ike & Tina Revue was their favorite. That sounded great for the grown-ups, but all I cared about was swimming in the hotel pool.

In the early 1970s, there was not much for a kid to do in Las Vegas. This was years before theme parks and zoos made the desert town family-friendly. Back then, Las Vegas was principally an adult playground. But that did not matter to me. I had all I needed just a few feet away from our hotel room. Almost, anyway. Not many children my age were around, and while I was comfortable playing alone, I wanted a companion. My wish was answered the second day of our vacation when I spotted a girl on the other side of the pool. She seemed friendly, if a little lonely like me, so I bounced through the warm water to introduce myself. It seemed to me we had a lot in common. We appeared about the same age and were dressed in the same swim gear: colorful one-piece suits, white rubber swim caps, and blue goggles. Within minutes, we were friends, giggling until our sides ached and playing in the pool until our finger and toe tips looked like bleached prunes.

But even with that much fun, I probably would have forgotten the afternoon had it not been for what happened next. We were doing underwater somersaults when the lifeguard made everyone get out for the pool's chlorine treatment. My new friend and I be-grudgingly complied, agreeing to meet as soon as the guard gave the signal that the pool was ready. The girl climbed out on one side of the pool and I on the other, wrapping ourselves in towels and tak-ing our places beside our moms in their plastic lounge chairs. What seemed like an eternity was likely only fifteen minutes, so as soon as the guard gave the "all clear," I wasted no time jumping back into the crisp, clear water. I waded toward the center, eagerly waiting for my new friend to join me, and feeling a bit bewildered when she did not. I looked at her still sitting with the towel wrapped around her thin body. Come on, I exuberantly gestured, the water's warm. It feels great! She did not move.

Undeterred, I kept trying, twirling in circles to show how much she was missing. To my dismay, I watched her stiffen even more. Come on, I mouthed, with ever-diminishing enthusiasm, having noticed her swim cap was off, revealing her dark, straight hair.

She finally moved, slowly and subtly shaking her head—back and forth, side to side. Her gaze moved shyly toward her mother, sitting rigidly in her plastic chair, a magazine or book in her hand. But the woman's eyes were on me, cold as a shark's. Stunned, I saw something I had never seen before: hate. I shivered in the warm water, as I slowly grasped what was happening. The woman's cruel eyes and the little girl's mortified expression said it all: *You're differ-ent. Stay away.*

What I had overlooked when the girl became my playmate was her race. She was white, but I barely noticed because it didn't matter to me. Race had only recently become a part of my consciousness, but not in a political or social way. I knew I was Black, but I didn't feel that made me different, just different looking. Until that day in the Las Vegas pool.

I don't think race mattered to the girl either. But it did to her mother. I turned my back to the woman's piercing eyes and resumed bouncing about the pool but without a friend. Like insults I would endure in the future, I pretended that nothing was wrong. That day, a coping mechanism I would employ throughout my life took root.

I did not tell anyone what happened until almost fifty years later. But I will never forget how the woman made me feel—alone, abandoned, and a little sad. Until Las Vegas, I thought race indicated color, not opportunity and privilege. In fact, for many years, I thought Dad and Jan, with their light complexions, were white. Race was not a topic we discussed with family, friends, or teachers. At home, school, and church, we pledged our allegiance to the same God and country.

4

WASHINGTON, DC:
THE JEFFERSON QUESTION

1970–1972

For many years, family elders, especially my parents, effectively sheltered me from the caprice and humiliation of race and discrimination. It helped that we lived in Washington, DC, a majority Black city steeped in middle-class comforts and conformity. But they could not protect me forever.

Of course, I knew about Dr. Martin Luther King Jr. Mom insisted that I watch his last speech, "I've Been to the Mountaintop," delivered April 3, 1968, the day before he was assassinated. And I could not have missed the riots in Washington and in urban centers across the country that followed his death. Crowds looted businesses on the main thoroughfares of the DC Black community and burned hundreds of buildings to the ground in an outpouring of rage and grief. More than a dozen people were killed. The military was called in to quell the violence, and machine guns were mounted at the White House and the Capitol. But it didn't affect me very much. I always felt safe.

Appearing unalarmed, Mom reported that tanks were rolling down Rhode Island Avenue past my school, St. Francis de Sales. She chuckled when confiding that Dad had a sign in his car that announced "Soul Brother," protecting it and him from rioters. He often complained that Mom didn't take life seriously enough, and during the 1968 riots it certainly seemed that way.

I found her laissez-faire posture reassuring, which might have been her intent. At that point, she was still mother-henning. As a result, rather than absorb the chaos unfolding around Washington and cities across the country, I retreated to my bedroom with a book, my stuffed animals, and my recently installed private-line, pink "princess" phone. Adopting Mom's disposition, I ignored the violence and the racial strife at the heart of it.

But two years later in that Las Vegas pool, I encountered for the first time what racism felt like, and I did not like it. That was the first shock to my otherwise stable world. But worse was to come.

Back home a few weeks later, another intrusion punctured what had been a tightly spun cocoon. I know it was a Saturday morning because I didn't have school and was sleeping late, or at least trying to. I was a light sleeper—still am—but the noise I heard that morning would have awakened a drunk. Mom was shouting, and so was Dad. They were saying horrible things, even attacking each other's families. Stunned, I left my bedroom, climbed down the center-hall staircase, and turned left toward the dining room to face my parents.

Dad was sitting at the head of the French provincial table Mom had proudly purchased with the money she earned taking care of working mothers' children. He was wearing large, square-framed reading glasses fashionable in the 1970s and often required by people in their mid-fifties. In front of him was *The Washington Post*, which he read daily from front to back, and a cup of coffee. Mom was sitting catty-corner to him, her pretty face already made up but lined with the fury she felt. They both seemed surprised to see me, as if they had forgotten they had one last child living in the house who still needed parental assurance.

Uninvited, I plopped down into one of the dining room chairs, whose brocade-patterned cushions Mom had upholstered herself. Their argument was so heated that they could not unplug, even with me sitting there. I watched, dismayed; picked up my cat, a black-and-white tuxedo named Cleo; and placed her on my lap. I stroked her and prayed for courage. If the cat stayed in place, and generally she did not, it would be a sign from God that I should intervene in my parent's war. I was still a good Catholic girl then. I believed it was up to me to save them and to save our family. Miraculously, Cleo sat placidly, purring with each stroke. I had my sign. With tears streaming down my cheeks, I pleaded with my parents to end their fighting, if not for their sake, then for mine. My words were like a prayer, sweet, sincere, scared.

I looked at Mom, watching for an indication that I'd made a connection and expecting her to shed a few tears of her own, even though she rarely cried. Instead, I saw her large eyes narrow, as she turned to my dad and said, "Do you see what you've done, Cedric? You've upset Gayle." Discouraged, I looked at Dad, wondering whether I had influenced him, even a small bit. I did not expect what happened next. To my horror, I watched as Dad lowered his head into his hands and wept.

It didn't take long for my father to compose himself. He apologized, assuring me that everything would be all right, and their fight ended. I was relieved to see the self-possessed, autocratic visage Dad ordinarily displayed at home and in public return. I was also deeply disturbed by what I'd witnessed. I felt scared and insecure. Yet I recognized that something transformative was happening.

My *Father Knows Best* Dad, who in our family was almost as omniscient as God, was human after all. The moment he let his emotions go changed the way I saw him, and for the better. His sensitive display for my feelings would make it easier for conversations we would have in the future—ones where we would both reveal our vulnerabilities.

But that would come later. At the moment, witnessing my parents unravel, I felt exposed, as another layer of my innocence was stripped away. And my season of revelations was not over. There was another shock on the heels of Las Vegas and my parents' fight—this time from my oldest sister, Janice.

I had not seen her for three years. Janice was back in the States after having moved halfway around the world with her husband, Wallace Terry, a correspondent for *TIME* magazine. She and their three small children lived in Singapore while he covered the Vietnam War as the magazine's deputy bureau chief in Saigon. After marrying Wally, Jan gave up her teaching career for what she anticipated would be an exciting adventure as a foreign correspondent's wife. She was not wrong. More than once, she traveled to the war zone to be with her husband. Wally's reporting became a 1967 *TIME* magazine cover story, "The Negro in Vietnam," and eventually a book, *Bloods: An Oral History of the Vietnam War by Black Veterans.*

Even though Jan was my sister, we were not very close. She had been a college sophomore when I was born, married with a family of her own when I was six years old, and off to Asia when I was ten. By the time she returned to the States, I was a blossoming thirteen-year-old and very curious about the sister I barely knew.

When she visited our tidy brick colonial in the fall of 1970, I was enthralled and at the same time intimidated by her. She was like no one I had ever seen, aside from in the pages of a fashion magazine. Tall, slender, and very glamorous, to me, she looked like a model. Her smooth complexion was light, like vanilla custard and her straightened hair was almost black. Her sophisticated good looks were a contrast to my own. Just shy of five feet, six inches tall and tannish, I was still a somewhat awkward teenager. In spite of the fashion magazines that cluttered my bedroom, I had not yet developed a "look." Not so for my sister. She accented her large, brown eyes with heavy eye makeup and her full mouth with red lipstick. The dress she wore that day was a skinny, burgundy knit that hit her mid-thigh, a radically different look from the ladies-who-lunch ensembles complete with pearls, matching shoes, gloves, and handbags that my mother preferred.

Having lost my childhood shyness and most of my baby fat, I was an outgoing if bookish kid with a group of neighborhood and school friends whose families shared the same values and goals: hard work, education, family, and God. I thought that my trips to places like California, Nevada, Mexico, and New York had given me some insight into the adult world, but nothing in my youthful experience prepared me for someone like Jan. She seemed so cosmopolitan. I had no idea what to say or how to act in her presence, so I just hovered around her and the rest of the family, watching and listening.

As Jan sat on the sofa in the living room, her long legs crossed at the knee, she regaled my parents with stories about the past three years. She had been to places all over the world I had learned about in geography class—France, India, Lebanon, Thailand. It was impossible to keep up. She spoke quickly and with an accent that matched her sophisticated appearance, her vowels stretched, so that *a* sounded like *ah*. France, for example, became *Fraahnce*. Brown University, her husband's alma mater, became *Brouwwn*. As the conversation sprawled, I eventually retreated to the kitchen for a snack.

Peering into the well-stocked refrigerator packed with processed American cheese, sliced deli meats, eggs, leftovers, and lots of salad dressing (I don't know why, but we always had so much salad dressing), I listened with a little less interest than I had when the conversation had begun. Janice had been talking for hours.

I had just found a cold can of grape soda, the less expensive generic brand my dad bought when he did the grocery shopping, when once again, she had my attention. She and Wally were the guests of honor (and the only Blacks) at the American ambassador's home in Saigon. When the dinner table conversation turned to family lineage, the other diners (all white) began claiming illustrious roots, "like royalty," I heard my sister say. "So I told them, well, I'm descended from Thomas Jefferson."

I stood in silent disbelief, drawn back into the conversation, and strained to hear what might follow. Mom had left the room, probably to entertain Jan's children, leaving my sister and Dad sitting alone on the sofa. I listened closely, hoping for an explanation and feeling as if I had just overheard something forbidden. "How dare they?" she demanded with a rhetorical sweep. "That is not what America is supposed to be about. We don't have royalty here. So, I told them." As I peeped into the living room watching Jan and Dad, his expression was unchanged as my sister seamlessly moved to the next topic. I, however, was flummoxed. I thought, *What in the world is Janice talking about? Related to Thomas Jefferson? No way.* That was not the kind of thing families hide. Or was it? I was too timid, too nervous around her to ask what she meant. Whatever questions I had would have to wait. Meanwhile, I thought, in spite of the improbability, wouldn't it be exciting to be descended from my favorite president?

I had been captivated by American history ever since that visit to Mount Vernon when I was ten years old. Of the founders, the one I admired the most was Jefferson because he had written the Declaration of Independence. Even as a young girl, I understood the document's weight on American history. Of course, July Fourth picnics and fireworks helped to reinforce my appreciation. We usually spent the holiday with neighbors who had an annual cookout. I loved the handheld sparklers almost as much as I loved America. And I really did love America! I thought it was the greatest country in the world. Since first grade, we had said the Pledge of Alliance to start our school day. I proudly recited the words "one nation, under God, indivisible, with liberty and justice for all," and *believed them*. I thought the lyrics of "The Star-Spangled Banner" were poetry: "O say does that star-spangled banner yet wave o'er the land of the free and the home of the brave?" My idea of a good time was visiting the Smithsonian Museum of American History. I trusted that my country represented liberty and justice for all. Nothing I experienced in my young life had shown me otherwise. Even the incident in Las Vegas had not changed my mind. That, I told myself, was an anomaly.

Ignorant of Jefferson's status as one of Virginia's wealthiest slave-owners, I placed the third president on a pedestal, a superhuman of almost mythical stature. I thought being descended from him was tantamount to being related to Zeus.

However, no matter how intriguing, Jan's claim seemed unlikely. As a naive thirteen-year-old, I could not imagine under what circumstances my hero would have Black descendants. Besides, one thing that became demonstrably clear during my sister's visit was that she had a flair for the dramatic. I considered the possibility that she had made up the entire story.

Still, I could not ignore the physical evidence right in front of me—my dad. Like Jefferson, he was six feet, two inches tall. His face was freckled, his nose long and pointy. Before he started going grey and then bald, his hair had been reddish, the color of a rusty bucket. I thought about the images I saw of Jefferson in my textbooks, an aristocratic-looking man with auburn hair. Yep, in my adoring, girlish eyes, that was what my dad looked like, too. With my head spinning, I needed to get answers. I decided to go to the person I trusted most, the person I believed could separate fact from fiction, the person who always told me the truth—my father.

Like many fathers and daughters, Dad and I shared a special bond. I was his baby girl, and although my dad could be reserved, and even aloof, we were close. And after the argument I saw between him and Mom when he had let his emotions show, we grew even closer.

It was also a relationship born out of necessity. Mom was drifting away from us. She was often gone from home, working as a substitute teacher, shopping, or volunteering on political campaigns. She stopped cooking regularly, serving up TV dinners with shriveled "fried chicken" and dried-up "mashed potatoes." Sometimes we had Chinese carry-out or hamburgers from the Hot Shoppe. She had even stopped going to Sunday Mass with us.

Because Dad covered all household expenses—the mortgage, the utilities, the cars and their maintenance—the money Mom earned was completely hers. Although she was generous with her children, she used most of her income to build a queenly wardrobe, including diamonds, leathers, and furs—all the luxury items she imagined a doctor's wife would have. There were plenty of lunches, club meetings, and dances to attend to show off her pretty things. To this day, people marvel at how well put together my mother was. "Everyone knew about Billye Jessup. She was always dressed up and very social," one of her old friends told me when I called on her ninety-sixth birthday. "Some people thought she was a muckety-muck," she added, perhaps indiscreetly.

Eventually, Mom would leave us for days and weeks at a time while on trips that took her to Europe, Asia, and the Caribbean. Her excursions allowed her to meet celebrities like Sidney Poitier and Lena Horne. Mom was intent on pursuing the life she felt she had lost when she became a teen bride. Dad and I were collateral damage. We filled the vacuum her absence left with each other's company.

I knew Mom loved me, loved all of us, but I missed her and resented her absences. I was a young girl experiencing all that young girls encounter—physical changes, an infusion of hormones, boys. As close as Dad and I were, these were subjects I did not want to discuss with him.

I was also struggling with my religious faith. After eight years of Catholic school, catechism lessons, confessing my so-called sins— *Bless me, Father, I said a "bad" word*—and regular church attendance, I was having some doubts about Catholicism, and even about the existence of God.

All that logical thinking the nuns taught us had unintended consequences. Nothing I learned about God seemed logical to me. For example, I wondered how the God we were taught loved us allowed so much suffering in the world, even among innocent children. "Eat all your food," Mom would say. "Children are starving in India." Why would God let children starve? And closer to home, I wondered why God allowed so much pain in my life. Surely a loving Father would not allow the discord that threatened my parent's marriage and my continuing happiness. But even as my faith floundered, I longed for something to hold on to, something grounding. Finding out whether I was actually descended from Thomas Jefferson, who was for me godlike, would give me purpose. Dad, I felt, was almost as infallible as the Pope. Surely, he would know.

"I overheard Jan say we're related to Thomas Jefferson," I eased into the conversation one afternoon when we were alone. "What was she talking about?" We were in his basement lair watching TV.

"That's what they say," was his matter-of-fact response, his eyes glued to the football game on his floor-model Zenith color television set. The Washington Redskins, as DC's team was then called, were having a winning season and we were both huge fans.

I probed, "What do you mean 'that's what they say'? Who is 'they'? Is it true? Are we really related to Thomas Jefferson?"

Appearing mildly annoyed, Dad looked at me and shook his head—"I don't know, Gayle"—then turned back to the game, making it clear that he would not be interrogated.

However, his reticence only fueled my interest. I wondered whether he was hiding something, another secret perhaps, like the reason he had dropped out of college or that one of the Jessup children was intellectually disabled or that racism existed. As close as we were, as much as we talked about religion, politics, football, and a plethora of other topics, he had never mentioned the Jefferson connection. Dad was holding something back. I just knew it.

As a teenager, I began developing the relentless determination that would one day lead me to Monticello and to my ancestors. Perhaps Dad didn't want to talk about his family's ties to Jefferson, but that was not going to stop me from probing. However, I needed a strategy. It was not long before I devised a plan that would suit us both. Every Sunday and many weeknights, I climbed down the basement stairs to join him while he watched his favorite TV shows. I settled into what was then a fashionably sleek, orange, leather loveseat near his cushiony La-Z-Boy recliner. Only an end table hosting his pipes and the paraphernalia that went with them separated us. During commercial breaks between the *CBS Evening News*, *The Carol Burnett Show*, *The Mary Tyler Moore Show*, and *Gunsmoke*, I nudged, poked, and pushed, day after day, week after week. For the longest time, he just chuckled and tried to ignore me. "There's nothing to tell, Gayle," or, "I don't know any more than what you heard from Jan," he insisted.

Then one afternoon while the two of us were alone watching golf, he broke. "You know my mother was from Charlottesville," he said, a hint of slyness in his voice. I was flabbergasted. "Jefferson was from

Charlottesville," I practically shouted. "I know," said Dad, the glimmer of a smile on his narrow lips. Then he turned back to the match
we were watching, signaling that he was done with the subject—at
least for the time being.

I still felt Dad was keeping something from me. The bombshell
that his mother was from Charlottesville was proof that he knew
more than he was letting on. I was not going to give up. But Dad
was as stubborn as I was relentless. I had to be patient, stick to the
strategy, and keep watching TV shows on that floor-model Zenith.

"Tell me about your mother," I sweetly cajoled one Sunday afternoon after serving him his favorite—a bowl of Breyers vanilla ice
cream. Dad was no fool. He knew what I was doing. He had been
thinking about what he would say long before I tried to bribe him
with dessert. He took a last swallow and started talking.

"My mother's name was Eva Jessup," he said. How beautiful, I
thought, wishing it were mine. "Gayle" was a cute name and sounded
up-tempo, like me, so it suited. But "Eva," I thought, sounded sym-
phonic, like the languid notes of a cello. I was already imagining what
my grandmother looked like. In my mind, she was as beautiful as her
name, slender, I was sure, with a heart-shaped face, a warm complexion, and soft, gentle hands. "Tell me about her," I implored. "What
was her maiden name? What did she look like? Was she kind or funny?
What was she like?" He picked up one of his pipes and filled it with
tobacco. As he lit it with a disposable BiC lighter and took a puff,
he seemed to consider how much he was ready to disclose. Once his
mind was made up, he turned to me, the pipe resting in his left palm,
and said, "I don't know, Gayle, I don't know much about my mother.
I'm not even sure of her name."

THAT MY FATHER DID NOT KNOW A FACT AS BASIC AS HIS MOTHER'S
name was to me unfathomable. I finally blurted out with unmasked

incredulity, "Daddy, how can you not know your own mother's name?!" Suddenly, what felt like a light-hearted conversation turned gloomy.

"I don't know my mother's name or much about her because she died when I was five years old," he said. "I don't know what my mother looked like. I can't remember her face or the sound of her voice." He faltered, but just a bit. And then, like a tragic hero, he confessed his darkest agony, "I never knew a mother's love."

I didn't know what to say. Legs crossed like a sitting Buddha, I sat upright in the orange loveseat, twisting strands of curly hair around my finger. It was difficult to imagine my dad, stalwart husband and father of five, as a motherless child. I wanted to comfort him but wasn't sure how. At the same time, I wondered whether my badgering opened a painful past that he had tried most of his life to forget.

I managed a weak "I'm sorry Daddy." A minute or so passed before he responded. Then, taking his eyes off the TV, he turned to me and repeated, this time with greater emphasis, "I never knew a mother's love. Imagine that, Gayle, *never knowing a mother's love.*" I took that as a cue that he wanted to talk, that he wanted my sympathy and support, that he wanted to share the grief he carried from his childhood with someone who loved him unconditionally.

Had my mother been at home, he might have confided in her. Perhaps he already had long ago. Whatever the case, she was not there when my questions pushed Dad's memory back to the nightmare that was his childhood. She was off on one of her escapades, and Dad and I were alone. I couldn't understand what it was like to lose a mother, but I knew what it was like to miss one.

As I unfolded and stretched my limbs and sank into my chair, I waited for Dad to continue. He might not have known his mother's name, but surely he knew how she had died. Unflinching, he kept

talking. "My mother died from TB—tuberculosis. And she wasn't
the only one." I braced myself. "All of my sisters died from tuberculosis too," said Dad, stiffly belying the emotion he must have felt.

I was familiar with the disease. As a fan of classic black-and-white
films, *Wuthering Heights* and *Camille*, for example, I had watched
Hollywood stars stricken with "consumption" waste away in ethereal
beauty. As I listened to Dad, I romanticized my grandmother's death,
envisioning her fading, like Merle Oberon or Greta Garbo, in her
husband's arms.

However, what my father described was anything but romantic.
What happened to his family was nothing short of carnage.

"I had five sisters. I don't remember much about them, but I
was told they were sweet girls. One after the other, they died," he
shook his head. Again, almost dumbstruck, I offered a meek "I'm
sorry, Daddy." I was fourteen and had no experience confronting
such incomprehensible loss. What ran through my mind was what
parents tell their children with a scraped knee, "Let me kiss it and
make it better." That's what I wanted to do for my daddy, kiss it
and make it better.

From that moment forward, I promised that I would take care
of him, that I would give him the love he had lost, that I would kiss
it and make it better. I got up from the chair, walked over to him in
his La-Z-Boy, and kissed his bald head.

During the weeks that followed, Dad was more forthcoming,
showing the eagerness for storytelling that I had been trying for
months to tease from him. Most of the stories he shared were of
hardships, but there were lighter moments. Like the time he and his
buddies, caught splashing in a brook behind a fire station, were spotted by neighborhood "cops." The boys ran, but one, Henry Hill, got
caught. Dad said he and his friends feared the boy would be locked
up. Instead, he was spotted later that day with an ice cream cone, a

gift from the policemen. "That's how it was in those days," Dad chortled. "The cops were all right."

But mostly he talked about his losses, especially the death of his mother. He finally explained to me as best he could the mystery of her maiden name. "It could have been Eva Robinson or Eva Taylor," he said. "I don't know which. That's just what I heard people say." Dad had few mementoes from his mom, only a set of pastel-and-cream-colored fine china dessert plates his father had brought back from his naval service in the Philippines, and an elegant hand-painted porcelain tea set. The floral pieces were also decorated with graceful-looking women in red kimonos and stored in Dad's workshop. As a child, I occasionally got a glimpse of the set when, like a puppy, I followed him from room to room.

All he knew of his mother's family was that she had two brothers, both of whom shed their Black identities. "I know I have white cousins out there somewhere," he confided. He also had an aunt, a woman everyone called Aunt Peachie. "Who was she?" I asked, having never heard of her. "My mother's half-sister," Dad said nonchalantly, as if he hadn't just dropped another bombshell.

Aunt Peachie, I learned, lived with the family for several years before I was born. Dad didn't have much to say about her, only that he was her favorite. He didn't remember her speaking of Jefferson, although he acknowledged hearing the family lore from somebody, somewhere. "That's what they say," is all he was able or willing to muster.

He did, however, talk about his brother and five sisters, especially the one he remembered well, Cary. She had been a lively girl who loved to joke, he said, and the only female in the family to survive the scourge's first wave. She was eleven when their mother died, six years older than Dad.

A faded photo taken in the mid-1920s shows a slender teenage Cary in a print dress and with a fashionable "bob" haircut, surrounded by friends. Eyes squinting in the sun, she displays a mischievous smile.

But whatever hopes the family had were dashed when Cary was also stricken with TB. Summoning all their emotional and financial resources, the family sent her to a sanatorium, and prayed. Hospitalized for weeks, Cary seemed to rebound. She was well enough for company on her sixteenth birthday and well enough to show off her spirited personality. "I'll never forget it," Dad recalled fifty years later. "'Sweet sixteen and never been kissed,' she said." Two days later, Cary was dead.

Dad and his older brother escaped death, but not hardship and horror. The emotional toll on them and on their father was devastating. "I'd trade both my sons for just one of my daughters," his father would tell them. If that was not cruel enough, after a house fire, he sent them to live with relatives they barely knew.

Separated from their father and from each other, the boys were shuttled from house to house, as one relative after another cast them out. Dad was only ten, scared and often alone. He said he walked miles to school, sometimes in the dark and through mounds of snow.

When their father remarried, there was hope his new wife would bring a mother's love and warmth to the reunited family. But that did not happen. "Cold and indifferent," was how Dad remembered her. On the other hand, my mother's family was warm and welcoming—just what Dad needed. "The Greens were great people," he often said. With my mother, he acquired more than a wife; he also got a wonderful family.

If the notes my parents exchanged early in their marriage are to be trusted, they were very much in love. A few survive, including a postcard Dad wrote to Mom during World War II:

March 24, 1942

Dear Mrs. Jessup,

Times have changed. The world is at war. Spring is in the air. The birds are chirping. The bees are buzzing. The trees are budding. The time has come when one must declare himself. In these words I would like to say, "yo-te-amo."

Lovingly,
C.B.J.

Mom would tuck similar notes, along with homemade sandwiches and snacks, in the lunch box he took to work when he was still a mail carrier.

But by the mid-1970s, whatever affection she had for him was apparently gone.

"So, what?" she said when I asked her what she knew about Dad's childhood. "My father died when I was six years old, and you don't see me moping about it." I pushed back.

"But you had your brothers and sisters. Most of Dad's family died. And besides, nothing seems to bother you. You laugh about almost everything—except when it comes to Daddy."

She shrugged her shoulders, saying, "Your father loves being unhappy."

I did not believe her. One year after the spectacle of the big fight that brought their marital discord out of the shadows, I felt that I had gotten to know Dad pretty well. It was true, he was not like my mother. He did not laugh as easily as she, or want to dance, or go to parties, or travel, or do many of the things that Mom thought made life worth living. But he didn't want to be unhappy either. Unlike Mom, he was not having a midlife crisis, but he still faced a reckoning.

His marriage was unraveling, and he felt partly to blame. He admitted that he had disappointed my mother, that he was not as sociable as she wanted him to be, that he did not like traveling unless it was for work, and that he could lose his temper. Like the time Mom was playing Sammy Davis Jr.'s "I've Gotta Be Me" for the umpteenth time. Dad hated that song, that and Otis Redding's "Try a Little Tenderness" and Frank Sinatra's "My Way." They were Mom's theme songs and her way of getting a not-so-subtle message to him. Enraged, he snipped the head off the stereo's electric cord, and for good measure, the radio's too. My parents had unique methods of torturing each other.

But Mom's biggest complaint—that he had not gone to med school—he felt was unfair. He provided a good life for her, he said, built her a brand-new house when she was only nineteen. She didn't have to work outside of the home, unless she wanted to. For goodness sake, he said, she even had a housekeeper.

They both had grievances, and appropriate or not, shared them with me. More than anything, I wanted the parents I loved to be happy. If it meant hearing marital issues that should not have been my concern, so be it. I would do whatever it took to keep them together.

Meanwhile, my conversations with Dad continued, sometimes about his childhood, sometimes about his wife. We talked about Jefferson, but Dad was not as consumed about knowing the truth as I was. He was more interested in the family he knew than the family he had lost.

Still, I was convinced that if I could prove our Jefferson lineage, I would give Dad something to be proud of—and Mom, too. So what if Dad was not a doctor? He was something better—a descendant of one of the most famous men in history.

As it turned out, my interest in Dad's clan only made matters worse with Mom. "It was my family that was accomplished," she said. "My father was a White House chef, not his." And the perennial, "Your father was supposed to be a doctor." I wanted to cover my ears and scream, "Enough!"

But instead, many mornings and nights, I lay in bed listening to their fights, most of them wrenching. One was so outlandish, however, that even Mom laughed about it—eventually. After traveling to Italy, a colleague of Dad's, a white woman, sent our family gifts: a tie for him, cameo earrings for me, and a potholder for my mother. Sizzling with justified anger, she tore the offending object to shreds, its cotton fibers floating through the kitchen like down feathers.

Other than that, the household's instability was no laughing matter. I felt like I was living on a fault line, fearful of the earthquake that would one day swallow us. The time I spent with Dad quelled my unease. As long as he was around, I knew everything would be okay. So I kept joining him in the basement, crawling into the orange loveseat, watching TV—and talking.

The best were Sunday afternoons during football season. He taught me to love the "Skins" as much as he did. However, his admiration for the team's legendary coach, Vince Lombardi, had as much to do with racial equality as it did with skillful team management. "He stood up for the race," Dad said of the man who, as longtime head of the Green Bay Packers, had insisted on equal treatment for his Black and white team members, including the same hotel accommodations in the segregated South.

There was not much Dad and I didn't discuss, from how to

shake hands ("with a firm grip and looking the person straight in the eye"), to what to read ("*The Washington Post*, every day, front to back, including the comics"), to religion ("you just have to accept the Bible on faith, even if some of it doesn't make sense to you"), to interpersonal communication ("never let people know what you're thinking. Remain stoic. If you don't know what that means, look it up").

As I matured, so did our conversations. Race was no longer a taboo subject. "You have to be twice as good to get half as far," Daddy counseled, an adage many Blacks passed down to their children. The principle seemed to work for Dad and our family. By most material measures, we had a good life.

However, there were times he acknowledged the challenges Black people faced, even in a family like ours that seemed to have so many advantages. "If I had my druthers, I'd rather be white," he said one day, to my shock and dismay. I loved being Black. I felt like a princess, never wanting to be anyone else aside from Gayle Louise Jessup. But I guess for Dad, it was different.

His ambiguous looks—"Some people think I'm Greek or Italian," he told me—exposed him to uncomfortable situations. Like the time he was playing golf with white colleagues who commented that a coworker was "smart for a nigger."

"I'm a Negro," he announced to the unsuspecting and embarrassed offenders before recording the breach in their employment records. This was years before diversity training. Back then, it was the job of human resource managers to train an integrating workforce. Dad said one of his responsibilities was to make note of race-related insensitivities and insults.

Before Dad became a Post Office "big shot," back when he was still delivering mail, he stopped eating watermelon because of the distorted, racist postcard images of children devouring the fruit. "It was shameful," he said in disgust. But after a few years of deprivation, he changed his mind. "I decided not to deny myself something I love so much because of people's racism," he said.

Dad retired soon after I started high school at the all-girl Notre Dame Academy near the US Capitol. With time on his hands, he became my chauffeur, driving me to school, to concerts, and to sleepovers. While Mom was sporting about town in a striking, crystal-blue Buick convertible, he was driving teenagers in his lack-luster white Rambler. Often, after dropping my friends and me off at an event, he would park until it was time for us to go home. One night, he waited five hours outside a concert venue, Constitution Hall, while my best friend and I and a thousand other fans waited for the perpetually late R&B group Sly and the Family Stone to show up.

Although I was at a Catholic high school and still attending Mass, my faith continued to stumble. The beginning of ninth grade marked the end of my years as a devout Catholic. By the end of my first year in high school, I announced to my parents that I no lon-ger believed in Catholic doctrine. I did not believe that Moses had parted the Red Sea or that Noah had built an ark or that God had turned Lot's wife into a pillar of salt. "Nonsense," I told Dad during our many conversations about God and faith. I wasn't even sure if I was a Christian.

Rather than chastising me, he listened patiently, explaining that the Bible was meant to teach us lessons. "There're things you just have to accept," he said. "It's a mystery. That's why you need faith." But my faith was like an old fluorescent lightbulb. What was once so bright had begun to flicker and die.

Sick of religious education, nuns, and uniforms, I asked to be released from Notre Dame, as if I were seeking a prison probation. My parents agreed, and the next year, I started tenth grade at a new public school, H. D. Woodson. Ironically, the concrete, eight-story high-rise building with its black asphalt parking lot looked more like a prison than a school.

On the edge of far Northeast Washington, Woodson was promoted as an oasis in an urban desert. The state-of-the-art building was equipped with an indoor swimming pool, elevators, and escalators. The best teachers were recruited from high schools across the city. Exceptionalism was expected. In spite of its Brutalism-inspired architecture, it seemed like a good fit for me.

Eager to become popular, I sought extracurricular activities, joining the band, becoming a majorette, and singing with a choir. Beyond football—specifically the Washington team—I was not a big sports fan. But I tried to develop school spirit, attending basketball games and track meets after school. I dated a couple of guys and even got caught skipping class once. None of that endeared me to my less affluent classmates, however, many of whom lived in low-rent or subsidized housing. My first exposure to children from a different socioeconomic background than my own left me emotionally and, after a fight, physically wounded.

I just did not fit in. For one thing, my clothes were all wrong. After years of wearing a uniform, I invested in a fashionable wardrobe purchased at expensive Georgetown shops. I traversed Woodson's halls in bright-colored, flare-leg pants, stretch tops, and platform shoes. Many of my fellow classmates didn't have the resources to buy clothes like mine.

Some kids ridiculed the way I walked with my eyes focused and head held high, and even the way I talked. "You sound like a white girl," they taunted. I was devastated. But it wasn't all bad. One smiling girl with a neat afro greeted me with "Que pasa?" at the beginning of every Spanish class. We never became friends, but I always remembered how she made me feel: welcomed. And I was a hit when I won for the girls' history class team, correctly answering how Socrates had died.

"He drank hemlock," I shouted as the down-to-the-knuckles contest ended to the applause of my classmates. However, those enchanting days were few, and I often avoided fellow students altogether, skipping class and studying alone in the school's library.

Weekends were a reprieve and a chance to spend time with Dad. For a while we felt like a family. Mom, while still frequently out and about, was spending a little more time at home, and my brother Bruce was back from military service in Vietnam. He had his own place but was at our house almost every day. Bruce was the sibling chronologically closest to me—only nine years older—but still too distant for us to be buddies. After he returned from Vietnam, we became friends. Bruce, a cinnamon colored version of Dad, came home with an afro, bell-bottom pants, and an irreverent attitude. He once dropped by the house wrapped in an American flag. My brother taught me how to swear, appreciate rock and roll music, and smoke a joint.

In the 1970s, we were not the same family that once had held nightly prayers in front of Jesus's bleeding heart. In fact, Dad, who had moved into his own bedroom, had taken the statue under his protection. It sat atop his dresser beside a dish that held his keys and small change.

In spite of my parents sleeping in separate rooms, their marriage appeared to be on the mend. On at least one occasion, when I broke curfew, they were a united front, grounding me for two weeks. In an odd way, I didn't mind. Their attention felt like a security blanket. If a little acting out on my part helped us feel like family, the crime was worth the punishment.

I was beginning to feel safe again, that no matter what happened between them, they would stay together, and we would remain a family. Until one day after school, I came home to my worst fear.

Nothing looked different as I walked up the cement path toward the front porch steps. Dad's well-manicured lawn was like green velvet, the waist-high shrubs like leaf-covered boxes. To my right, the old-fashioned yellow-and-white metal porch swing was motionless, the matching chairs on the opposite side empty. Dad's car was gone, but I assumed that only meant he was running errands, perhaps to the grocery or hardware store.

However, I knew something was amiss when Mom opened our onyx-painted door before I could insert my key in the brass lock. "Where's Daddy?" I asked. Her face looked worn, gnarled like an old oak, not like Mom's at all. "Your father left," she angrily spat, "he moved out."

I didn't believe her. Dad would never have left. He loved routine, his big Zenith color TV, his backyard pear trees, his home. He loved us. Why would he leave? However, Mom persuaded me that he was indeed gone. I was too angry to cry—angry with her for chasing him away and with him for leaving us. I refused to discuss the acrimony that must have preceded his departure and went straight to my room. I didn't even want to talk on the phone. One of my favorite science fiction writers—George Orwell or Kurt Vonnegut—would be my companion that evening.

Dad called before bedtime to check on me and to say good night. He had a furnished apartment in Bethesda, Maryland, a ritzy DC suburb. A two-bedroom, nice enough, he said. I heard the local TV news in the background. If I closed my eyes, I could imagine him watching his preferred station, channel 9, as if he were downstairs in his La-Z-Boy. If I squeezed them hard, I could see myself plopped in the orange leather chair next to his while we reviewed the day.

What I couldn't imagine was Dad living alone in a furnished Bethesda apartment.

I never saw his place. He came back home in less than a week as stealthily as he had left. I arrived home from school, and he was standing at the front door, as if it were business as usual. Feeling bruised that he had been gone, even for a short while, I gave him a perfunctory hug and ran upstairs to my room. We never talked about it, ever.

The only hint Daddy ever gave came several days later. We were back in our usual post in the basement—him in his La-Z-Boy, me in the pumpkin leather chair. "You never know what goes on inside a marriage," he counseled. It was a lesson I would recall many times in the years to come.

5

HOWARD UNIVERSITY

1974–1976

During the three years after my sister Jan's return from Asia, my world began to change. As I matured, she and I grew closer. I admired so much about her—the way she dressed, and spoke, and moved elegantly about the townhouse she shared with her husband and their three children. I spent hours at their place, listening to music, laughing, learning. To my teenage eyes, they were so sophisticated.

Their stylish home was in Southwest Washington, a section of town that redevelopment had transformed into a trendy neighborhood. Like Foggy Bottom where Dad had spent his nightmarish childhood, Southwest had been a "slum" until so-called urban renewal swept away old neighborhoods and the Black people who lived in them. Families who had lived in the area for decades were forced to move out. The government's answer to displacing Black homes and businesses was to corral poor people into public housing—in some cases, right next to high-end apartment complexes and townhouses, like my sister's.

Even though federal government jobs and well-paying professions supported a large, affluent, and well-educated Black professional class, Janice and her family among them, the city had huge pockets of poor Black people. Many lived in tension with their better-off Black neighbors and the affluent whites who moved into their gentrifying neighborhoods. Sometimes resentment spilled over, manifesting in petty crimes—burglaries, thefts, and robberies at gunpoint.

But at my sister's, no one seemed to notice. Jan and Wally's was a home buzzing with dizzying activity. The attractions were many— good food (homemade pizza, for starters), interesting people, and provocative conversations at all hours of the day and into the night.

Wally was president of the Capital Press Club, an alternative for Black journalists kept out of the segregated National Press Club. His position gave him entrée to Washington's most powerful players. In 1963, President John F. Kennedy sent greetings to guests at the club's first banquet where Vice President Lyndon Johnson announced the birth of Jan and Wally's first child. Among the political and social elite that they entertained at their home were Johnson's vice president, Hubert Humphrey; Supreme Court Justice Thurgood Marshall; and CBS's Dan Rather.

I was too young for their parties, but I remember spending an evening with Justice Marshall and his wife, Cecilia. "Uncle Thurgy," Jan's children called him. Unmindful of his stature as an associate justice and the role he played in ending legal segregation in the landmark 1954 *Brown v. Board of Education* decision, I was unimpressed when we visited his Virginia home. I saw only a scowling old man wearing ill-fitting clothes. Had I understood who the man was, I would have been too nervous to breathe, let alone speak. As it turned out, the evening was most memorable for his retiring early while the rest of us watched slide projections of Jan and Wally's adventures overseas. That's how ordinary our visit was.

At age fourteen, I was better versed in racial identity than I had been after being dismissed and rendered invisible by the white mother at the Las Vegas hotel pool. I had a floppy afro and wore a

"Free Huey" pin advocating the liberation of jailed Black Panther Huey Newton. But I still had a lot to learn. Jan and Wally became my tutors. By the time I was fifteen, race tinged almost every conversation with them. "When white people get together, they talk about art, literature, and music," Wally would say. "When Black people get together, we talk about white people. Think of all the valuable time we're losing." Everyone would fall out laughing, but it was true. I'm pretty sure the first time I heard "white people" used derisively was at their house, even though some of their closest friends were white.

But at that time, white people were not my problem. The Black people at my high school were. It was a rare day that I did not hear, "You think you cute" or "You ack like a white girl." It was not that I was the only middle-class student. There were others with similar backgrounds. I was just an easy target, walking around in fancy clothes with my nose in the air. As I approached the end of the eleventh grade, I didn't think I would survive my senior year. Luckily, I didn't have to.

Thanks to Dad insisting that I attend summer school to learn typing, all I needed was one course, senior English, to graduate. There would be no senior year, no prom, no senior trip, no graduation, no celebration. As it turned out, there would not even be a diploma, only the required credits. But I didn't care. I would be free from the torture that was high school.

I was seventeen when I finished the summer course that was my ticket to a new beginning. I just wasn't sure where that ticket was taking me. I had taken the College Board's PSAT, a primer for the SAT. But because completing high school happened so suddenly, I had not considered where I wanted to go to college, let alone applied to one.

However, I did know what I wanted to be: a journalist like my brother-in-law Wally and like *Washington Post* reporters Bob Woodward and Carl Bernstein. I devoured their stories about Watergate, the political scandal that unraveled Richard Nixon's presidency. I shared my ambitions with my sister, who took to calling me "Brenda Starr," after the red-headed, glamorous comic strip reporter. Then she and her husband went to work toward making my dream of becoming a reporter a reality.

A few weeks later, I was a college freshman, following the same path Dad had taken forty years earlier. Thanks to my brother-in-law, who was appointed the Frederick Douglass Journalism Chair at Howard University's School of Communications the same year I finished high school, I was easily enrolled at the country's most prestigious historically Black university. He walked my application through the admission process with barely any input from me. All he needed was my signature and a check from Dad.

In 1974, I was a seventeen-year-old college freshman with a shiny new red Mustang, a credit card, and all the earnestness of youth. It was not long before Wally, who had been more of a stranger to me than my sister, became a best friend.

I had still been in kindergarten when Wally, a young *Washington Post* reporter, courted and married my sister. He was a Brown University graduate and had studied theology at the University of Chicago. She was an elementary school teacher with an adventurous bent and a habitual byline reader. She was also beautiful. When Wally became one of the first Black correspondents for *TIME* magazine, he joined the ranks of the journalistic elite, covering two wars, the civil rights movement, and Vietnam. Returning from Asia, he added to his journalistic bona fides, becoming a Harvard Nieman Fellow. When I was at Howard University, he became my mentor.

Unlike at Woodson High School, at Howard I was with my own. Black royals came to Howard from as far away as California and as close as Northwest DC. In fact, among the sons and daughters of doctors, lawyers, and engineers, I, the daughter of a civil servant, was of lower rank. The distinction, however, was negligible, especially since I had a car, Dad's credit card, and a family member on the faculty.

I chose commuting over dorm life, a decision I came to regret, mainly because it was hard to find campus parking. I accrued hundreds of dollars in tickets from parking illegally. Dad paid them all. He did not want anything like worrying about money (or parking tickets) to interfere with my academic success.

Although I had the polish (from years of observing Mom and my older sisters) and, according to admirers, the looks for TV, I wanted to be a newspaperwoman. I believed real reporting happened at newspapers, places like *The Washington Post*, where Wally had cut his journalistic eyeteeth and where Woodward and Bernstein's exploits had brought down a president. So, I joined *The Hilltop*, the college paper.

Jan and Wally were now living in a section of Northwest DC called Cleveland Park, where I spent more time than I did at home.

During my freshman year a book about the nation's third president and the man I presumed to be my ancestor scandalized a cross section of people—historians, scholars, publishers, and the public. *Thomas Jefferson: An Intimate History* by biographer Fawn Brodie was the first scholarly exposition of Jefferson's relationship with Sally Hemings. At the time of its publication, few scholars acknowledged that Jefferson had a relationship with an enslaved woman. I didn't know the history, but my sister did.

In the years since I first overheard her say "We're descended from Thomas Jefferson," I had devoted more time to questioning Dad than Jan, assuming he would have the answers I needed. When I thought I had mined all I could from him, I turned to my loquacious sister.

"Aunt Peachie told me," she said. "I heard it all the time, 'You're descended from Thomas Jefferson, I'm not, but you are.'" Dad had mentioned Aunt Peachie a few times, explaining that she was his

mother's half-sister, but offered few details about her life or her relationship with the family. Wide-eyed, I waited for more from my
sister. Unlike Dad, when it came to family stories, she did not need
a lot of encouragement.

"She lived with us for twenty years," Jan explained, "and was
practically Mom's maid. She washed clothes, folded diapers, whatever she could do to help around the house. I guess you don't remember her. She was old and sick and died soon after you were born. Poor
Aunt Peachie. Anyway, she's the one who told me that we're related
to Jefferson."

I wondered why Dad had not told me more about his aunt, why
I knew virtually nothing about a relative who had lived with our family for twenty years. As my sister continued to talk, a clearer picture
emerged. "She was completely illiterate," Jan said. "She couldn't read,
write, or spell her own name. Her signature was an 'X.' She worked
as a domestic for a wealthy white family who let her go after she had
a stroke. That's when she moved in with us. Poor Aunt Peachie," she
said again.

I began to understand. During one of our many conversations,
Dad said with apparent pride that no one in his family served tables or
waited on other people. Now, I was discovering from Jan that not only
was his aunt a domestic, she was also illiterate. That was the kind of
information my father would have preferred to keep to himself. I don't
think he was judging. Dad readily acknowledged that his father had
only an eighth-grade education. "But he had a thick dictionary that he
read every day," he often told me, using his thumb and middle finger
to demonstrate the book's density. He never said it, but I think it was
the image of a member of his family serving white people that he resented. Dad was as straightforward and honest as any man I have ever
known, but sometimes you had to read between the lines.

Jan was delighted to describe the woman whose meanderings

were the only clue we had to our family's past. Her real name was Virginia Robinson. No one knew when she was born or where she acquired the nickname "Aunt Peachie," but we assumed that since she moved from Virginia during President William McKinley's administration, she was probably born in the 1870s.

She had a penchant for telling tales, said Jan, some of them tall. One that was likely true involved a tip of the hat from President McKinley during one of his strolls near the White House. Aunt Peachie claimed he looked her way as she walked her employer's baby, and well, tipped his hat. It was a nice story.

Her tales left an indelible impression on Jan, like the catastrophic 1922 "Knickerbocker Blizzard" that killed 98 and injured 133 Washington, DC, theatergoers. "Roof fell in at the Knickerbocker Theater. Snow on the roof. Killed a lot of people," Jan recalled her saying over and over again. It was true. A former US congressman and several prominent local political and business leaders were among the dead and injured. Because Washington at that time was a segregated Southern town, all the victims were white.

Another was about Ku Klux Klan parades in the nation's capital. "Ku *Kluck* Klan marched down Pennsylvania Avenue," she would say, mutilating the name of America's deadliest terrorist organization. Indeed, tens of thousands of Klan members dressed in white robes and hoods had marched down America's most famous street on August 8, 1925 and September 13, 1926. President Calvin Coolidge refused to review the back-to-back parades but that was far shy of a condemnation.

Some of her ramblings were old wives' tales or superstitions. For example, pigs squealed during thunderstorms, she told Jan, because they saw blood in the clouds. She was sure of it because she knew a man who had extracted fluid from a pig's eye to prove it. Or the luck of a child born with a "veil" or caul over its face.

But the story that captivated Jan more than any of the others was about the author of the Declaration of Independence. "You're descended from Thomas Jefferson. I'm not, but you are," Aunt Peachie repeated, as she did everything, over and over again.

Jan was apparently the only one in the family who heard our great-aunt's reminiscences. When I grilled my other siblings, neither could recollect her saying anything substantive, let alone comments about Jefferson. Pat recalled that she always played with her and shared what little she had. "Aunt Peachie was the sweetest person I've ever known," she said. Bruce remembered just wishing she would stop talking. Even though she lived with our family for years, Mom and Dad had almost nothing to add about Aunt Peachie, just that she was Dad's aunt. Like Dickie, she was someone they loved but didn't talk about. Neither one fit in with the healthy, middle-class image our family had of ourselves.

It would have been easy to doubt Aunt Peachie. She was sweet, everyone told me, but superstitious, uneducated, and childlike. However, Jan chose to believe her, and I chose to believe Jan.

With Fawn Brodie's 594-page book, I had even more reason to believe that what my sister and great-aunt said was true.

Brodie brought to the 1970s what was gossip and newspaper fodder in Jefferson's lifetime: that he had children with one of the women he enslaved, Sally Hemings. It was a charge that established Jefferson scholars vehemently rejected, as did much of the public. But that did not stop Brodie's book from making the *New York Times* Best Seller list or the publisher from selling 350,000 copies.

"What do you know about Sally Hemings?" Jan asked one afternoon as we sat in the kitchen of her new house in Northwest DC. Sitting at Jan's white kitchen table while enjoying a Perrier, a beverage she of course introduced to me, I confessed that I did not know much. I had not read Brodie's book and had certainly not learned of Hemings in my American history classes. "She was Jefferson's slave, his lover, and his wife's half-sister," said Jan with typical dramatic flair. "It was no secret. Everyone in and around Monticello knew. It was even in the newspapers. They called her 'Dusky Sal.' What an awful thing," Jan said of the racist, nineteenth-century description of Sally Hemings. "It's all in this book," she said, placing her hand on a copy of Brodie's volume lying in front of her. "You can borrow it," she said. "It's fascinating, and of course, it's true. Why would Jefferson be different from any other slave master?"

With that, my sister and I locked eyes, sharing the same thought—we must be the Black descendants of that union. Aunt Peachie had never mentioned how we were related to Jefferson, just that we were. Jan and I surmised that we'd figured it out. Sally Hemings was our ancestor. All we had to do now was prove it.

6

ROOTS

1977

Roots: The Saga of an American Family, Alex Haley's bestselling book adapted into a TV miniseries, was an unexpected sensation. When it aired on ABC in 1977, to everyone's surprise, including network executives, *Roots* became one of the most successful television programs of all time and a national phenomenon. The miniseries also sparked the multibillion-dollar genealogy industry. Haley's chronicle of kidnapped Kunte Kinte—his African ancestor—and Kinte's descendants was viewed by 130 million people. My Dad and I watched together. Every evening over the eight consecutive nights the program aired, we sat in front of his Zenith TV, eagerly awaiting to see what travails the Haley clan would face in America, and how they would overcome them. Even Mom watched a few nights, not wanting to miss what everyone was talking about.

To me it seemed impossible that such a story could be true, that word could be passed from one generation to another, that oral history could be interpreted as fact. But Haley's account, true or not, was familiar to us, because something similar was unfolding in my own family.

Dad and I had not talked about our lineage for a while, but while we were watching *Roots*, the conversation took its natural course. Maybe the miniseries stoked Dad's memory because at some point during those eight nights, he delivered a whopper.

"About twenty years ago, your mother got a long-distance call from a woman in New York, so she assumed it was important. I was at work, so your mother took a message. The caller claimed that she was caring for an old woman who was sick and senile. She was very wealthy, she said, and people were taking advantage of her."

From there the story turned from bizarre to tragic. The caller said her ailing friend had a nephew named Cedric Jessup who worked at the Post Office. Mom confirmed that she had reached the right household, but she had a question: "Is the woman you're calling about white or Colored?" The answer seemed to settle the issue: *she's white.* "Well, she can't be related to us. We're Negro," Mom said, but she told the fretting woman that she would convey the message to Dad. She passed the word along as promised, encouraging him to return the call. He never did.

Had he responded to the mysterious caller, he might have betrayed the sick woman's secret, that the woman the caller believed was white was actually Black. Dad revealed that for years he had heard rumors that his mother had a sister who passed for white and married a wealthy Englishman. They lived in New York. That's all he knew. Another bombshell.

The possibility of kinship with a dying woman and the prospect of inheriting her money held no allure for my father. He was not going to acknowledge or care for a woman he did not know, a woman he felt turned her back on her family and her race. He didn't know his aunt's name or her fate. However, my father was not one for second-guessing his decisions. He buried the memory of the call until *Roots* resurrected it.

Dad was not done with his surprises. "You know, there's a portrait of my mother in the attic," he also volunteered. All the years we had talked about his family, about his mother and sisters, about how he could not remember her voice or face, about how bereft he was when everyone died—and now suddenly there was a picture of her in the attic, along with one of his father? For a second, I thought he was pulling my leg. But he assured me it was true and that when he got around to it, he would retrieve them. I knew what "got around to it" meant. I could be waiting until the next time Mom needed something stored up or retrieved from there—clothes, Christmas decorations, or an antique lamp that was back in her favor. Climbing up the rickety ladder that he pulled from the ceiling to get to the attic was one of his least favorite activities.

Why he waited so long to tell me about the portraits was a mystery. It could have been that he was protecting himself, that seeing his parents' faces conjured sad memories, just as seeing Dickie, my disabled brother, did. It was also possible that he simply had forgotten the portraits existed. I would have to wait a few months before I saw them. When Dad collected Mom's spring wardrobe from the rafters, he brought his parents' portraits down the wobbly ladder with him.

I hated to admit it, but when I finally saw the images of my grandparents, I was disappointed, not because they weren't a distinguished-looking couple. They were quite elegant, he in his US Navy uniform and she in her high-collared blouse. But the portraits were in awful condition, torn and battered from years of neglect. They were massive things, twenty-four by eighteen inches, and looked more like paint on canvas than photographs on paper. I later learned that they were hand-colored photos, a common nineteenth-century portraiture technique.

Early in their existence, the portraits must have hung in some hallowed place, perhaps in the parlor of my grandparents' home or in a hallway. Who knows how many years they had lived in our attic, buried beneath cast-off toys, books, old furniture, and whatever else was stored up there? Yet, in spite of the pictures' deteriorated condition, I could see what a beautiful couple they had been.

There was my grandmother, her image enhanced with touches of blue, grey, and dusty rose. Dressed in a "Gibson Girl" shirt adorned with a bow and buttons, her dark hair was pinned up in a blue bow, and a hint of blush adorned her cheeks. She looked young, perhaps eighteen, the age she was when she married my grandfather. Studying her face, I was sure I recognized characteristics I saw in Dad, a self-assured presence—a quality that cannot be taught. You had to be born with it.

My grandfather's visage was also impressive. Sporting a handlebar mustache, he looked dashing and strong, very much the "leader of men" that my dad frequently described. He had helped found a church, Zion Baptist, was a commander of the Spanish American War Veterans, and an exalted ruler of his Order of Elks lodge.

I studied my grandmother's face, looking for what might have passed down to me—perhaps the eyes that slanted just a bit or the small mouth. I wanted to make a connection, maybe even feel something spiritual. I stared at Eva Robinson Jessup, and she stared back. But nothing happened, or at least not that time.

One day, the pictures would be mine, but meanwhile Dad gave them to Jan for safekeeping.

•   •   •

As a Howard University student, I had access to the Moorland-Spingarn Research Center, one of the world's finest libraries of African American history. One day when I had a little extra time on my hands, I decided to take full advantage of the extraordinary resources that my tuition helped to support. If any place had information about Sally Hemings, Moorland-Spingarn would.

I had no trouble making my way over to Founders Library, which housed the research center. It was my favorite hangout on the main campus. The Georgian-style brick building featured a clock and tower modeled after Philadelphia's Independence Hall. I loved the smell of the leather-bound books in the library's stacks. I got to know the staff and even volunteered there one semester. Yet during my stint as a volunteer, I had never taken the time to venture into the research center.

However, in 1977 on the heels of *Roots*, my interest in finding my connection to Thomas Jefferson and Sally Hemings was reinvigorated. I breezed by the reception desk at the library's entrance and through the hall that led to the reference room. I had no idea where to begin, so I headed to the librarian's desk where a middle-aged woman was intently organizing. She looked up as I approached. "How can I help you?" she asked pleasantly.

"Have you heard of Sally Hemings?" I asked almost timidly. I was not sure how much people knew about Jefferson and the enslaved woman I suspected was my ancestor. "Of course," she said, rising from desk. "Right over here. Follow me."

She pulled a few thick volumes off the shelf and handed them to me. They weighed heavily in my slender arms, but I cradled the books as if they were chunky gold bars. Pointing to a table, the kind woman issued instructions, "You can't check these books out, so have a seat and bring them back to me when you're done." She smiled again, very politely, and returned to her desk and to her papers.

I sat down and appraised what lay before me, three books that might hold the key to information about my past. One reminded me of a volume from the *World Book Encyclopedia* that composed part of our home library, except the book now in front of me was about Black people.

My heart pounded as I respectfully opened the leather cover and turned the pages. If our inkling was right—Jan's and mine—that Sally Hemings was our forebear, the answer might literally be at my fingertips. I flipped through the alphabetized catalogue, *h*—*ha*—*he*—*hem*, until I saw her name. *Hemings, Sally.* I started devouring the words like a child eating a thick slice of birthday cake.

But what I read only partially fit with what I already knew. The entry confirmed the assertion's in Fawn Brodie's book. Sally Hemings was not only Jefferson's enslaved "concubine" but his dead wife's half-sister. She and Jefferson had several children, three boys and a girl. Two of the children, a son and a daughter, disappeared into white society, while two sons moved to Ohio. The account I was reading was based on the recollections of one of the Ohioan transplants. But what I couldn't make sense of was where my family line fit.

I tried to connect the dots tracing a possible route from Virginia to Ohio, back to Virginia, and finally to Washington, but there was no evidence Hemings's sons returned to Virginia or moved to Washington. Then I remembered what Dad once said during one of our more revelatory conversations. He hinted at his "shameful past," that he believed his grandmother had been "taken behind a woodshed" by a white man, that she might have been raped, and that she had never married. Through no fault of his own, he felt disgraced. "Why do you think I look like this?" he asked, his cheeks reddening with disgust.

Sitting at the rectangular table at the exalted Moorland-Spingarn Research Center, my mind raced toward the salacious. What, I wondered, if there was yet another family secret, one that explained why my father was not sure of his mother's name? "It could have been Eva Robinson or Eva Taylor," he had said. What if she was the abandoned love child of one of the Hemings's before the family migrated to Ohio? What if my great-grandfather was not white, as Dad seemed to believe, but instead was a Black man who looked white, like Dad?

My father was a devout Catholic who believed that the confessional absolved the contrite. Yet he still felt the burn of his grand-mother's scarlet letter. If his mother had been born out of wedlock and abandoned by her father, that would have been a burden for him, another part of his past that he preferred to forget, another secret.

I left the library and rushed to Jan's house, eager to get her take on my theory. It was customary for the back door to remain un-locked for the stream of children, friends, and family in and out of the Terry household. As always, we greeted each other with air kisses and a hug before settling down at the kitchen table. No matter how comfortable or inviting the rest of the house, the kitchen was always the place for gatherings, even large ones.

I lit a cigarette pulled from a green-and-white pack of Newports (everyone smoked back then) and took a sumptuous drag, inhaling the mentholated tobacco into my lungs. Jan already knew as much as anyone about Sally Hemings—that she was enslaved by Jefferson, that she was his wife's half-sister, and that she and Jefferson had sev-eral children. But she had not considered that one of the sons might be our ancestor. We had no idea how we were related to Jefferson, only that Aunt Peachie said it was so. We assumed it was through Sally Hemings but could not prove it any more than we could kin-ship to Jefferson.

"I'd love to rent a pied-à-terre in Charlottesville and spend my days poring through everything I could find. That would be heav-enly," Jan mused. With a husband and three children, that was not going to happen, at least not any time soon. So, the two of us agreed that we were likely the descendants of an out-of-wedlock relation-ship, that one of Jefferson and Hemings's sons was the forebear, and that we would probably never be sure of the identities of our an-cestors. "That's our story and we're sticking to it," my sister and I laughed. We then shook on it.

I felt like we were partners in crime.

7

CHICAGO

Howard's commencement is always the second Sunday of May—Mother's Day. Mine was May 14, 1978. Like church on Easter Sunday, Howard's commencement was as much a fashion show as it was a celebration of academic achievement. From grandmas in wide-brimmed floral hats and grandpas in spiffy pin-striped suits to teens sporting afros and pantsuits, the latest fashion trend, families packed the stands of the campus's outdoor stadium. The weather was accommodating, a comfortable mid-70s, balmy enough for me to wear a flower print sundress underneath my black commencement robe.

Since 1924, when Calvin Coolidge became one of the first of several US presidents to speak at Howard's commencement, the university has attracted political and entertainment celebrities. The year I graduated, civil rights activist and Health, Education, and Welfare Assistant Secretary Mary Frances Berry was the keynote speaker. But R&B superstar and honorary degree recipient Stevie Wonder was the headliner. He didn't perform, but at my 1978 commencement, he became Dr. Wonder.

Of course, my family was there—Mom wore a white blouse, black blazer, oversize sunglasses, and her trademark smile. Dad opted for a grey suit, a broad tie, and his patrician look. My siblings, brother-in-law, nephews, and niece completed the celebration. I was not the first in our family to finish college, but I was the first and only to graduate from Dad's alma mater, the place where he had abandoned his dream of becoming a doctor in order to care for his family. If that was on his mind, or Mom's, neither showed it. As was their custom, my parents put on a show in public. No one would ever have guessed that theirs was a splintered marriage.

Yet for all the household tension, I did not want to leave home and set out on my own, nor did my parents want me to. We all had our reasons. For me, it was watching over them. I felt that as long as I was at home to mediate, their arguments would not get out of hand. Illusionary or not, I believed I was the glue that kept their marriage together.

For their part, they likely suspected that at twenty-one years old, I was not prepared for independence. The entire time I was in college, Dad paid all of my expenses—car maintenance, gas, clothes, parking tickets, of which there were hundreds of dollars worth. Any money I made from working was mine to spend as I pleased, just like Mom.

I had good summer jobs, usually arranged by family connections, doing administrative work for government agencies. "It's who you know," Mom always said. The experience illuminated what I already knew—I did not want an office job, especially working for the government. I thought the work was respectable, but to me, it looked predictable and unstimulating. And while all it would take was a phone call from Dad to secure for me a "good government job," I was not interested. Besides, I had trained to be a journalist.

I could not have known then what a pivotal decision that was. Had I followed my father's path and become a bureaucrat, I would have had financial security. But it is doubtful that I would have found the route to our ancestral home. The skills I honed as a journalist helped unearth that passage.

After a few nondescript temporary jobs, I scored my first, and only, with a newspaper—working in the Washington bureau of the *New York Times*. I had my brother-in-law, Wally, to thank. He made a call to his buddy, the *Times*'s DC bureau chief, and I was in.

My new job as "desk clerk" or "copy girl" was not glamorous. In the days before computers, reporters banged out stories on typewriters. When they were done, they yelled "Copy!," and a young apprentice would pick up their finished product and move it through the newsroom, from editing to the presses, as quickly as possible. Today, it seems archaic, but in 1979 when I was an aspiring journalist, jobs like mine helped "put the paper to bed."

No matter how mundane, I was lucky to have a job in the newspaper business, especially at the *Times*. I may have been a lowly clerk, but I was working at the highly regarded "newspaper of record." And for many would-be reporters, a copy job was entrée into the big leagues.

One of my proudest moments in journalism happened on January 8, 1980, with my first *New York Times* byline. The story, bearing the headline "Network of Learning," was about a national program that allowed high school students to travel well beyond their school districts for jobs or special courses in, say, political science or forestry. Dad, knowing the value of the written word, added his. On a Xeroxed copy of the piece, he wrote, "Congratulations!! Your Daddy is very proud!!" I framed the autographed article and hung it on my bedroom wall.

By 1980, I was twenty-three and had been at the *Times* for two years and was still living at home. It was time to move on, away from the paper and from home. I just didn't know what road to take. I considered law school, and I even took the LSAT, the Law School Admission Test, and did well. But I did not have a passion for law. I loved journalism. Good reporting had the power to change history. Watergate had proved that.

There were advocacy journalists who fomented change, addressed social injustices, and exposed political corruption. I longed to be a member of that league of crusaders. As I struggled to find the right course, once again good fortune and great connections provided the direction I was seeking. This time, it was a scholarship to a prestigious university.

After years of negotiations, in the early 1980s the *Times* settled a racial discrimination suit with its Black employees. One of the provisions was a scholarship for minority employees at one of four college journalism programs: Howard University School of Communications, Columbia Journalism School, Missouri University School of Journalism, or Northwestern University Medill School of Journalism. As one of the first recipients of the scholarship, I chose Northwestern, in part because I wanted to see Chicago. But also, I knew it was time to put distance between my parents and me, not because they were fighting, but because they were not.

During the two years that followed my graduation from Howard, Mom and Dad appeared to be in a good rhythm. They were working on home improvements, getting together with friends, and even planning a trip to Europe. My relationship with Mom improved as well. She became more of a friend than a mother, even accompanying me to parties and bars. She often had more fun than I did! For example, there was the time in 1979 Mom went with me and a group of friends to the Super Bowl in Miami. The Dallas Cowboys, the Washington team's nemesis, were playing the Pittsburgh Steelers. As it happened, we were staying at the same hotel as the Cowboys.

Our first night there, I went to bed relatively early, before midnight. But Mom stayed up. In fact, she went out. I don't know what time she returned to our room, but the next day we were on the elevator when three muscular men got on with us. "Hey, Billye," they cheerfully greeted my sixty-one-year-old mother. She flashed her winning smile. "Good luck at the game," she said with a wink. "Who was that?" I asked when we were once again alone on the elevator. "Oh, just some Dallas football players I met at the bar last night," Mom blithely answered, as if nothing extraordinary had just happened.

Indeed, by 1981 Mom and I were in a good place, and it appeared that she and Dad were as well. I no longer felt that I had to stay at home and referee or felt fearful that everything would disintegrate if I was not there. Without guilt, I boarded the plane for Chicago's O'Hare airport that summer. I was free.

Northwestern, of course, is actually in Evanston, a suburb north of Chicago. The sprawling campus gracefully banks Lake Michigan with a beach, green space, and walking paths. When I first saw the campus, I thought it was a little slice of heaven. I shared a campus dorm room with another graduate student, a business major from Philadelphia. But that did not last long. I was too much of a princess for dorm life. Sharing a room, communal space, and a bathroom was not for me. So I moved off-campus into a large apartment with another princess, a Jewish one. She was pleasant, pretty, and easy to like. But I still had to share a bathroom, so that did not work out either. I had plenty of money saved from working and gifts from relatives, plus Dad was sending me his entire Social Security check every month. Besides, I had not moved to Chicago to live in Evanston. That fall, I moved into my own place, an efficiency apartment on the city's North Side. My place, appointed with poster art, oversized pillows, and an antique desk, became the hub for a tight-knit group. We were male, female, straight, gay, Black, and white. I loved hosting, employing skills I had acquired from hanging around Jan and Wally's home. My friends took to calling me "The Queen" or "Queeny." Race never seemed to be an issue. We were simply friends trying to make it through a grueling graduate program and one of the coldest winters on record in the Windy City.

The temperature on January 16, 1982, dropped to minus 26 degrees Fahrenheit. I was awestruck to see steam rising from frozen Lake Michigan. But the cold never stopped us from making a deadline. When my car was towed for being illegally parked in a snow lane, I took care of my class assignment before retrieving it.

Even though I had always wanted to be a newspaperwoman, school advisors agreed I had the goods for TV reporting. Following their advice, I enrolled in the electronic journalism track. From the moment I held a mic in my hand and looked into a camera, I knew it was the right choice. Talking into a lens was second nature for me, like conversing with a best friend.

The year-long program was as physically demanding as it was intellectually challenging. We had to lug around heavy camera equipment all day and work to make deadlines all night. It was tough, especially for me, a spoiled twenty-four-year-old with a homesick heart. On the most exhausting days, I called home and talked to Mom for hours. This was before cheap cell phone service. The daytime, long-distance calls in the 1980s cost my parents who knows how much. But they never complained. They did whatever it took to support me.

The year I lived in Chicago was apparently a quiet one back in Washington. Not once did my parents indicate discord between them. For the first time in years, I did not hear Mom's refrain, "Your father was supposed to be a doctor" or Dad's *tsk-tsking*, "Your mother just wants to have fun." Instead, I heard from both of them, "Are you okay? How can I help? Do you need money? We're proud of you." I dared to hope my parents' marriage had mended.

In 1982, I graduated from Medill with a master of science degree in journalism, ready to begin the next chapter in my life.

8

GEORGIA

1983–1987

I made a big scene when I left for my first TV job. Just weeks after graduating from Medill I landed a post in Augusta, Georgia, a town of about one hundred thousand people. It was an industry practice for young reporters to begin their careers in small or medium-size TV markets. The ABC affiliate I would be joining was a respectable start.

Preparation for my departure was a whirlwind—finding an apartment in a town I hadn't yet seen, shopping for clothes and furnishings with Mom, mulling over advice from Dad, drinking with friends. There was an alcohol-infused going-away party that packed all three levels of a friend's townhouse. It felt like everyone I had ever known was there, even Dad, who hated crowds and parties. I was twenty-five years old and still at home with my parents. When it was time to launch, I should have been ready.

When the day arrived, the family came to Mom and Dad's to see me off. We gathered as we had for years and on hundreds of Sundays, birthdays, holidays, and just about anytime we felt the need to get together. We laughed and joked on the front porch while my boyfriend waited in the car to chauffer me to my new home.

And then it was time to leave. I swallowed. I choked. I burst into tears. "No! No! No! I don't want to go," I wailed, wrapping my fingers around the black wrought iron railing that trimmed the porch and planting my feet on the concrete floor. "No," I screamed loud enough to bring neighbors to their own porches. "No!"

My parents, at once amused and exasperated, tried to soothe me, but it was useless. My sobbing just grew louder. When persuasion failed, they tried force, prying my fingers one by one from the railing. And one by one, my fingers snapped back, gripping the wrought iron bar as if it were a life raft. I just kept crying, "I don't want to go." Janice, Bruce, and Wally stood mute, stunned by the spectacle.

It was only after I noticed the neighbors gawking that I ended the embarrassing outburst.

Dad gave me the handkerchief he always had in his pants pocket. I didn't bother to inspect the white linen cloth, gratefully using it to wipe my runny nose and dab at my ruined makeup. I finally surrendered.

My family escorted me to the car, and my boyfriend, who had been watching and waiting, started the engine. Wearied, I climbed into the passenger seat, prepared to finally say goodbye.

As the car rolled slowly down Forty-Second Street, I peered through the rear window for one last look at the people I so dearly loved. They were waving and blowing kisses. We were halfway to Georgia before I stopped crying.

• • •

The most exciting attractions in Augusta were James Brown—he was born there—and the Masters Golf Tournament. Of course, there was the routine stuff—fires, traffic accidents, and drug busts. But for a young woman looking to nourish her journalistic chops, there was not much to feast on. When a job offer came to join a friend working in nearby Savannah, I jumped at the opportunity.

A coastal city of about 130,000, Savannah was a charmer. Dripping in Southern tradition, it also had an edgy side. John Berendt's 1994 bestseller *Midnight in the Garden of Good and Evil*, also made into a Clint Eastwood film, perfectly captured the city's eccentricities. Savannah's St. Patrick's Day Parade rivals Chicago's, the day ending with beer-guzzling and music-infused parties at bars along the Savannah River.

The people were idiosyncratic too. There was a man who daily walked a leash around one of the city's lush parks—no dog, just a leash. But the town's greatest attraction was its history. It was awash in it, from the Revolutionary War to the Civil War to the civil rights movement.

Aside from the richly treed parks throughout historic downtown, there were cobblestone streets, historic homes, and centuries-old houses of worship, including the historic First African Baptist Church, first organized in 1773.

Like the tourists who converged on the quaint and quirky city, I explored Savannah's history. I spent much of my spare time visiting house museums, strolling the parks, or looking for threads to the past in secondhand shops. I even moved into one of the historic downtown homes that was converted into multifamily housing. Even then, when I thought my calling was journalism, I was drawn to another vocation, one that would not be clear for another thirty years.

Savannah thrived on tourists and the Black people who served them—hotel maids, cooks, porters, street cleaners, and trash collectors. Many African Americans were on the city's social and economic bottom, the lowest caste in the lowest caste. To be sure, there was a thriving Black middle class—educators, school principals, doctors, lawyers, government bureaucrats, and a university president. But compared with Washington, DC, their numbers were small. Many Black people lived in underserved communities plagued by crime and neglect.

I started out as a general assignment reporter, often covering events that involved the Black community, such as NAACP meetings. Eventually, I became the education reporter, sharing an award for my coverage of Savannah's public schools. I was pleased to get the education beat. At the time, I didn't want to be the Black reporter covering only "Black" issues. One of my mentors, who happened to be white, warned me against that direction. "You don't want to get pigeonholed," he said.

I would recall his advice decades later when, as Monticello's Community Engagement Officer, I explained to colleagues that Black people could discuss other topics aside from enslavement, systemic racism, and historical trauma.

In spite of my apprehensions about covering segregated issues, I thought it was my job to combat the stereotypical coverage of Black people that dominated the media. At times the newsroom chatter felt like an assault on African Americans, especially Black men. For instance, there was a practice of describing white crime suspects in detail—age, height, hair color, wardrobe, vehicle, if they had one. Not so for Black suspects. There was always a truncated description, "a Black man was seen running from the scene," or "two Black men robbed a convenience store." Those description theoretically made every Black man a suspect.

One day during newsroom banter, I couldn't take it anymore. Displaying the kind of justified indignation that would have impressed my Howard University professors, I took up the issue with the news director. Bracing for a rebuke, I steadied myself. The silver-haired, silver-tongued news director was a "good ole Southern boy," who also was Savannah's number one anchor. But he surprised me. "You're right, gal," he drawled with beguiling Southern charm and changed the practice.

Savannah was a good experience, another step toward discovering my purpose. However, after two years, I wanted to anchor the evening news. The co-anchor spot was locked in by another woman, a former model with little TV experience but lots of charisma, so I looked elsewhere. A friend recommended me for an anchor position at a fledgling ABC affiliate station in Macon, Georgia. There was a little bump in salary, a contract signing bonus, and a wardrobe allowance. I took the offer but regretted the decision almost immediately.

Macon was another midsize Southern town but lacked Savannah's charm. Nor did it have the historical gravitas that I found so stimulating. There was not much news to report either—just the usual fires, car accidents, robberies, and cats stuck in trees that were standard fare for local newscasts. Mirroring my Augusta experience, I found myself in a town and a newsroom that did not match my temperament or ambitions.

But I had friends. Like Savannah, Macon had a small but growing Black middle class. I took up with an influential clique that included an attorney and his city government-employed wife. They were about my age and seemed to have it all—a lovely suburban home, great careers, and an excellent network. She became my dearest friend in Macon. Confident that I was among the town's Black elite, I felt safe and secure—until one day between newscasts, I got a call.

"Ms. Jessup, this is officia so-and-so of the Macon Police Metropolitan Enforcement Group. Can you come down hereya to the station for questionin?"

Standing at my desk, heart and head throbbing, I asked why.

"Uh, we have reason to suspect you in a drug investigation. Ah think it would be wiize for you to come hereya raight away."

Unnerved equally by the Southern drawl and the allegation, I immediately thought of Dad. *Never let people know what you're thinking*, he always counseled. "Yes, of course, I'll come to the station," I told the officer, trying to hide my alarm.

I was no illegal drug user, let alone drug dealer. But I was afraid that would not matter. I was a news anchor, a public figure. Just being a suspect could ruin my career and—worse—shame my parents. Frightened and unsure of how to proceed, I confided in a colleague. "Call a news conference right away," he urged. I dismissed that idea without a thought and decided to face my accusers. It did not occur to me to call a lawyer, even though my closest friend was married to one. I grabbed my purse and suit jacket and rushed out the TV station's glass door to the police station—alone.

The two white officers were polite when they invited me to have a seat in a small, fluorescent-lit room. I slid into the chair, working overtime to appear relaxed and confident. In good-cop, bad-cop fashion, they laid out their case. First to speak was the bad cop: "We been watchin someone who's suspected of dealin drugs, alota drugs. Got his phone wyer tapped. Saw calls goin'in and outta youra news station. And one on youra house phone. We thought, dang, we got ouraselves a news ankah!"

Then, the good cop: "Now, Ms. Jessup, therya maight be a reasonable explanation for these calls. And if, so we'd laike to heara it." They both sat back looking like hunters who had just made a kill.

Then it was the bad cop's turn again: "Why don't eye jes play th' recordin for ya raight now." He switched on a cassette recorder resting on the desk. I recognized the upbeat voice of my girlfriend. On the other end of the line was the suspected drug dealer. I wanted to tell the officers that I did not know the woman's voice, that it belonged to a stranger. But I could not lie. I surrendered her first name, confirming what the policemen already knew. I started feeling sick to my stomach. I had just thrown my girlfriend under the bus, and now the cops were trying to get me to ID a suspected drug dealer.

"What 'bout this guy? You reknize that voice?" I did not, I told them.

"We don't know his name," said one of the officers. "Jes that he goes bye 'BoBo.'"

With those words, I began feeling the color flow back to my cheeks. I gracefully interlaced the fingers of my manicured hands, straightened my back, and leaned ever so slightly toward my interrogators. Looking from one man to the other, I settled my gaze on the bad cop.

"Do I look as if I know someone named—'BoBo'?" I challenged him with a news anchor's authority and a Jessup's imperiousness. The officers' grasp was immediate. Both dropped all pretense of professionalism and burst out laughing. No, they admitted, I did not. I walked out of the station, never to hear from the Macon Metropolitan Enforcement Group again.

While the ordeal ended quickly for me, it was just beginning for others. My friends were caught in the investigation's net, their lives and careers ruined. Like thousands of African Americans during the 1980s, they were victims of President Ronald Reagan's "war on drugs." As usual, African Americans bore the heaviest burden, with suspected Black drug users arrested at five *times* the rate of whites. Prisons started filling with African American men and women accused of drug offenses, some of them as minor as possessing a small bag of marijuana.

My girlfriend and her husband were among the big losers. They lost everything—their home, their livelihoods, their social standing, and their friendships. A political aspirant, his fall was such a big deal that it made one of the news weeklies. He ended up spending years in prison. Decades later when I was representing Monticello at an NAACP conference, I learned from someone who knew him back in Georgia that he had died in prison. And even though I had long ago put Macon behind me, I was saddened to know that a Black man who once showed great promise had such an ignominious end. I don't know what happened to his wife. I guess she just disappeared.

9

WEDDING OF THE YEAR

1987

Nothing happened in Macon without the news director knowing about it. He never said anything to me, but there was little doubt that he heard about the drug squad's newsroom call. There was an investigation of station personnel—"Bobo's" calls were going to somebody. But not, thank goodness, to me. Nonetheless, it became apparent that it was time for me to leave when the news director recommended that I step down from anchoring to become the station's "chief correspondent" in Atlanta, which included a salary cut.

I regularly received on-air job offers, but always from midsize markets, and after Macon, I was done with small cities. Atlanta, one of the country's largest TV markets, was eighty-four miles up the road. It was almost commutable, but I could not see myself driving almost three hours each day for a job. I had to get out of Macon, so I cast a net in Atlanta and came back with a decent catch—a job as a producer at one of the network affiliates.

I had been hearing about Atlanta being called "Hotlanta" by fans for years. People compared its burgeoning Black middle class and social elites to Washington's. Civil rights icon Andrew Young was mayor, and the town was a thriving "Chocolate City."

I should have felt at home, but like in DC, success in Atlanta meant breaking into the right clique, and I never did. There were three factors for my unusual failure: (1) after what happened in Macon, I had an aversion, albeit a temporary one, to hanging out with members of the Black bourgeoisie; (2) I was dating a white guy, an attorney but one with little social capital; and (3) I inadvertently insulted one of the station's anchors, a woman who was a favorite of Black Atlanta's coolest clique. It happened when I made a derisive comment about BMWs, a preferred mode of transportation among the young and hip. I thought "Bimmers" were great cars but was wed to a black Ford Cougar at the time. And in 1987 I was rebelliously rejecting the status symbols of the Black elite. Foreign cars were an easy target. (For the record, I've since been driving BMWs for decades.) I was flushed with embarrassment when the woman and I were heading to lunch and she pointed to hers.

I was not having great social or professional success. The job was not exciting. I was mostly confined to the newsroom and writing copy for the anchors to read. Sometimes I was in the field reporting, but I was no longer working in front of the camera. And I missed it.

Additionally, I was feeling pressured to get married, thanks to a report that caused a lot of consternation among Black women. The study, which made sensational headlines, claimed that thirty-year-old, college educated white women had a 20 percent chance of getting married. Stories began circulating that it was even worse for Black women, who after thirty had a better chance of getting struck by lightning than finding a husband. At the time, I was twenty-nine and unattached, having ditched the white guy I had dated for several months. I assessed that, specious or not, if the study had any degree of credibility, I had better find a suitor fast. My thirtieth birthday was just around the corner.

As usual, my luck was good. I was at a Howard University alumni party in Atlanta when I ran into a man I had dated ten years earlier when I was nineteen and he was thirty. The age difference was too much to overcome when I was a college junior, but ten years later, I was looking at Prince Charming. His name was Chuck, and he was very good-looking—a smooth mahogany complexion; dark, silky hair; and a solid, square jaw. He was not tall, five feet ten or so, but his body was well proportioned—no belly hung over his belt. People said he looked like Billy Dee Williams, but I thought he was far more handsome than the screen idol.

Chuck was from DC, divorced, and had two daughters. And the coup de grace: he was a doctor. Reacquainting ourselves at the party, we chatted and sipped champagne. I smiled confidently at him and thought, "Mom will be over the moon." We had a brief long-distance courtship that included several trips between Washington and Atlanta. Within a few months I had moved back home with my parents, and we were planning a wedding. Chuck and I had dated only ten months.

The midafternoon August ceremony was lovely. The weather was temperate for a summer day in Washington, a little overcast but no rain and unusually low humidity. Although Chuck was Lutheran and I was a nonpracticing Catholic, in deference to my parents we were married in a Catholic church. We chose St. Francis de Sales, the church affiliated with my elementary school. It seemed only fair since Mom and Dad were footing the bill.

The scent of roses and white lilies lofted through the church, packed with 250 guests. We had seven bridesmaids, including Chuck's two daughters and my sister Pat, who was my maid of honor. There were seven groomsmen, most of them doctors and lawyers. Our colors were a delicate peach and cream. The men wore morning tuxedoes, the bridesmaids, lacy, peach cocktail dresses. Mom was stunning in a peach silk and satin tea-length dress. Everything looked sumptuous, like a porcelain bowl of peach and vanilla ice cream.

Nervously clutching Dad's arm as we walked down the aisle, I wore a bare-shouldered designer ballroom-style wedding gown, layered with white tulle, pearls, and crystals and accented with a short train. My puffy hair had been trimmed and styled that morning to fit into the tulle headdress, but I refused to hide my face behind a veil. I had turned thirty two weeks before the wedding, and the accessory denoting innocence just seemed like too much.

Janice chose the music, mostly Bach, and read from 1 Corinthians 13: "Love is patient, love is kind. It does not envy, it does not boast, it is not proud. It does not dishonor others, it is not self-seeking, it is not easily angered, it keeps no record of wrongs. Love does not delight in evil but rejoices with the truth. It always protects, always trusts, always hopes, always perseveres." Pat sang a solo, "Evergreen," and a friend, an opera singer, performed Schubert's "Ave Maria." It was lovely.

Still, as I sneaked a glance at Chuck standing next to me, I was filled with trepidation. Showing off a toothy grin and the latest haircut trend, cropped close on the sides and full on top, he looked sharp in his morning suit. We appeared to be the perfect couple.

But I was not sure if I actually loved the man who was moments away from becoming my husband. Nor was I confident that he loved me. Both of us were desperate to get married—me from feeling the pressure of age, and him because he was lonely. And for him, I was also the one who got away. If there was anything Chuck hated, it was losing. So marriage was something we both wanted—and what my mother wanted too. Still, I had my doubts, and with good reason.

The night before our wedding day, Chuck had presented me with a prenuptial agreement. The subject had come up before, but I refused to sign. Our marriage should be built on trust, I argued. Besides, he didn't have *that* much money. What exactly was he trying to protect?

However, at the rehearsal dinner, he handed over a document and insisted that I sign, or the wedding was off. It was crushing. Family and friends had flown in from all over the country, my parents had forked out tens of thousands of dollars, and the wedding was just hours away. I felt coerced into doing something that seemed fundamentally wrong to me. However, the alternative—calling off the wedding—was just as unacceptable. I felt it too risky to call his bluff, so on the advice of one of my bridesmaids who was an attorney, I bitterly signed the papers. The act set the tone for our entire marriage.

I displayed no sign of the hurt churning inside as we took our vows and I became "Mrs. Doctor." In front of the church after the ceremony, I heard my favorite aunt's exuberant voice above the din of the crowd, "It was a beautiful wedding!" I thought so too. But the greatest pleasure was my parents' joy, especially Mom's. Since college, she had been living vicariously through me—attending parties, taking trips, and just for fun, sitting at the anchor desk when I was a TV reporter. She even considered skinny dipping with my buddies and me at a Hilton Head resort. I quickly put a stop to that idea. My marrying a doctor was Mom's ultimate vicarious thrill. I was living her dream.

The reception was at one of Washington's most expensive hotels in Northwest, a location where we would not have been welcome a generation earlier. Inside the grand ballroom, waiters served champagne and light hors d'oeuvres, the light from crystal chandeliers bouncing off their silver trays. And that was before a multicourse sit-down lunch for 250. The live band played a variety of music from jazz standards to R&B hits. Mom chose "Tenderly" for the first dance. It would not have been my choice, but the wedding and reception were as much her celebration as they were mine. At day's end, my beaming mother confided that her friends had said, "It was the wedding of the year."

After a Caribbean honeymoon, I moved into Chuck's townhouse

located not far from his office in the DC suburb of Silver Spring, Maryland. Meanwhile, I settled into a new job, working at Howard University's public TV station, WHMM. The news director was one of my new husband's patients. Once again, for me to get a good job, all it took was a phone call.

Within a year, we had built a new house, a four-bedroom, brick front colonial with hardwood floors, a sunken living room, and a kitchen with a center island. I danced from one spacious room to another as if I were in a disco, so excited to have a home of my own. But beneath the revelry, I also knew that for us it was just a starter house. Even as we unpacked the moving boxes, I had my eyes on one of the area's most prestigious addresses, Potomac, Maryland, the region's Beverly Hills.

It was home to many of Chuck's colleagues as well as pro athletes, CEOs, political royalty (one of the Kennedys had a house there), diplomats, TV celebrities, millionaires, and a few billionaires. The idea of one day moving to Potomac was not just an aspiration for me but for my mother as well.

Eastland Gardens, the neighborhood in which I grew up, had long ago lost its cachet. The cozy neighborhood saw its polished image dulled because of urban renewal. For example, twenty houses and buildings were lost to construction of a multilane highway. Like many urban communities, we experienced petty crime—burglaries and robberies. There was the Christmas that thieves broke in our house while we were celebrating the holiday at Jan's house. And the time Dad awakened to find boys in his bedroom. He chased them away with a baseball bat. During another confrontation, he was robbed right in front of the house! He was forced to put bars on the basement windows and bolted locks on all the doors.

Yet he refused to move. He had built that house, he said, planted apple, pear, and plum trees in the backyard, raised chickens during

World War II, and brought up five children. He still took pride in the flower and vegetable gardens he cultivated every spring and summer. The thieves were just kids, he said, assuring us that they would not be a threat for long. And he was right. Maybe it was the baseball bat that scared them away. Whatever the case, the burglaries stopped.

But that did not end Mom's desire to move. Many of her friends had relocated to desegregated neighborhoods with more status in Northwest Washington or to the city's suburbs. She had taken to calling the folks left behind in Eastland Gardens "country."

My new suburban house wasn't "country," but it wasn't Potomac, either. I knew that one day I would be moving to area code 20854 and giving my mother another vicarious thrill. It was just a matter of time.

10

A PRAYER AND A POEM

1992

Working at Howard University's public TV station was like going to a family reunion every day. Many of my colleagues were Howard alum, including a few from my class. I produced and hosted TV shows, on-air fund-raisers, and special events. Many of the guests were people I knew. Unlike the newsrooms where I had spent the first years of my career, WHMM was a very Black environment. Only one person on staff was white. The programs we produced were about Black people and Black culture. I felt at home.

The pace at Howard's public TV station was not nearly as demanding as that of commercial news, but I was still very busy. I did a little acting and modeling on the side for extra money—TV commercials; feature films, including speaking parts in *Contact* and *The Jackal*; and print jobs. I also shared an active social life with my husband. He loved going out, partying, and dancing. Sometimes we took Mom with us.

But even with a busy professional and social life, I was still drawn to the mystery surrounding my father's family. It had been twenty years since I had first heard of our connection to Jefferson. Yet I was no closer to knowing the truth. Since I was back home in DC, I started looking for new opportunities to uncover the past.

It made sense for me to talk with the oldest living member of Dad's family, his brother. Uncle Eugene had been at my wedding, but we hadn't visited him since I could remember. He and my dad had their differences and would go for years without speaking. For one thing, Dad was buttoned-up and arrow straight, while Uncle Eugene was the kind of guy who liked to have fun, lots of it. But the brothers were getting up in years, and it was time to put whatever disagreements they had to rest. Daddy and I set aside a Saturday afternoon to visit my uncle.

At seventy-six years old, Uncle Eugene was as jovial as I remembered him, with a round belly that reminded me of Santa Claus. He was also just as generous as the fictional character, always pressing coins in my hand when I was a child and twenty dollar bills as I grew older. But during my last visit with him, he gave me the best gift of all.

Relaxing in his armchair, my uncle was eager to answer questions about the mother and sisters he remembered more vividly than his younger brother did. Their mother was tall, he said, six feet tall, and slender. She had straight, dark hair and a pretty voice. "She was always in the kitchen singing," he recalled, his eyes dancing the way I imagined a real Santa's would. There was a piano in the parlor that the family played, including a brother-in-law who was a professional musician. His mother, he said, was happy, the best mother a boy could have. "My father called her his angel," Uncle Eugene said, smiling at me.

He then turned his attention to a green photo album resting on a side table. "Would you like to see some pictures?" he asked, his eyes still twinkling. Yes, would I ever! Uncle Eugene opened the book to pages of black construction paper with pictures glued on them. He turned from photos of his children when they were young to pictures of an earlier generation of Jessups, his sisters.

There were four palm-size, black-and-white portraits of angelic-faced babies. The firstborn was Louise, he said, followed by Thelma, Artie, and Cary. There was no picture of a fifth child, Helena, who died in infancy. I turned with wonderment from one page to another. Dad was just as curious. Until our visit, he had not known these pictures existed. Like the portraits of my grandparents that were for decades stored in the attic, the pictures of their dead children must have been packed away, as if hiding them would also obscure the pain of the family's losses. But Dad and his brother were getting old. I think they wanted to share their memories before it was too late.

As I continued examining the photo album, Uncle Eugene picked up from the table a small frame with the picture of a young woman dressed in a silk gown and a plumed hat the size of a silver serving platter. "This is my aunt," he said. "She used to visit before my mother died. She wanted to take your Dad, Cary, and me to live with her in New York after everyone else died, but my father did not want us to go. She was rich, you see, married to a man from Great Britain. She promised to take care of us and give us a good education. She told him if he refused her, she would never come back. He said no, and we never saw her again."

I could not believe what I was hearing. Could the woman in the picture Uncle Eugene held be the same one who, many years later, was dying in New York, the same woman a friend made a desperate call to my dad for help, the same woman described as senile, elderly— and white? Because she lived as a white person, had she cut herself off from her family, even her beloved sister's children, when she could not have her way? As a result, had she died alone? After talking with Uncle Eugene, I felt confident that the answers were "yes."

But my uncle wasn't done. He reached to the table for two more objects, small Bibles, one with an elegant wood-grain cover, the other bound in black leather. "This one belonged to my father's mother," he said handing the wood-grain book to me. "And this one," he continued, "belonged to my mother." I inspected both books, handling them with care reserved for the most fragile of objects. One Bible preserved my grandfather's meticulous handwriting, "To my mother, Virginia." The other carried a date, 1821, and the initials "D:T." engraved in gold. The book was practically ancient. "It was passed down to my mother from her mother," said my uncle.

They were precious heirlooms that also conjured speculation. Could the initial "T" have anything to do with Thomas, I wondered, forgetting that one of my grandmother's names was Taylor. My uncle had no idea. In fact, he knew less about the Jefferson family lore than Dad.

However, he did promise to bequeath to me both Bibles, the old photo album, and the picture of his aunt. When Uncle Eugene died the following year, his children honored his promise.

A few people from my parents' old Deanwood neighborhood were at my uncle's funeral, among them a woman named America Crew Nelson. Miss America, as some folks called her, was in her eighties with bright eyes and cocoa-colored skin. She was short, and not round, but not slender either. She reminded me of a Russian babushka nesting doll. Miss America, who liked to talk and had a reputation for having a sharp and creative mind, had known three generations of Jessups—my grandparents', my father's, and mine. Four, if you counted Jan's kids.

She was all hugs and warm smiles at McGuire's Funeral Home, where the family was saying our last goodbye to Uncle Eugene. She pulled me close to her and said with characteristic ebullience, "I have something for you," and handed over several lined pages of hand-written notes. I thanked her and tucked the papers in my purse to read later. "It's a poem about your family," she said, beaming with pride. "Your grandfather, your grandmother, all the Jessups. They were great people." She was irresistible, and so was her poem.

I found a secluded hiding place and unfolded several pages of careful penmanship. The title, "The Silent Great: An Ode to the Jessup Family," was captivating. Iambic dimeter, it was not. It was better, for Miss America's poem was more than verse; it was about my family's character and a lost generation of Jessups. She even alluded to the Jefferson connection, which she claimed to have heard from her childhood best friend, one of my long-departed aunts.

The five Jessup girls had been gone for seventy years, yet Miss America remembered them and the rest of the family adoringly. They must have been impressive—my grandfather, "a leader of men," as Daddy always said; my grandmother, "an angel," according to Uncle Eugene; and the girls, lovely, as described by Miss America.

With new bits and pieces of data—the Bible, photos, and the poem—and the memories of the elders, I was making more progress than I had in twenty years. Still, no one knew how the family was related to Jefferson or whether it was even true. It was pretty much as Dad had said when I first queried him years earlier, "That's what they say." At this point, I didn't know what steps to take next. Besides, I had more immediate concerns demanding my attention.

11

AN ODE TO THE JESSUPS

1901–1926

America Nelson's poem was a gift to our family, one of remembrance and of love. Her recollection of my grandmother and aunts fired my imagination, as I tried to envision them vibrant and alive. I will forever be grateful to Miss America and to her family for sharing her artistry, her heart, and her radiant memory.

The Silent Great:
An Ode to the Jessup Family

It is trite to say that an Ode is written to persons in praise,
That to others is tribute and song their voices might raise.
But this Ode to Jessups is sung from the heart,
because fond memories from the writer will never depart.

There was Louise, eldest child of the lot,
Whom Janice today looks alike as if it were a planned plot.
We do not this moment see flowers at her feet.
But Louise was pretty, and very neat.

Whenever one sees Janice with the beauty that nature did her endow,
One can think only of Louise and to this, take a deep bow.
Louise was gracious and very sweet,
since she used good manners wherever one she did meet.

Now let us think of Thelma, the second child of the group,
whose long curly hair behind her eyeglasses did loop.
Always ladylike, attractive, quiet and serene,
her behavior was never base or mean.

Artie came next, and because with me she did play,
Sometimes her best behavior had a delay.
If any descendants, as children acted "fresh,"
maybe from Artie and me they inherited,
because we were that way . . . with zest!
Thelma and Louise were of the dating age, as we know.
Then Artie and I, mentally, began dating too!

Artie would find out the name of one beau,
and this would mentally be her love, you know.
Then she would get from the other sister, the name of another,
and he would in my thoughts be mine,
but not as a brother.

Artie and I never spoke of this
in a manner loud and bold.
And I hope as an angel, she forgives me,
now that the story I have told.
Because those big sisters, quiet and demure,
never guessed that from their innocence,
our "freshness" grew.

When in the classroom, we did our work well.
And no one to us the answers ever had to tell.

With the proper attitude of good breed,
our eyes met only to get the laughter
the thought we did need.
But, little did we know that at the age of eleven,
my dear Artie would be going to Heaven.

At the age of eleven, in the eighth grade,
our minds were overwrought,
because preparing for high school
was our only thought.

Artie was ill for a long, long time,
but often, I went to visit her with a rhyme.

Then, once a week during my days of woe,
I was allowed to walk Artie to school,
so she could hear and see
all that she wished to know.

Then, one day when I was feeling forlorn,
I was thinking of Louise and Thelma,
who long ago had passed on.
This was the day I knew Artie would leave,
and for her already, I had begun to grieve.

Parents, neighbors, faculty and peers
extended empathy to keep me calm and without tears.
Like a princess, I was treated at home and at school,
which helped to keep me pleasant and cool.

To the funeral everyone in the class did go.
My assigned seat by the teacher gave me strength to grow.
Handkerchiefs large or small were used by one and all.

From hindsight, I can truly state,
well do I remember the very date.
With my pursuit of visits, to keep Artie in shape.
I witnessed her suffering that she could not escape.
Then God had called her with her "Humanity of Love,"
to live beyond the skies of above!

Cary was the in next line;
so cute and very fine. With hair curly and brown,
she had natural pink cheeks and wore nary a frown.
My sister Estella and Cary were best friends,
which lasted to Cary's very end.

Whenever I see Gayle, always at her best,
I immediately think of Cary, who is now at rest.

Beside the sisters, one remembers two brothers.
Ever smiling Eugene and another.
Dear Family, not just because you are descendants of Thomas Jefferson
you should walk with pride you know.
But your own aristocracy does surely show.

We have not mentioned the other brother Cedric by name.
But he was the youngest of the family,
and he remains the same.
However, he was not too young for the best to select,
because into the highly esteemed Green Family,
queenly Billye for a wife he did get!

Now, the love in the Jessup Family was dignified and rare.
and to what others thought, they did not care.
The mother, Eva, being tall and fair
easily accented the beauty and her long, straight hair.
The father in his stature, stout and round,
with a loyalty to his unprecedented and sound.

The family as a whole was benevolent and caring,
because to those in need, they did their sharing.

Let us not forget Aunt Peachie
who would with this family stay,
rather than with other relatives or friends
who were not far away.

The nephew and cousin Arthur,
handsome and tall, in the family was loved by all.

A superior good behavior showed
that the Jessups did pray.
Since to the Catholic Church every Sunday
they were on their way.

The Christian parents have long ago gone
to their Heavenly home,
leaving the religiously trained descendants happy
in Earthly homes of their own.

Sincerely,
A. C. Nelson
1992

12

MARRIAGE

I should have been happy married to Prince Charming and playing Mrs. Doctor. But it did not take long for fissures to appear. Because of the prenup, our marriage was built on a shaky foundation, so even small incidents could cause a tremor. And when it came to money, we did not function the way I thought a married couple should. He managed the budget, doling out whatever funds he thought were necessary for household purchases. On the other hand, the money I made, which was not much, given my working at a college public TV station, was mine to spend as I chose.

Admittedly, the creature comforts were persuasive. The house was nice, and so was the white convertible in the driveway that he helped me buy. And my parents were happy. I kept hoping that would be enough and that eventually, I would forgive the prenup debacle. But the rehearsal dinner episode stuck to our marriage like leeches sucking blood.

My parents' marriage, on the other hand, appeared to be thriving. Of course, I was not living at home, but they were not ones to keep their disagreements to themselves.

They were probably getting along because Mom was approaching seventy and slowing down. She still haunted the malls almost every night, lunched with friends, and attended club meetings. She even performed with a dance ensemble, a chorus line of spunky senior women called the "Funtastics." Costumed in fringed skirts, feather boas, and top hats, the ladies were a hit at community centers, senior citizen homes, and social events around the city. But she was not traveling as much, and most Sundays she was at home for the family's weekly get-together. On those days, she was especially happy to see Chuck.

Mom really liked him. He was everything *she* had wanted in a husband—social, gregarious, a doctor. Dad liked him too. They were both fans of the Howard University and the Washington football teams. However, Dad also understood when I started sharing with him my disillusionment with the marriage. He knew about the prenup and did not like what it portended. Nonetheless, his advice was dispassionate. Marriage is a business arrangement, he told me. Chuck was looking out for his interests, and I should look out for mine. "You never know what the future will bring," he cautioned. It was not exactly romantic, but my astute father recognized that my marriage was one of pragmatism. He advised me to try to make it work. "Chuck is a decent fellow," he said, even though he was not the ideal spouse for me.

I usually heeded my father's advice, and this time was no exception. But the marriage was not easy. My resentment simmered at a low temperature, always ready to heat up and boil over at even the smallest provocation. It could be over what to watch on television, or where to have dinner, or more seriously, what friends I could have. But the stickiest thorn was the prenup. Even after five years of marriage when he tore the thing in half, I was unable to forgive or forget.

Still, I stuck with the marriage. My parents were my role models, an acrimonious marriage, my norm. Chuck was not happy either, but having been divorced once already, he did not want another failed marriage. We committed to persevering.

After a few years, we left our first house, the cookie-cutter suburban brick colonial, for the community I (and Mom) had long set my sights on: Potomac. We moved into a custom-built five-thousand-square-foot tan-colored stucco house with a red tile roof, marble floors and bathrooms, and the model train room Chuck had always wanted. The house also featured an elegant curved staircase, black granite kitchen countertops, and a chandelier that hung from a two-story ceiling. Changing bulbs was no problem, as the fixture included an electronic lift that lowered it to ground level. I thought the house was an architectural masterpiece.

I was several months pregnant when we moved into our new home. The baby I was carrying was no accident. I was already thirty-four years old when a dream convinced me that it was time to conceive. During a midday nap, I had a vision of my aged maternal grandmother, Christine Green, that was so real I could smell her arthritis cream. I barely remembered my grandmother, who had died when I was four years old, but in the dream, I recognized her soft, grey hair and narrow, mud-brown face.

She was clearly on a mission, as her remarks were limited to a single directive. "Hurry up and have that baby," she said. "What do you mean, Grandma?" I asked, mildly mystified at having a conversation with a dead relative I barely knew. "I have to go, child," she chortled. "Just hurry up and have that baby." Who was I to say no to my grandma, even though it was just in a dream?

Move-in day was predictably hectic, but fun. Mom and Dad came over to help unpack the kitchen boxes. I had several sets of china, one of many small indulgences, like the Waterford crystal, fine art, travel art, seashells and decorative glass, bowls, and vases I enjoyed collecting. We didn't have much furniture—certainly not for a great big house—but there were plenty of objets d'art.

Mom spent a lot of time with us, even before we moved into the new house. In fact, for a few days, she moved into the new house *with* us. It was after a fight with Dad. She showed up in a cab, with her suitcases, a small plant my brother had given her, and a deep frown. To believe that my parents' squabbling was past was too good to be true.

"I'm not going back," she declared and proceeded to make herself comfortable in one of our bedrooms. To his credit, Chuck did not object. But I was worried. I didn't want to find myself back in the middle of my parents' vitriolic marriage, especially when I had my own fragile relationship to attend to. However, it turned out my fretting was unnecessary. After three days, Dad showed up to take her home. She left smiling as if no disruption had occurred, blowing a kiss as they pulled out of the driveway.

• • •

The stomach pains started at 1:00 a.m., but no one, including my doctor husband, thought it was labor. The baby wasn't due for two weeks, and I had just stopped working the day before. I had not even begun to "nest," the process of getting the house settled for the new addition.

We were so confident that the gnawing I felt was from the crab cakes I'd had for dinner that I went back to sleep. The next morning, Chuck and his daughters, who were staying with us for the summer, left town for a funeral. I was alone, and my husband was 124 miles away in Philadelphia when it became apparent that what I was experiencing was no stomach ache.

I tried not to panic, but it didn't help that Mom was hospitalized for treatment of a blood clot. I called my sister, who confirmed that I was likely having labor pains and advised that I call my doctor. Then, I called Dad. "Don't worry, Sweetie," he said. "I'm on my way."

In fewer than thirty minutes, he was letting himself into the house with the spare key. He helped me dress and collect my bag, assuring me all the while that everything would be okay. Daddy, who unbeknownst to me at the time was being treated for prostate cancer, steadied me as we walked down the curved staircase to the marble foyer and to his car. He gave me a photo album filled with fresh family pictures to distract me as we drove to the hospital. The ploy worked for a while, but as the pain increased, I closed my eyes and prayed.

Mom was being treated at the same hospital and was almost fully recovered. She met us there, dressed not in a hospital gown, but in casual street clothes. The nurse wheel-chaired me into a private suite—one of the privileges of being married to a staff doctor—and the wait began.

Jan and Wally arrived while someone tracked down Chuck and his daughters. When they arrived by late afternoon, the suite was so full, it felt like a family reunion. But as evening approached, the doctor asked everyone to leave, except Mom and Chuck. The wait, he said, was about to end.

Charles Jessup Franklin arrived at 5:52 p.m. on June 27, 1992. He weighed six pounds and was nineteen inches long. Aside from the drama of not knowing if his dad would make it back in time, it was an easy birth. After a few days we took our baby home, hopeful that he would bring the stability that we both wanted to our marriage.

For the first few months, our little family thrived. Chuck, who usually worked well past 7:00 p.m., arrived home in time for dinner and to put "Little Chuckie" to bed. He sat in a rocker and read *Milk and Cookies* to our baby every evening. Observing his love for our child made it easier to forget the indignities that had once threatened our marriage.

However, with the baby new issues emerged, this time about child-rearing. I was more lenient. For example, I gave in to Chuckie's wailing when he was left alone in his crib at bedtime. Much to his dad's disapproval, I let him sleep in the bed with us.

As our baby grew, so did the conflicts over how to discipline him. The tension was on full display at an Episcopal church christening. Chuck and I were the godparents of a friend's newborn baby boy. By this time, Chuckie was three, old enough I thought to accompany us to the altar. However, it was not long before he became restless. He squirmed and fidgeted and finally dropped to the floor for a hearty roll. I was amused. Chuck was mortified. Neither of us hid our feelings from the congregation.

Chuck practically dragged the child from the church, insisting that he be punished for what I considered normal toddler behavior. If anyone was to blame, it was me for allowing Chuckie to join us at the altar. I stopped Chuck from imposing the hour-long timeout he planned to inflict on our three-year-old son. I might have lost the prenup battle, but I was not going to lose the one over how to best raise our child.

Even as the marriage strained, I started looking for another house because I believed the one we had was no longer suitable. In fact, I thought it was dangerous. Though elegant, the house was built near high-voltage electrical wires. They were eyesores I was at first willing to tolerate to move into the zip code I desired and a house we could easily afford. "I'm not going to be house poor," Chuck said, turning down possibilities in prettier but more expensive communities.

However, now debunked news reports from the mid-1990s that the electromagnetic field the wires generated caused cancer changed my mind about the unsightly wires. If they were a threat to our health, we had to move. Besides, our house was in a less-than-desirable location near a busy street and a strip mall. I wanted a home with a big yard for Chuckie in a quiet community, perhaps gated. Chuck resisted, but I was going to have my way.

Within a few months, I found the perfect place—a Potomac golf course community with horse stables, a country club, parks, and swimming pools. For a girl from Eastland Gardens, it was paradise. I persuaded my husband that the flat, one-acre lot on which we would build our next house offered the best prospect for our marriage's success.

The problem was that he said he didn't have the money for the down payment. His resources were tied up in his practice, the stock market, and the house we had purchased only three years earlier. So I sought the funds from another source—my parents.

Without hesitation, they wrote me a check for $50,000, which I handed over to the builder. I promised to pay them back as soon as Chuck and I were able. Soon after, I was watching the construction of another new home—one, though capacious, I hoped would feel cozier than the marble palace next to the high-voltage wires. The five-bedroom, redbrick colonial had a hip roof, burgundy shutters, a double front door, and a three-car garage. Gone were the marble floors and bathrooms, vaulted ceilings, curved staircase, and other luxury appointments. This house, with its honey-colored hardwood floors, wall-to-wall carpeting, and center staircase, had a warm, welcoming aura. Unlike our first Potomac house, this one felt like a family home, not a feature for *Architectural Digest*. The conditions seemed right to preserve our marriage—we had a bright little boy, a family-friendly community, an unpretentious house, and a good nanny. But nothing worked.

When Chuck balked at how to pay my parents back, I knew the marriage was doomed. He wanted Mom to join him in a multilevel-marketing scheme selling vitamins to pay off the debt. Mom, always willing to try something new, was game, but I would not hear of it. Our fights reached a new level. Finally, after almost ten years of marriage, I was ready to quit.

Chuck, ever the fighter, tried to dissuade me. So did my parents and every close member of my family, even Bruce, who I always thought didn't like my husband. But I was determined.

I had to break the mold. I did not want to end up like my parents.

We negotiated what I thought was a reasonable settlement, including paying back the money we owed my parents. We had joint custody of Chuckie (who would soon insist on being called Charles); however, he lived with me and spent every other weekend and summers with his dad. I also insisted that Chuck take out an insurance policy with our son as the beneficiary. Chuck had longevity in his family—two grandparents lived to age one hundred—but I was not taking chances. I did not want anything to happen to Chuck, but if it did, insurance would guarantee that our son's education would be paid for. And if I had learned nothing else after living forty years, it was that the future was unpredictable.

13

DEATH ALWAYS COMES IN THREES

2002–2006

Whatever my mother felt she lacked in social status, she made up for with an abundance of confidence. She even compared herself, without irony, to royalty—and on national television. The declaration came after Mom met Queen Elizabeth when the queen and Prince Philip visited Washington in 1991. While there was the usual pomp, including a dazzling White House state dinner, there were also sidebar trips. On the queen's itinerary was a visit to an affordable housing project in a less, shall we say, regal section of the city. Mom, because of her community work, was part of the delegation greeting Her Royal Highness.

Interviewed by network TV after the event, Mom, always immaculately dressed, quipped of the queen that she might be extraordinary, "but then, so am I." That was not bravado. Mom had a very high opinion of herself. She had lived through a lot, including the loss of a son to institutionalization and a disappointing marriage. Even though she had not finished college, she managed to accumulate a modest fortune, independent of Dad. She owned a three-unit apartment building and had an impressive stock portfolio. My mother was not intimidated by anyone, not even royalty.

So when Mom started showing signs of mental decline in her early eighties, the family was not sure how to handle it. Especially Dad.

I was living in a place I had purchased not far from Charles's school, a private institution I believed would stimulate his obvious intellect and inquisitiveness. We were still in Potomac, but no longer in a grand house. In fact, the small collection of townhomes that made up our development was sardonically called "divorce court."

I was still acting and modeling, but the bulk of my income was from a publicly funded training program I had created teaching TV production to at-risk young adults. My work schedule offered plenty of flexibility to care for my son and my aging parents. Still, I was not prepared for the call from Dad one afternoon in 2001.

He was almost frantic. Thirty thousand dollars had gone missing from a joint account he shared with Mom. Getting answers from her was impossible. She could not seem to grasp what he was talking about. It was the first time I saw my dad unsure of what to do. He was eighty-six years old, and although his mind was sharp, serious illnesses, including cancer, shingles, and surgery after a ruptured appendix, had left him physically weakened. He did not have the energy to investigate what happened to the money or to confront bank officials who would be able to tell him. So he turned to me. I promised him I would take care of everything.

Dressed in my best black suit and with my sternest expression, I made a trip to their suburban bank. A middle-age white man escorted me into his office and tried to explain away what had happened to my parents' money. He had persuaded Mom to invest in a long-term plan that was plainly ill-suited for elderly people. It seemed obvious that he was taking advantage of my mother. By this time, she was repeating herself and moving with the rigidity of an arthritic body. Even for people who did not know her, it was plain that she was failing mentally and physically. The bank officer couldn't have missed it.

I accused the man of preying on my elderly, Black parents and threatened go public with my media connections. My charge was not unfounded. The history of the unscrupulous taking advantage of African Americans was as old as the nation. From enslavement to share-cropping to lower wages to higher interest rates, too many white people saw Blacks as prey, minnows in a vast ocean. I was not going to allow my parents and their savings to be gulped up. The man didn't know whether I was bluffing, so he took no chances. Their funds were immediately released.

However, our problems were just beginning. As Mom's mental capacity continued to decline, so did her physical health. Some days she was in so much pain that she couldn't walk. Yet she never complained. In fact, my mother, who was usually disarmingly glib, became as quiet as a cloistered nun.

During a visit to their house, I noticed that she was drinking an unusual amount of water and eating a lot of sweets. I think that Dad, who was dealing with his own health issues, was in a state of shock. It must have been hard to believe that his wife of more than sixty years—the "pistol"—was failing so rapidly. I knew it was time for an intervention.

I took Mom to see my doctor, who diagnosed her with diabetes and spinal stenosis, a painful deterioration of the spinal cord. He also recommended we see a specialist, someone who dealt with Alzheimer's disease.

Even though I knew Mom was having memory issues, I did not want to hear those dreaded words. In fact, for a long time, Dad and my siblings denied what was evident. There were so many signs, such as the time Mom got lost driving to my house. Or when she refused to come indoors from the front porch even as night descended. Or when she allowed her best St. John knits to pile up, soiled, on the floor of her room like little dirt mounds. We did not want to believe that our vivacious mother was the victim of such a cruel disease.

However, the specialist's exam confirmed my doctor's suspicions. Mom had dementia. He was confident of the diagnosis because his own mother was suffering from the same illness. She no longer recognized him, he said, before putting his head on his desk and weeping.

It was up to me to give Dad the horrific news. He held steady as I explained the experience we had in the doctor's office and what the prognosis meant. There were some meds that might help for a while, but eventually Mom would lose her memory and control of her bodily functions. She would need more care than Dad would be able to give her.

Confronted with a problem he never expected, Dad proposed two possibilities: we could hire someone to care for Mom at home, or we could put her in a nursing home. Of the latter, I responded "over my dead body," so we decided to give in-home care a try. When that didn't work out—Dad was doing more work than the caregiver— there was only one other option. I brought Mom to live with me. I found a good caregiver—an easy task in wealthy Potomac—and cut back my business activities. With Mom on one end and ten-year-old Charles on the other, there wasn't much time for anything or anyone else. I was sandwiched.

But I didn't mind. I loved having Mom with us, and so did Charles. When she felt up to it, we took her to dinner and for car rides. However, we never took her back home, believing that would have confused her. Sometimes, she showed sparks of her old self and we laughed like teenage girls. But too often, she was in a zombielike state, having little concept of place or time.

One snowy afternoon, she wondered how her mother was doing "over on Gault Place," her childhood address. There was no explaining that her mother had been dead for forty years.

That was in 2003, a tough year made worse by the untimely death of my brother-in-law, Wally Terry. He died unexpectedly of a rare disorder that causes inflammation of the blood vessels. The disease is treatable if caught in time, but if not, it is fatal. Unfortunately for our family, Wally's was not caught in time. He died at the age of sixty-five.

Even as we mourned Wally's death, we had to address another concern—Dad. He was living alone in the house and unhappy about it. The family decided the best thing to do was sell the house and move him and my mother into a complex designed for senior living. We found a brand-new, two-bedroom condo in Northern Virginia, with a den and an enclosed balcony; sold their house; and got rid of much of their furniture. Dad bought a Cadillac pretty much just to watch it on the parking lot below his sixth-floor apartment. In 2004, my parents were reunited after being separated for more than a year. For a while, they were content.

They had lived in their new condo for eighteen months when I got a call from their caregiver. It was two days after we had brought in a new year—2005. "Mr. Jessup is in a lot of pain," she said. "I think you should come over right away." By the time I got there, an ambulance had taken Dad to the hospital. As we had done too often recently, Janice, Bruce, and I convened in the emergency waiting room. The news was not good. Dad had an intestinal blockage that required immediate surgery. At age eighty-nine, he was frail, but the doctor was reassuring. He promised to do all he could for our father.

The surgery was successful, and we were soon able to visit Dad as he recovered in the hospital's intensive care unit. He looked thin and whiter than ever, but he was alive. Pat flew in from LA, and my sisters and I made the hospital a daily vigil. Even Dad's surgeon commented on the loving presence of his patient's "three beautiful daughters."

Over the next six weeks, Dad seemed to rebound. He refused to eat the hospital food, so Jan made him soup. He struggled to feed himself, so we fed him. He left the hospital for a rehabilitation facility and continued to show signs of recovery. Pat brought flowering plants like the ones he once had cultivated in his backyard on Forty-Second Street and set them at the foot of his bed.

We asked whether he wanted a priest, and he said no. A devout Catholic his entire life, Dad might have lost his faith toward the end. If so, the child abuse scandals that had plagued the church since 1990 were to blame.

We began to consider how to care for two ailing parents once Dad was released. Would they stay in their condo? Should they move in with one of us? Even as we fretted over what to do, Dad was making up his own mind.

He stopped eating. But even as his body weakened, his mind remained sharp. He was in command as he neared his last breath, ordering us to leave the room as he felt death approach. "Go, go," were his barely audible words. He did not want us watching as his life ebbed. My father, who always kept his own council, chose to die alone.

On February 15, 2005, six weeks after surgery, Cedric Benedict Jessup departed the Earth. He was three months shy of his ninetieth birthday. One of the last things he said to me was, "I'm proud of all of my children."

• • •

The family was now enduring two deaths in as many years. For me, Dad's was a devastating loss. Since I was a little girl, I had depended upon his strength and steadfastness. There was no problem my dad could not solve, no question he could not answer. I struggled to imagine what the future would be like without him. But once again, there was little time to mourn.

My mother needed more attention than ever. We were not sure if she could fully comprehend that her partner of sixty-six years was gone. "Cedric must be at church," she said, noticing that his new leather easy chair was unoccupied. No, Dad has passed away, we told her. For a moment, she looked stricken. Then, a short time later, the scene repeated. "Cedric must be at church." We finally stopped explaining that her husband would not be coming home.

Once again, I brought Mom to live with me. When my parents moved to Virginia, I had bought a house to live closer to them. It was another oversize five-bedroom, which I shared with Charles and my new beau.

His name was Jack White Jr., and he was a retired *TIME* magazine correspondent and columnist. The first time I saw him was on TV when he was a panelist on the 1984 vice-presidential debate with Representative Geraldine Ferraro and Vice President G. H. W. Bush. I was a young reporter in Savannah and quite infatuated with the urbane Black man shooting questions to the candidates. From the first moment I saw Jack on television, I had begun to imagine what it would be like to be his wife.

We finally met in 2000. I was touring Howard University's TV station, my former employer, with my production students. He was at the station taping a talk news show. I gasped when I spotted him— "There's Jack White." I could not let the opportunity to meet my idol slip by, so I decided to introduce myself. Approaching him with my hand extended for a firm shake, I looked him right in the eye (as Dad had taught me) and said, "Jack White, my name is Gayle Jessup, and I think you're really smart."

I don't remember what he said, just how he looked—flabbergasted. Later, once we became an item, he told me that my introduction was "brash." It was a compliment. We were smitten from the moment we met; however, both of us were already committed. (He was married, and I was engaged.) Adding to the awkwardness of a potential future was his acquaintance with my first husband. They were high school classmates.

But after a series of chance meetings—at movie theaters, soccer games, and restaurants—it seemed that fate was pushing us together. Four years after we met, we had our first romantic date. We chose Monticello.

In the many years that I had talked about my family's kinship to Jefferson, I still hadn't visited the Virginia mountain plantation turned museum. It got in my head that I wanted my first visit to the place that I had long dreamed of to be with the man whom I had long dreamed of.

We rendezvoused in Charlottesville on a sunny Saturday afternoon in March 2004. Jack arrived first, eagerly waiting for me at Michie Tavern, a colonial-era restaurant just down the road from Monticello. After a buffet lunch of fried chicken, green beans, stewed tomatoes, and peach cobbler, we headed up the mountain.

I was flushed with excitement when I laid eyes on the house. It bore all the elegance and grace I had always imagined. The red brick, the white columns, the domed roof—it was picture perfect. When we entered the "Entrance Hall" filled with artifacts from the Lewis and Clark expedition, I wanted to shout, "I'm here!" In fact, in a less conspicuous way, I did.

As we left the hall and entered a smaller room where Jefferson's daughter Martha had taught her eleven children, the guide unintentionally offered an irresistible opportunity. Some historians, she said, believed that Jefferson and his "slave," Sally Hemings, had several children. She did not dwell on the subject, but I did.

My hand shot into the air. "I'm related to Thomas Jefferson and Sally Hemings," I announced, displaying the brashness that Jack admired. The guide, however, barely acknowledged me. Neither did other members of our tour. No one seemed interested. As we walked quietly to the next room, I thought to myself, "You'll believe me one day."

A few months after our Monticello visit, Jack moved in with me.

Our house felt as busy as a bus depot. Someone was always coming and going. Mom had a room and full bath on the main floor. Her caregiver arrived early every day and stayed late. Twelve-year-old Charles and his buddies made happy noises playing games and watching TV. My family—Jan, Bruce, and their kids—were regular guests. The housekeeper was there weekly. We also had animals—Charles's cat, Jack's dog, birds, fish, and any uninvited creature that might sneak indoors.

Sometimes, a glimmer of the old mom shone through, especially with Jack. He was good-looking, like Dad, in that racially ambiguous way. Except Jack was tanner and had a headful of dark hair. Mom could never resist flirting with a handsome man. When Jack came in the room, her eyes sparkled and her lips puckered, as if she were ready for a kiss. I couldn't help but think of the teenage girl Dad told me about who put her straw in his milkshake so they could drink from the same glass. Inside her shrinking brain was that enthralling girl. Something about Mom, no matter her declining condition, was still a "pistol."

Jack and I were married on October 1, 2005, five years after we met. It was a civil affair in front of the courthouse in the quaint colonial town of Leesburg, Virginia. Unlike my first wedding, the only guests were close family and friends. Afterward, we had a reception at our house for about fifty people.

It was a great party with lots of champagne and good food—shrimp and grits, ham biscuits, salad, and a yellow-and-white, triple-layered cake baked by Charles.

Pat sang, as she had at my first wedding, but this time instead of the reserved "Evergreen," it was a boisterous rendition of "And I Am Telling You I'm Not Going" from *Dreamgirls*. I joined her. We were the hit of the party.

Mom, who loved to dance so much, was locked in a wheelchair. Nonetheless, she clearly enjoyed herself, smiling and rocking her head to the music's rhythm. She was living, quite literally, in the moment. She was no longer asking about Dad, or about anyone for that matter. She recognized those closest to her—my siblings, Charles, and of course, me. But when Jan's granddaughter came to visit, a child she knew well, Mom asked, "Who is that pretty little girl?"

Throughout the holidays of 2005, she seemed to be doing okay, getting a little tipsy when Pat, who was visiting, slipped her a glass of eggnog and delighting over a champagne-filled chocolate candy. But as the one-year anniversary of Dad's death approached, her health visibly deteriorated. Her hospice counselor advised that we get prepared. "Dying is as beautiful as being born," she explained in a voice trained to comfort.

It was approaching mid-February, and forecasters were predicting several inches of snow. I called Pat and suggested she get a flight from LA as soon as conditions allowed. Bruce and Jan were on notice that our mother could go soon. Meanwhile, Mom hadn't left her bed and was eating very little. She stopped talking completely.

The evening of February 12, I sat alone beside her as she lay in her bed, her arms occasionally extended upward, as if she were reaching for something or someone. Worried, I called the hospice nurse. "She's seeing loved ones who have already passed away," the nurse tried to soothe. "They're calling for her. It won't be long now."

I took a deep breath and sat back in the chair. Her favorite, Frank Sinatra, piped through the speakers in her room. When "My Way" came on, she frowned, her eyes visibly darting back and forth. She could hear. I yelled to Jack to change to the next song. It was Antônio

Jobim's "Wave," a tune Mom and I loved. She stopped frowning and soon dozed off. I went to bed after midnight. Pat managed to get a flight and would be arriving in the morning. The family would be together the next day to be with Mom.

But around 4:00 a.m., I woke up and sat upright in a move so jarring it startled Jack. "I have to be with Mom," I said, and bolted downstairs. As I entered the dimly lit room, I could see Mom's chest moving. Her breaths were rapid and shallow. I stared at her for several minutes and let her know I was there before going to the kitchen for a cup of tea. By the time I returned, Mom's breathing had slowed. And then stopped.

There was no death rattle, just silence. And her face seemed to collapse before my very eyes. I stared at the shell that just a second before had been my mother, then called upstairs for Jack. "I think Mom just died," I said, almost as if I were announcing that someone was at the door. It was important to remain steady, for myself and for my son, who adored his grandmother. I didn't want to upset him.

Jack came downstairs, looked at his watch, and made note of the date. It was February 13, 2006, almost exactly one year to the date that Dad had died—February 15.

For all the fighting, all the recriminations, all the disappointments, my parents stayed together until death. They were married sixty-seven years and died within a year of each other, separated by one day, February 14, Valentine's Day.

PART TWO

PART TWO

14

RICHMOND

2006

Months after Mom died, I did what I swore I would never do again—I left the Washington, DC, area. There were many reasons for me to leave my beloved hometown. The main one was Jack's new job teaching at Hampton University, in Hampton, Virginia. He was making the three-hour commute from DC several days a week, and sometimes not coming home at all. I hadn't waited all those years for my dream man to be separated from him so much of the time. So we decided to move closer to his job.

Hampton, while invitingly located near Atlantic Ocean beaches and the Chesapeake Bay, was for me a great place to visit but not to live. Its population was small—about 135,000 people—and too far away from DC. I wanted to be able to get home pretty quickly on a regular basis. Our best option, we decided, was Richmond. The state's capital city was a mere hundred miles from Washington, had a metropolitan area population of more than one million, and housing in charming neighborhoods far more affordable than those in the Washington area. As a bonus, it was only seventy miles east of Monticello.

The house we purchased, a two-story midcentury modern design with as many windows as walls, was in a leafy Richmond suburb. Not as posh as Potomac, but comfortable. Built on a wooded hill, the house was open and filled with light. The floor-to-ceiling windows looked out onto lush treetops. The place felt like a luxurious tree house. We hoped the in-ground pool that came with the large back-yard would help Charles make new friends. The house was more in line with my taste than the other places I'd lived. We looked forward to moving in.

In spite of my eagerness to begin a new life, I held back tears as Charles, Jack, and I stuffed the car with what we considered essential—suitcases filled with clothes and boxes of framed pictures and photo albums. Moving vans would bring the rest. DC the Cat, the only pet who was still part of the family, occupied the backseat with Charles. So did a box with Mom's ashes. Dad's cremated remains were preserved in a hand-painted box at Jan's house.

"It's very strange, Gayle, the way you carry your mother's remains around with you," Jack commented as we packed the car. It was, ad-mittedly, a little weird. But having Mom's ashes with me was comfort-ing. Earlier that summer, I had taken the metal container—about the size of a shoe box—with us on a weeklong Rehoboth Beach vacation.

As we drove down Interstate 95 and past familiar landmarks—a huge discount mall, Quantico Marine base, and the National Mu-seum of the Marine Corps—we chatted about our new home. Charles would be starting ninth grade at a prep school less than one mile from the house. I would be getting to know parents and the community. And Jack, whose job at Hampton was the principal rea-son we decided to move, would be looking for work.

By the time we moved to Richmond, he and Hampton had agreed to a parting of the ways. The reason he left was of no consequence to me. What mattered was that we had upended our lives unnecessarily. However, once he decided to leave the university, it was too late for us to reverse course. The house was purchased, and the school had accepted Charles. There was no turning back. Although as we drove onto Richmond's main drag, Boulevard Avenue, in May 2006 and surveyed our surroundings, I wanted to.

We entered a part of the city we had not seen before—one that might have influenced our decision to move there. Cruising down Boulevard, we rotated our necks from right to left, like oscillating fans. On one side of the street were vacant lots covered with dry, mud-cracked sidewalks, blades of grass pushing through split seams, like sharp needles. On the other side were abandoned storefronts next to decrepit-looking businesses with smudged windows as dark as storm clouds.

But what practically gave us whiplash was the city's aging baseball stadium. The "Diamond" was home of the Richmond Braves, a minor league baseball team. While their mascot was a duck, it was the shoulders and head of a giant Indian that loomed over the side of the stadium. It reminded me of Washington's football team.

Like most fans, for years I cheered for the "Skins," insensitive to how indigenous Americans might feel about a team whose name was a racial slur. But by the time the team's Black quarterback Doug Williams took Washington to the Super Bowl in 1988, I was beginning to understand that "redskin" was akin to "blackface."

The Indian sculpture's artist said he had created the work to honor native culture. But no matter the intent, it was offensive to many, including me. Eventually, it would come down, and the team would change its name to the Richmond Squirrels, long before the Washington team dropped its name. But in 2006, it was still the Braves.

We kept driving until we arrived at the intersection of Boulevard and Monument Avenue, Richmond's Champs-Élysées. If we were shocked by the stadium's statue, we were appalled by what we saw on the city's most prestigious street.

On a verdant and vast median strip, bounded by cobblestone-paved streets and million-dollar mansions, were larger-than-life tributes to America's most notorious traitors. There was Confederate president Jefferson Davis; rebel army commander Robert E. Lee; his right-hand man, Thomas "Stonewall" Jackson; and two others towering over this otherwise beautiful boulevard.

The only challenge to the failed rebels was a statue of the late Richmond-born tennis star and civil rights activist Arthur Ashe. Holding a racquet in one hand and books in the other, the twentieth-century social justice advocate seemed out of place with the traitorous nineteenth-century rebels.

Looking at the behemoths, one might have thought the Confederates had won the war. That, of course, was the whole idea. Early twentieth-century promoters of the "Lost Cause," the South's revisionist history, wanted to create the illusion that in a way they had. African Americans were among their most insidious targets. Statues like the ones on Monument Avenue rose up throughout the South during the Jim Crow era to remind Blacks to stay in their place. Erected between 1890 and 1925, the Monument Avenue statues would remain in *their* place for about one hundred years until a summer of unrest brought them down in 2020.

But in 2006, there was no indication that would ever happen. At that time, Richmond, the Confederacy's former capital, stood by its statues.

Jack and I brushed aside our reservations. There were solid indications that Richmond was making strides. The city had a Black mayor, a Black school superintendent, and Black representation on the city council. While much of the city's African American community was poor, there was a substantial Black professional class. Jack's sister was among them. She was a doctor at one of the city's best hospitals and had lived in Richmond for many years. Besides, we rationalized, after all the trauma, including my parents' deaths and Jack's divorce, Richmond would give us a fresh start. We moved into our "tree house" and began making ourselves at home.

Our new neighborhood was typically suburban—stretches of lawns, mature trees, driveways, and no sidewalks. Unlike newer communities, the houses were not cookie-cutter homes. No two were alike. A testament to the city's entrenched racial divisions, the neighborhood was all white. Until we moved in. We had not set out to integrate the suburban hamlet; I just wanted to live near my son's school.

While our neighbors were accustomed to having Black help, they weren't used to having Blacks living "next door." But most were friendly, especially when they learned that Jack had been a *TIME* magazine correspondent. We smiled and waved as we drove by or passed each other while taking a stroll. Occasionally, we struck up a conversation about the weather.

However, there were times when the conversation got more personal, such as when I politely admonished a few of our new associates not to call the police when they saw a Black boy walking down the street or cutting across someone's lawn. "It's only Charles," I would say. They would laugh, not recognizing that I was not joking.

15

THE DOME ROOM

2007–2010

One year after our move to Richmond, Charles was settled in school, Jack was doing freelance writing, and I, well, I was looking for a job. The country was in a recession and "good jobs" were hard to find. It did not help that I was a Black woman in my forties. I scoured the internet, built up a network, and interrogated acquaintances, with mixed results.

I picked up a few acting gigs doing corporate training films, taught journalism as an adjunct college professor, and landed a decent contract marketing for a local architectural firm. For a while, I was a US Census taker, and when Barack Obama ran for president, I lobbied people to vote. It was a hodgepodge, and nothing comparable to the business I once had generated in DC.

With more spare time than I had had in years, I made the most of it. I took a cooking class, joined a gym, and dug into my genealogy. I had a subscription to Ancestry.com, the online service that has amassed official documents, such as census records, in an electronic archive. For less than $20 a month, I could search for my ancestors without leaving my house—or bedroom.

And when I did leave the house, Monticello was a preferred destination. It was as if I were making up for all the years I had not visited. It was always on the itinerary of out-of-town guests who wanted to see Jefferson's home as well as Charlottesville. A sophisticated college town, it was gaining a reputation for its scenic views, wineries, and fine dining.

I never tired of the seventy-mile drive, passing exits with names that, unbeknownst to me at the time, would one day prove significant in my research. Names like Goochland and Shadwell and Keswick. They all played a part in my family's history.

Touring the house at Monticello was never the same experience. Certain basic facts during the tour were required—the house has thirty-three rooms, for example, or is eleven thousand square feet. But guides were allowed some prerogative, perhaps choosing to focus on one of Jefferson's many interests, such as architecture, the natural sciences, philosophy, or horticulture. What remained consistent on every tour I took was reference to some kind of relationship between Sally Hemings and Jefferson. And just as consistent was my reaction. As I had during my first Monticello tour, I would shoot up my hand and make my claim, "I'm a descendant." Although the guides' responses were different, what they telegraphed was always the same—*Who cares?*

Since I was a part-time actor, my visits to Monticello felt analogous to repeatedly auditioning for the same part and never getting the role. And while I had this fantasy of being "discovered" and working there, I didn't know what part I could play. I didn't feel qualified to be a guide or inclined to work in the gift shop. Besides, the salary would barely cover my gas expenses. I had good communication skills but was not a historian, curator, or archeologist. Still, I was not willing to give up on my fantasy of working at Monticello.

So in May 2010, I "auditioned" one more time.

Charles had never been to Monticello. He was a high school senior and would soon be leaving for college—the Massachusetts

Institute of Technology. We didn't know if there would be another chance to make the trip, so on a perfect May day, the two of us headed to Charlottesville.

The day was cloudless, fragrant, and shimmering with the freshness of spring, the temperature a perfect mid-70s. Charles had heard the family saga many times, but on the way, I recounted for him once again the oral history—that Aunt Peachie swore to Jan that we were descended from Jefferson, and that Jan had passed it down to me. Now, I was passing it down to him. I told him that we also believed that we were related to Sally Hemings but did not have proof of kinship to either her or Jefferson. My son, a burgeoning scientist, wanted evidence. I hoped that on this idyllic spring day we would find some.

By this time, I was familiar with the tourist's routine: the walk through the Visitor Center and up the blue stone stairs to the shuttle bus, the ride up the curved road to the mountain, and the walk up the redbrick path to the mansion's East Portico.

We waited with the other tourists for our turn to enter the building. Per usual, we were the only Black people on the tour. Our guide was an older woman with silver hair and a jaunty step. Like her colleagues, she demonstrated in-depth knowledge about her subject—Jefferson and his house. And, as always, when the liaison with Hemings and Jefferson was mentioned, I thrust my hand into the air. This time, I pointed to my son, already six feet tall, and as I had many times before, announced, "We're related to Thomas Jefferson and Sally Hemings."

I waited for the silence that usually followed. But what came next was a stunner. With the warmth of a gracious hostess, the guide extended her arms to us and said, "You're family. You're dignitaries. If you would like, meet me when we're done, and I'll take you on a private tour upstairs to the Dome Room." The other guests—all white—turned to see who was getting the special treatment. I smiled coyly and thought, *At last.*

As promised, the guide, whose name I will never know, took us on a steep and narrow staircase to the second floor. There was not much to see, just several small bedrooms, some of which were used for storage or office space. And then up to the third-floor Dome Room. I was expecting something grand, but instead saw an empty octagonal room with large, round windows and a skylight. It was pretty but apparently without function. I would learn later that the Dome Room, architecturally unique in nineteenth century America, was just as impractical during Jefferson's time.

Our guide took us back downstairs to one of the bedrooms-cum-office. A desk was strewn with papers and photos, like a pile of leaves dusted by the wind. A woman sitting at the desk looked up as we entered, her face as welcoming as her colleague's.

Our escort introduced us—descendants, she said, interested in learning more about Monticello's work. This was my chance to tell someone "official" about the family lore. Like a griot repeating an often-told legend, I recounted the story of Aunt Peachie and Jan, my grandmother's Charlottesville roots, and my father's red hair. I described his height, his freckles, and the slope that was the bridge of his nose. I explained that my grandmother and all of her daughters had died, and much of what we might have learned about our family had died with them. I talked about the old photos of my dead aunts and of my grandmother's sister who had passed for white. We hadn't a clue what her name was, so Jan and I had nicknamed her "Lucy" after the 3.2 million year old fossil of a female found in Ethiopia in 1974. (I would later discover that my grandmother actually had a sister named Lucy!) I even mentioned the 1821 Bible with the initials "D:T."

By the time I was done, my audience of two knew the story I had been waiting years to tell. The woman sitting at the desk searched through the pile until she found a picture of Jefferson, pointing to his nose. It looked like Dad's. "It's the 'Jefferson nose,'" she said. I nudged the arm of my son, who was looking for proof.

The women nodded assuredly before offering a suggestion. They had a colleague, they told us, who was an expert on slavery at Monticello. Her name was Lucia "Cinder" Stanton, and she was researching the descendants of people enslaved by Jefferson. She was on vacation, but when she returned, she would definitely be interested in our story. I collected Cinder's email information, thanked my new best friends, and made my way back down the skinny staircase, gliding on air.

Charles and I, full of enthusiasm as we left the house, decided to walk down the mountain instead of taking the shuttle back to the Visitor Center. The path down took us past Mulberry Row, where we saw the remnants of living quarters and workshops. We kept walking until we reached the family cemetery where Jefferson, his wife, and their descendants are buried. Charles and I stopped outside the seven-foot-tall wrought iron fence that stood between us and the final resting place of our presumed ancestor. Studying the obelisk that marked Jefferson's grave, I felt a tingling sensation that would become familiar to me many times in the future when I was close to learning about my ancestors. It was exciting that we might soon know whether the family lore was fact or fiction.

16

EVA TAYLOR—MYSTERIOUS AS EVER

2010

In an unusual moment of doubt, I did not contact Cinder right away. The possibility that the foremost expert on enslavement at Monticello could confirm—or obliterate—my family's long-held beliefs made me hesitate. In the back of my mind was the fear that we might be wrong. After a few months, I finally summoned the courage to send her a carefully crafted email. I had to make sure I set the right tone as I presented the facts, as I knew them. I wanted, no, *needed* her to believe me.

The July 16, 2010, message was only two paragraphs:

Cinder,

My name is Gayle Jessup White and I was very excited during a recent visit to Monticello to learn about your research into the Jefferson slave family descendants. If my family's oral history is to be believed, we should be included in your study. According to long deceased family members, my paternal grandmother,

born in Charlottesville in 1883, was a descendant of the
Jefferson/Hemings liaison. I have no way of proving the story,
but it's family lore that I embrace and hold in high regard. My
grandmother did resemble Sally Hemings' description, tall (my
grandmother was 6'), with fair skin, and long dark hair. Like
Sally, my grandmother was very "handsome" indeed. I have
a beautiful restoration of a late 19th- or early 20th-century
drawing of her. My father, also tall, had red hair and freckles,
as do I. He also had a nose that was remarkably similar to
Jefferson's.

I would like to learn more about your research as I continue my
attempts to confirm what my family has long believed. Please
contact me at your earliest convenience. I'd enjoy talking with
you. Thank you.

I wanted my tone to sound confident. Had I conveyed my true
feelings, however, the email would have been more like this:

I have this crazy story I've been hearing since I was thirteen
years old—that we're related to Thomas Jefferson. It really
doesn't make any sense because I'm Black and from
Washington, DC. Except Jefferson did have children with an
enslaved woman named Sally Hemings, right? And maybe I'm
related to her, although I have yet to figure out how. But that
never stopped me from believing it was true—or from telling
people. I hope you can help. Please, oh, please write back—
and soon!

I heard from Cinder five days later:

July 21, 2010, 9:58 AM

Dear Gayle,

I'm excited to hear that you have a family story of connection to
Monticello. I'm just back after a week away so am racing to catch
up. I look forward to talking to you after the dust settles. In the
meantime, can you share the name of your paternal grandmother
and any of her known forebears? I and lots of others I work with
have been researching the history of the African Americans of
Charlottesville and Albemarle County, so we may have more to
add on that score.

Best wishes,
Cinder
Lucia Stanton
Shannon Senior Historian
Monticello

I could not wait to tell Jan that a respected Jeffersonian scholar
had offered to help us unravel our family lineage. As requested, I sent
Cinder my grandmother's name. However, I did not know the names
of any of her forebears—not her mother, her father, or her grandparents. I knew the names of two people: Eva Robinson, or Eva Taylor,
and Thomas Jefferson.

In just a few days, Cinder was back in touch with promising
information. She had found a seventeen-year-old Eva Robinson in
the 1900 Albemarle County Census. The girl was listed as a "servant"
living in the household of a seventy-two-year-old woman named
Carolina Ramsay Randolph. Cinder said the elderly woman was

Jefferson's great-granddaughter. She and her siblings were the children of Thomas Jefferson Randolph, Jefferson's favorite grandson.

With a few clicks on her computer keypad, Cinder uncovered what I had not been able to do in decades—my grandmother before she became a Jessup. And, just as important, she located her living with a Jefferson relative. It was not unusual, she said, for mixed-race children to live with and work for their white kin. It was a common practice during enslavement that continued for some families after Emancipation. It was quite plausible that Eva Robinson was working for her white father's family.

My head spun as I read the email, all the while imagining my grandmother as a teenager. Not only was she living with a Jefferson descendant, but she was working for a woman who was likely her white relative. The circumstances might have been typical of Southern mores, but that made them no less appalling. I needed fresh air to process what I was learning, so I retreated to the back porch.

It was hot, but not sticky—unusual for a Virginia summer. I stood on the screened porch, allowing the afternoon sun's warmth to drench my skin. Absently enjoying the view of the yard—the pool's glowing water, the blooming crepe myrtles, a few butterflies—I felt hypnotized. I closed my eyes and allowed my mind to drift. And then I heard her, a voice low and gentle but prodding. It was my grandmother's. *"Tell my story, Gayle,"* she said. *"It's all I have, tell my story."*

I had long ago separated myself from the Catholic Church and religious beliefs. After the deep hurt of my parents' deaths, I was not sure whether I still believed in God. Yet standing on my back porch, I heard my grandmother's voice as clear as the bells I heard every Sunday from nearby churches. It was not Paul's "Road to Damascus" conversion, but I definitely felt something spiritual. From that moment I knew I had an obligation to tell not only my grandmother's story, but that of as many Black ancestors as I could uncover.

• • •

Cinder instructed me to collect as many official documents as possible, beginning with my grandmother's death certificate. Some, she said, included the names of the deceased's parents. Anything else I could get my hands on also would be helpful—birth certificates, baptismal records, a marriage license—whatever I could find. Get back to her, she said, when I had something.

Jan was as delighted as I was with the new developments. We had collaborated from the start, partners in crime. Now we had a scholar who might be able to provide support for our speculations. It was imperative for me to include my sister, even as I began a relationship that would take me in a new and surprising direction. Besides, I didn't want to celebrate Cinder's discovery without Jan. It would have been like drinking alone.

My sister ordered our grandmother's death certificate from the DC Department of Health's Vital Records while I tried to track down ancient baptismal and confirmation records. She called a few weeks later, an air of suspense and gravity in her voice.

"Gayle, it's here," she said. "I'm holding in my hand an envelope from the Government of the District of Columbia. Shall I open it now?"

Speaking on my cell phone, I moved from the kitchen to the dining room. I wanted the surroundings of a formal setting as I prepared for what I might hear—the names of my great-grandparents. My sister was not the only one who could be dramatic.

"Give me a minute," I said as I a pulled a chair from the dining room table, allowing the anticipation to build. "Okay, I'm ready," I said once I was seated. I could hear the envelope rip as the letter opener slowly tore through its seam. Jan was methodical in everything she did, even opening an envelope. It was as if we were at the

Academy Awards, and the presenter said, "The envelope, please." I could hear paper rustling through the phone, like the sound of crisp, linen sheets.

"Okay, here we go," said Jan, setting the stage to read aloud a copy of the ninety-year-old document. A stickler for detail, my sister, the former elementary school teacher, proceeded to read every word. *Certificate of Death. District of Columbia. Date of this death, November 11, 1920. Full name of Deceased, Eva Jessup. Sex, female. Age, 37.* "She was so young," noted Jan. *Color, Colored.* "Not race, but Color. Interesting," she commented. *Conjugal condition, married. Occupation, housewife.*

Finally, midway through the document, Jan dramatically stopped at the section we hoped would reveal the names of our great-grandparents. She took a deep breath and continued. *Birthplace of deceased, Virginia. Birthplace of father, Virginia. Birthplace of mother, Virginia. Duration of residence in this district, twenty years.* Then, silence. I knew that could mean one of two things—nothing or everything.

A beat or two passed before my sister acknowledged what was a huge disappointment for both of us: the names of Eva's parents were not listed, only their place of birth.

However, we did learn where our grandmother was buried, Mount Olivet Cemetery, a racially integrated Catholic cemetery in DC founded in 1858. I had been there only once to visit the grave of my maternal grandmother. If our family had a tradition of visiting the dead, it ended soon after I was born. That Eva was buried at Mount Olivet was news to Janice and me.

I wanted to find out what the day was like when my grandmother was buried, November 13, 1920. My dad was only five years old when she died and did not attend the funeral. As far as I knew, no one still alive had been there. Literally, the very least I could do was check out the weather. Internet sites such as that for the National Weather Service made finding data pretty easy.

It was a Monday and cold, less than 24 degrees. A frigid air blast had descended on Washington, DC, earlier that week. Thanksgiving was just ten days away. I knew from Dad that my grandmother was a devout Catholic. No doubt, church members were at the gravesite. Her surviving daughters were probably there too. I imagined my grandfather, in a hat and heavy coat, silently weeping as her casket was lowered into the ground. I felt gloomy thinking about the broken hearts that mourned that day.

Cemeteries were never a place of comfort or solace for our family, never a place we visited. It is one of the ironies of my current preoccupations that gravesites are a big part of my consciousness.

Without the names of Eva's parents, I worried that we would never unlock the mystery of her lineage. However, per Cinder's instructions, I continued gathering documents that might deliver clues. A solid place to search was in church records, but I had no idea where my grandparents had worshipped. I decided to begin at the last place my parents had regularly attended Mass, the Church of the Incarnation in Deanwood. It was the church where they had met as teenagers, but the congregation didn't exist when my father was born. So where would I find his records?

Again thanks to the internet, that was an easy hurdle. A quick search offered a history of Incarnation's origins. It was spun out of what had been a predominantly white Maryland suburban church, St. Margaret of Scotland. At the beginning of the twentieth century, a number of Black Catholics who attended St. Margaret's wanted their own church, thus forming Incarnation. However, in the twenty-first century, St. Margaret's was still serving the faithful and the congregation that had become predominantly Black.

I had not been to Mass in years. I felt a hint of guilt when I called St. Margaret's asking for whatever documents they had about the Jessup family. But like those who serve, I had a calling. The woman who answered the phone, Carmen was her name, was graciously accommodating. She would look up Cedric Benedict Jessup, she said, and get back to me as soon as she found something.

A short time later, a packet arrived in the mail with a note: "Dear Mrs. White, I hope this information will help you. Be blessed." The packet contained a copy of a document almost entirely in Latin, including my dad's name: "Restirum Baptizatorum in Ecclesia" for "Cedric Benedictum" born "um die 18th Maii 1915." Another document was a copy certifying that he'd been baptized on June 13, less than a month after his birth. It was good information to have; however, what stood out was my grandmother's name. She was identified as "Eva Taylor."

It was another clue. On this sacred document, she chose not to use Robinson, the name on the 1900 Census record, but Taylor, the other name Dad associated with her. *It could have been Eva Robinson or Eva Taylor*, he had told me years before. On his baptismal certificate was evidence that what he said was accurate, albeit confusing.

St. Margaret's also sent me the confirmation certificates of my dad's sisters. From those documents I was able to glean that three Jessup girls were confirmed on the same day, April 15, 1915. Among the few photographs I had of Dad's family was of a group of children standing in front of a church, dressed in their Sunday best, their hands together as if in prayer. The Certificates of Confirmation verified that my three aunts were in the photograph. I recognized them because they were the only girls with light skin.

The church did not have a record of my grandparents' marriage, but I poked around the internet and found a newspaper announcement. Arthur Jessup and Eva Robinson had applied for a marriage license in 1901 according to the *Washington Star*.

Months had gone by since Cinder Stanton and I began exchanging emails. During those months, I learned more about my grandmother than I had in the previous forty years. But it was not enough to demonstrate how we were related to Thomas Jefferson. And now my emails to Cinder were going unanswered. I grew nervous that we had hit a dead end and that she had already moved on to a more promising family's lineage.

I sent a Hail Mary email in January 2011 with the subject line "Eva Taylor—as Mysterious as Ever," hoping to grab Cinder's attention. I filled her in on what we knew thus far—that my grandparents were married in 1901, that my grandmother used the name Taylor on at least one sacred document, and that she died on November 11, 1920—and what we did not know: her parents' names.

I received a response from Cinder within hours, but only with a message promising that she would soon have more time for my project. She was very busy, she said, working seven days a week.

I did not hear from her again for more than three months.

17

PATERNITY TEST

2011

The looming question of my grandmother's descent from Thomas Jefferson rested with the identity of her father. Without legal documentation, such as a birth certificate, or family records, such as a Bible (the one I had offered scant information), discovering paternity seemed an impossible quest.

However, when I finally heard from Cinder in April 2011, her news was tantalizing. I didn't have a job, so as usual I was at home in front of my computer when I got her email. Cinder believed that she had a lead on the identity of my great-grandfather—Eva's father. Recollecting that the 1900 Census had indicated that my grandmother was living in the household of Jefferson's great-granddaughter, a woman named Carolina "Carry" Ramsay Randolph, she pointed out that "Cary" was also the name of one of my grandmother's daughters, the one who near her death had wryly commented, "Sweet sixteen and never been kissed." Eva's "presence in the Edgehill household [where the Randolphs lived], as well as the passing on of the Cary/Carry name, tied her tightly to the extended Randolph family," speculated Cinder in our email exchange.

But the real intrigue rested with Carolina's siblings. She had several, including a sister named Martha. She was married to her distant cousin, John Charles Randolph Taylor, with whom she had twelve children. Among the youngest was a boy, Moncure Robinson Taylor, born in 1851. "Cure," as his family called him, did not get married until 1900, when he was almost fifty years old, during an era when most men married at half that age. The fact that he took a bride one year before Eva's December 1, 1901, marriage in Washington, DC, stoked Cinder's curiosity.

My imagination started racing as well. Did "Cure" remain single because he had a forbidden relationship with a Black woman, my Black great-grandmother? Were they in love? Did she die, freeing him emotionally to marry and their daughter, my grandmother, to migrate to Washington, DC? I had so many questions. It was best not to speculate too much, Cinder cautioned. "That won't get us far," she wrote. Still, it seemed that we were getting closer to identifying Eva's father and the link to my family's Jefferson lineage.

With Cinder's guidance, I was having more success finding US Census records and following the clues they provided. I traced Eva from the 1900 Census to Washington, DC, where in 1910 she was living with my grandfather, their four daughters, her mother-in-law, and a sixteen-year-old cousin named May Robinson. May's presence in the Jessup household would become an important clue in unraveling my father's familial relationships. By 1920, one of Eva's daughters was no longer listed—the family's first tuberculosis victim. By 1930, Eva and all of her girls were gone. The census record listed my grandfather, his new wife, and my dad and uncle.

While I was working my way forward, Cinder was reaching back. We knew that Eva was born in 1883, so the logical step *would* have been to look for her in the 1890 Census. Unfortunately, most of that decade's census data burned in a Commerce Department fire in

1921. We then went back another decade, knowing that she would not be listed, but looking for relatives who might be.

Cinder, a historian expert at culling through old records, unearthed a promising lead in the 1880 Census. It listed a thirty-one-year-old woman named Rachel Robinson—"Mulatto," single, and living alone with her two daughters, Lucy, age six, and an unnamed one-year-old. According to the record, her occupation was "domestic servant." A few "dwellings" from Rachel lived two sisters, members of the large Taylor clan. Their brother, "Cure," lived steps away.

"Do you think Rachel Robinson might be Eva Taylor's mother?" Cinder asked in her email. Yes, yes, I did. And since I did not have to follow a historian's professional protocols, I felt no qualms about making the next assumption—that Moncure Robinson Taylor was Eva's father and my great-grandfather. Cure was Jefferson's great-great-grandson, which meant that Jefferson was my five-times-great-grandfather.

After forty years of gathering shards of evidence, including a dubious oral history, an old Bible, fractured records, and faded recollections, it *appeared* that we had finally found the truth of Aunt Peachie's statement: "You're descended from Thomas Jefferson."

I was elated, but there was one disappointment. All those years, Jan and I had believed we were descended from the liaison between Jefferson and Sally Hemings. We were just as excited about being descended from Sally as we were from Thomas. Now, with the new discovery, it seemed that we were not Hemingses after all. But Cinder and I were not done researching.

Going back another ten years to the 1870 Census, we again spotted Rachel Robinson. She was twenty-one and living with her parents, Edmund and Sally Robinson, and several other family members. The names of four siblings—Peter, Anderson, Cary Ann (there was that name again), and Henry—would become vitally important as my search continued for Dad's family.

My grandmother Eva Robinson
Taylor Jessup, in her "Gibson
Girl" outfit, circa 1900.

My grandfather Arthur Eugene "Papa"
Jessup, circa 1900. He was a gunner's
mate in the Spanish-American war.

Dad's sisters: Louise Jessup (*left*), 1903–1920,
and Thelma Jessup (*right*), 1905–1921.

Artie Jessup, 1907–1919.

Cary Jessup, 1909–1925,
said on her deathbed,
"Sweet sixteen and
never been kissed."

Uncle Eugene, circa 1913.

Dad, 1915.

St. Margaret of Scotland Church, 1915; Thelma is on the photo's left, Artie is in the middle, and Louise is standing to her right in the back row.

My great-aunt, circa 1900; Jan and I called her "Aunt Lucy."

Dad (*first row on the right*) was an altar boy
at Incarnation Church, circa 1927.

Grandpa Delafosse Green, the "King of Cooks."

My maternal grandmother, Christine Hunt Green, in 1927. She always wore pearls.

Mom and Dad in New York
City during World War II.

Theresa "Billye" Green at
eighteen years old.

Janice, ten years old, and Pat, five, in front of the
fireplace where we said the rosary every evening.

Pat, Bruce, Mom, Dad, me,
and Janice, Easter 1958.

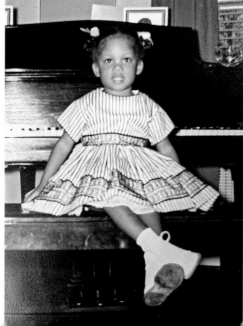

"Little Gayle" at home,
circa 1960. My godfather, a
professional photographer,
took this picture.

Mom and me at the poolside in Las Vegas, 1970.

Dad and Uncle Eugene during our last
visit shortly before Eugene died in 1991.

The Jessups, 1988. Pat, Dad,
Mom, me in the middle,
Bruce, and Janice.

Mom and Dad in 1990.

Jan and me in 2004.

My son Charles and other descendants doing an African dance on Monticello's South Lawn at a 2016 gathering.

Courtesy of the Thomas Jefferson Foundation

My cousins Velma (*left*) and Ruth (*right*) at the Goochland family graveyard the day after their Monticello visit.

"The Life of Sally Hemings" exhibition opened at Monticello during the 2018 Getting Word family reunion.
Courtesy of the Thomas Jefferson Foundation

The Robinsons at the Getting Word family reunion in June 2018; my cousin Andrew is on the left in the black shorts.

This 2018 Getting Word family reunion photo was taken on Monticello's West Lawn, where many of our ancestors were sold in 1827. I'm in the middle of the third row from the top.

Courtesy of the Thomas Jefferson Foundation

W. G. McADOO

NEW YORK

Santa Barbara, Cal.,
February 22, 1919.

My dear Delly:

Your letter received. The Big Four will probably not build any theatres themselves, but your proposition looks good, and I believe I can interest some people who can furnish the money in it.

It would seem to me that with only one moving picture theatre for colored people in Washington, there would be a good field for another, especially if we could put on a better show. I think that the serving of drinks and the dancing would be impracticable, but a good theatre with high-class shows ought to make money without any additional attractions. However, that could be looked into later.

I wonder if you can look the situation over quietly and give me the following information:

1. What do you think would be a proper location for such a theatre?

2. Is there any land available in this vicinity on which we could build, and what would the rent cost approximately?

3. What do you figure it would cost us to erect a modern theatre seating about 1,000 people? You might make some inquiries on this point.

4. Could you interest some of your friends in this proposition to the extent of investing from $100 to $200 each in it? You can see that if we got about twenty representative colored people interested on account of their investment, even though the investment be only a small one, we would have that many more rooters who would work hard to make the theatre a success.

I don't think that it is necessary to impress upon you the fact that all this work must be done quietly, and no information must leak out as to what we are contemplating doing.

Of course, I cannot assure you that we will go ahead with the project, but after you furnish the information I ask for above, and if it sounds reasonable, I could more easily get the proper parties interested.

With best regards, I am

Cordially yours,

Private Secretary.

Letter from Treasury Secretary William McAdoo
to my grandfather, Delafosse Green, 1919.

CERTIFICATE OF DEATH
COMMONWEALTH OF VIRGINIA
BUREAU OF VITAL STATISTICS
STATE BOARD OF HEALTH

1 PLACE OF DEATH

COUNTY OF _Goochland_

MAGISTERIAL DISTRICT OF _Byrd_

OR INC. TOWN OF ___

OR CITY OF ___

REGISTRATION DISTRICT No. _370 B_ (TO BE INSERTED BY REGISTRAR)

REGISTERED No. _5995_ (FOR USE OF LOCAL REGISTRAR)

(If death occurred in a hospital or other institution, give its NAME instead of street and number)

No. ___ St.: ___ WARD ___

2 FULL NAME _Peter F. Robinson_

(A) RESIDENCE. No. ___ _Fife Va_ St. ___ WARD. ___

(Usual place of abode) (If nonresident give city or town and State)

Length of residence in city or town where death occurred ___ yrs. ___ mos. ___ ds. How long in U. S., if of foreign birth? ___ yrs. ___ mos. ___ ds.

PERSONAL AND STATISTICAL PARTICULARS	MEDICAL CERTIFICATE OF DEATH
3 SEX _male_ **4 COLOR OR RACE** _colored_ **5 SINGLE, MARRIED, WIDOWED, OR DIVORCED** (write the word) _married_	**16 DATE OF DEATH** (MONTH, DAY, AND YEAR, WRITE NAME OF MONTH) _March 4_ 19_24_
5A IF MARRIED WIDOWED, OR DIVORCED HUSBAND OF (OR) WIFE OF _Billie Robinson_	**17 I HEREBY CERTIFY, THAT I ATTENDED DECEASED FROM** ___ 19 ___ TO _march 3_ 19_24_ THAT I LAST SAW H— ALIVE ON _march 3_ 19_24_
6 DATE OF BIRTH (MONTH, DAY, AND YEAR, WRITE NAME OF MONTH) ___ 19 ___	AND THAT DEATH OCCURRED, ON DATE STATED ABOVE, AT _3 a._ M. THE CAUSE OF DEATH* WAS AS FOLLOWS:
7 AGE YEARS _59_ MONTHS ___ DAYS ___ IF LESS THAN 1 DAY, — HRS. OR — MIN.	_Myocarditis Insuff[?] along with partial compensation_ 90
8 OCCUPATION OF DECEASED (A) TRADE, PROFESSION, OR PARTICULAR KIND OF WORK _farmer_ (B) GENERAL NATURE OF INDUSTRY, BUSINESS, OR ESTABLISHMENT IN WHICH EMPLOYED (OR EMPLOYER) ___	(DURATION) ___ YRS. ___ MOS. ___ DS.
(C) NAME OF EMPLOYER ___	**CONTRIBUTORY** (SECONDARY) _Rheumatism_
9 BIRTHPLACE (CITY OR TOWN) _Goochland Co_ (STATE OR COUNTRY) ___	(DURATION) ___ YRS. ___ MOS. ___ DS. **18 WHERE WAS DISEASE CONTRACTED IF NOT AT PLACE OF DEATH?** ___
10 NAME OF FATHER _Edmund Robinson_	**DID AN OPERATION PRECEDE DEATH?** _no_ DATE OF ___
11 BIRTHPLACE OF FATHER (CITY OR TOWN) _Albemarle Co_ (STATE OR COUNTRY) ___	**WAS THERE AN AUTOPSY?** _no_
12 MAIDEN NAME OF MOTHER _Sallie Simmons_	**WHAT TEST CONFIRMED DIAGNOSIS?** ___ (SIGNED) _John T. Wilson_ M.D.
13 BIRTHPLACE OF MOTHER (CITY OR TOWN) _Albemarle Co_ (STATE OR COUNTRY) ___	___ 19_24_ (ADDRESS) _Columbia_
	*State the DISEASE CAUSING DEATH, or in deaths from VIOLENT CAUSES, state (1) MEANS AND NATURE OF INJURY, and (2) whether ACCIDENTAL, SUICIDAL, or HOMICIDAL.
14 INFORMANT _Billie Robinson_ (ADDRESS) _Fife Va_	**19 PLACE OF BURIAL, CREMATION, OR REMOVAL** _Family Cemetery_ **DATE OF BURIAL** _Mar. 6_ 19_24_
15 FILED _Mar 6_ 19_24_ _Mrs. Annie W. Parrish_ REGISTRAR	**20 UNDERTAKER** _Edward Pannul_ ADDRESS _Elk Hill Va_

_5995_ _five_

•   •   •

In June 2011 Monticello hosted the Cabinet Retreat, an annual event for donors who contributed several thousand dollars. Jack and I were guests, thanks to a friend who was not interested in attending and passed her invitation to us.

A year earlier, I was raising my hand trying to get a guide's attention. Now, I was a guest, breathing the rarefied air of the donor elite. I was also more confident than ever that I had Jefferson's blood running through my veins. The day could not go by without my making attendees aware that I had arrived.

The retreat started Saturday morning with a meeting at the Visitor Center for an overview of the latest accomplishments of the Thomas Jefferson Foundation. When Jack and I arrived, the room was already filled with about a hundred people seated in white folding chairs. We found two seats in the back, which I preferred. Under some circumstances, and this was one, I felt it was better to observe than to be observed. Even so, we caught a few furtive glances as we walked in. Jack squeezed my hand and winked at me. Aside from one man sitting in the front, we were the only Black people in the room.

It was going to be an interesting afternoon.

The event began with staff remarks and acknowledgment of Board of Trustees members. Cinder wasn't present. We'd have to meet another time. To my surprise, the Black man sitting in the front row was a trustee. Not knowing what to expect, I was equally surprised that a substantial amount of the presentation was about enslavement at Monticello, including the reinterpretation of Mulberry Row, where the enslaved had lived and worked. Eventually, an initiative called the Mountaintop Project would raise millions of dollars to restore Monticello's landscape to what it would have been like during Jefferson's time. At a cost of tens of millions of dollars, the initiative sounded impressive. One donor, David Rubenstein, would provide most of the funding, $20 million. The billionaire businessman turned philanthropist began donating much of his fortune as part of an initiative among the very wealthy called the Giving Pledge. He has contributed millions not only to Monticello, but to the Library of Congress, the National Parks Foundation, the John F. Kennedy Center for the Performing Arts, and James Madison's Montpelier. He gave millions to repair the Washington Monument after an earthquake in 2011. Rubenstein also owns rare copies engraved by William J. Stone of the Declaration of Independence, the US Constitution, the Emancipation Proclamation, and the Thirteenth Amendment, which he has loaned to historical institutions, including Monticello.

Sitting from a rear-room vantage point, I detected a little fidgeting among the other guests. I leaned over and whispered to Jack, "I don't think these people want to hear this." My husband knew I meant "white people." In 2011, Americans—white and Black—still struggled to talk about the horrors of slavery and its legacies.

The tendency of some to dismiss the damage enslavement inflicted on Black people became evident when a white woman in the front of the room expressed her opinion. The slaves were better off in the United States than they had been in Africa, she said.

I practically gasped.

The woman, clearly privileged, had no idea that what she said was an affront to tens of millions of Black people and their enslaved ancestors. But just as I was about to raise my hand to object, a voice boomed from the front, "You don't know what you're talking about, so just stop." It was the other Black person in the room, the trustee. He was as confident in his rebuke as the white woman had been in her assertion.

The path was now laid for me to introduce myself to him. From the back of the room, I stood before going public with my Monticello bona fides. "As a descendant of the enslaver and the enslaved," I said, "I can assure you that my ancestors did not feel better off as captives." I resumed my seat, knowing that I had made an impression few in the room would forget.

I would later learn that the Black man with the booming voice was Judge John Charles Thomas, who in 1983 became the first Black (and at thirty-two, the youngest) appointed to Virginia's Supreme Court. In time, his family and ours would become close friends.

The week after the retreat, I finally met Cinder Stanton face-to-face. It was at another Monticello event, this time one that introduced Charlottesville's Black community to the planned restorations. Many of the guests were from the University of Virginia, "Mr. Jefferson's university." I was pleased to get acquainted with some of Charlottesville's Black influencers; however, for me the evening's highlight was meeting Cinder.

Physically, she was small and unassuming, with short hair, boxy bangs, and a shy smile. But to me she was a giant. Not only had Cinder unlocked the mystery of my grandmother's birth, which she tenuously confirmed that evening, but she also trained me to follow genealogical clues. We would continue our work together, but after a year of knowing her, I had many of the tools to make it on my own.

I soon made my first overture for a job at Monticello. I suggested that I produce a documentary about enslavement at Monticello as the foundation planned to restore Mulberry Row. Not right now, was the response from a leadership team member, but "keep the ideas flowing." That was fine. Meantime, I needed a job.

18

RIP, CHOCOLATE CITY

2012–2013

A late winter snow is not uncommon in the nation's capital. But in early March 2012, the weather was unusually balmy, hovering in the low 70s. I was temporarily living back in Washington where I had taken a development job at the national office of the YWCA. I was driving from its midtown office location headed to my mother-in-law's house when I spotted a middle-aged white couple walking along the median strip of a busy street. It was already dark, and we were in what I considered a sketchy part of the city, especially for naive white people. They looked lost. I pulled up beside them, rolled down my car window, and asked if they needed help. "Oh no," they said, pointing toward a block of brick row houses. "We're on our way home." Thus was the state of "Chocolate City" in the second decade of the twenty-first century. Black folk had sardonically taken to calling it "latte city."

I had moved back to Washington in the fall of 2011 for the YWCA job to take a break from Richmond, and because I was homesick. In the five years that Jack and I had lived there, I had not found suitable employment. There was a stint teaching journalism at Virginia Commonwealth University, another doing marketing for an architectural and engineering firm, and finally fund-raising for a foundering

HBCU, but nothing that enthralled me. Besides, I started missing my hometown from the moment we had pulled onto that dreary stretch of road leading into Richmond in 2006. With my husband's blessing, I accepted work in DC.

Washington was no longer the city I remembered. There was new construction everywhere—office buildings, housing developments, retail shopping, and restaurants. In Southwest, where there had once been windowless warehouses, vacant dirt lots, and strip clubs, there were high-rise condos and modern office buildings. In Southeast, white, green, and blue lights illuminated the new ballpark of the Washington Nationals baseball team. In Northwest, hip hotels and modern glass buildings stood next to squat brick structures that were salvaged because they were historical landmarks. And in Northeast, near my old neighborhood, a new trolley car system would soon deliver affluent whites to upscale restaurants and boutiques in buildings that used to house hair-braiding salons and fish joints. More than once I got lost in areas that were once as familiar to me as Eastland Gardens, where I grew up.

White people were moving into areas that had been at the heart of the Black community for decades, including my old neighborhood. In 2012, Washington was no longer majority Black. Whites were living throughout the city, even in places that a few years earlier had been fraught with poverty and crime. Laundromats were converted into restaurants and corner markets into coffee shops. Sections of town were given slick new names like NoMa—north of Massachusetts Avenue—or the Atlas District, named after a renovated movie theater.

I was at once repelled by and enchanted with all the changes. I loved what the city offered—the boutique shops, gourmet markets, and eclectic restaurants. But I hated that Black people and Black-owned businesses were pushed out to make way for the new developments. Further, why did it take whites moving into the city for such a renaissance? In a city dominated for years by Black leadership, many of its residents were still treated like second-class citizens.

A history of systemic racism was to blame. Redlining kept Black people out of the best neighborhoods, banks kept Black-owned businesses from getting the best loans, undersupplied schools kept Black children from getting the best education. Because of redlining, my parents had built their house in a section of DC populated by middle-class Blacks and poor whites. As a result, when they sold their home sixty years later, it was worth one-fourth the value of similar homes in white neighborhoods across town.

And this kind of change was not happening just in Washington. Gentrification was shifting political and population dynamics in cities all over the country. Ironically, years later as a Monticello staffer, I would witness firsthand the emotional indignation many Black people felt over the encroachment of white people in their communities, and I would be perceived as an instrument of that encroachment. It would happen in Detroit, another Chocolate City. Of course, cruising around DC in 2012, I had no idea what was in my future.

I was focused on what was in front of me. Whether I was on a bus, riding the Metro, or driving my nine-year-old BMW, what I saw was not the beloved city where I had grown up, not where I had learned to ride a two-wheel bike, shopped at downtown department stores, or danced the night away at a disco. Much of what I saw was as unfamiliar as a foreign land. I went from being homesick to heartsick.

Six months back in DC and working at the YWCA, I was beginning to wonder whether I had made a mistake. The job as a development associate gave me a chance to try something new, raising funds for a historical and highly regarded institution. "Eliminating racism" was one the YWCA's missions, a cause I supported. But the passion wasn't there.

I was still dreaming of a job at Monticello. "Your face just lights up when you talk about it," commented a colleague. "You'll be working there one day," she said with more optimism than I had. Having no experience in the museum world, aside from being a guest, I had no idea what kind of job would be possible for someone without a background in history or museum studies. My skill set was communicating, working in front of a camera, and connecting with people. If I could find a job doing that, it would be perfect.

The Great Recession of 2007–2009 burned a lot of people. At one point, the unemployment rate was 10 percent. Finding work was tough, especially for people like me, in their fifties. Many of my friends were considering retirement, even as I was thinking of a new career. However, I had a mission, a duty, a calling. The voice that was my grandmother's urging me to tell her story compelled me to work. But back home in Washington and employed at the YWCA, I had not yet figured out how to get where I needed to be. And as much as I hated to admit it, Washington did not feel like home anymore. By the end of the year, I was back in Richmond.

19

"A SLAVE GIRL NAMED SALLY"

January 2013

It was January 9, 2013, and I was driving to Charlottesville for lunch with Cinder. It would be our second meeting. This time would be different, more than just the several minutes we'd spent with each other two years earlier at Monticello. This time we would be spending the afternoon together at Hamiltons', a fashionable restaurant appointed with royal blue glassware and blue budding flowers. The menu, upscale Southern cuisine, included dishes like Crispy Carolina Flounder, Gin-Cured Braised Pork Belly, and Deconstructed Potato Salad. Located on Charlottesville's charming Downtown Mall, a pedestrian walkway several blocks long featuring sophisticated shops, bookstores, art galleries, and sidewalk cafes, Hamiltons' would become one of my favorite destinations. But on this January day, it was still a unique experience for me.

Cinder was already at the restaurant when I arrived. Seated at a table near the front, she seemed a little startled as I approached. Perhaps it was my irrepressible eagerness. I was so hungry, not for lunch but for her knowledge. With studious, brown eyes staring up at me, she offered a reserved smile and invited me to sit down. I liked her face and her manner. She seemed—calm.

We ordered lunch, nothing as heavy as pork bellies. For one thing, I don't eat red meat. But even my salad was too much. I was too excited to do more than pick at it. Cinder and I had not been in touch for more than a year. We needed to reacquaint ourselves with each other and with my ancestors.

A lot had changed in Cinder's life during the previous year. She was no longer working at Monticello; she had retired after forty years. She had also published *"Those Who Labor for My Happiness": Slavery at Thomas Jefferson's Monticello*, a book about several of the families held captive on the "little mountain." Still, she was never far away from Monticello and the seminal archive the Getting Word African American Oral History Project, which she had founded. The initiative, which collected the oral histories of descendants of people enslaved at Monticello, was indeed her brainchild. However, Cinder was white, and Black people have a justifiable history of not trusting white folk. Thus, much of the project's initial success was because of the contributions of two Black women, Monticello historian Dianne Swann-Wright and Ohioan Beverly Gray whose connections paved the way to people whose freed ancestors migrated to Chillicothe, who were able to establish relationships with the descendants. In time, faith would grow among descendants, and Cinder would become the patron saint of hundreds who recognize Monticello as their ancestral home. As for my own lineage, we hadn't uncovered enough for me to join the project. Nonetheless, I longed to be part of the group whose members I considered kin, even if I did not know yet *how* we were related.

I reached into my tote bag and pulled out a few family treasures— the photos of my grandparents and their young children, my grandmother's sister, and the freshly confirmed young people standing in front of the church. Examining the wallet-size image of my great-aunt, the one who had passed for white and whom Jan and I called

Lucy, looking splendidly well-to-do in her lace and silk gown and plumed chapeau, Cinder exclaimed, "Look at that hat!" She was clearly impressed with the material I had, and eager to help. She also held fast to her hunch that Moncure Robinson Taylor and Rachel Robinson were my great-grandparents. We ended lunch with a promise to stay in touch. I drove back to Richmond feeling like I had a new friend.

A few days later, I was at a lecture at the Virginia Historical Society by the author of a book about Martha Jefferson Randolph. After lunch with Cinder, I was more confident than ever that Martha, Thomas Jefferson's oldest daughter and Moncure's great-grandmother, was my four-times-great-grandmother.

Martha Jefferson Randolph, Daughter of Monticello: Her Life and Times by Cynthia Kierner portrayed a woman whose life was in many ways tragic. Ten years old when her mother died, she was the only person who could comfort her father. When he traveled to Europe to become ambassador to France, she accompanied him. In Paris, she socialized among the elite and studied at an exclusive convent school. She was smart, witty, and well educated. Unlike most of her peers back in provincial Albemarle County and Charlottesville, she spoke several languages. At balls and other social events, she was accompanied by a lady's maid. More than two hundred years later, the name of the teenager who saw to Martha's every need would outlive that of her mistress. She was Sally Hemings.

Some people (not scholars, to be sure) speculate that it was because of her father's relationship with Sally Hemings that Martha rushed into marriage when she returned to Virginia after five years in Paris. Whatever the case, she married her third cousin, Thomas Mann Randolph Jr., soon after returning to the United States. Randolph was from a prominent political family and a lineal descendant of Pocahontas and John Rolfe. He was smart, but troubled. Some historians believe that he suffered from mental illness.

While the couple had their successes, including twelve children, one of whom would become my three-times-great-grandfather Thomas Jefferson Randolph, the marriage floundered.

Randolph was unpredictable and held deep resentment toward his father-in-law, to whom Martha was obsessively devoted. Her loyalty to Jefferson put a wedge between the couple. And because Randolph inherited his father's debt while his own land values decreased, their finances were precarious. They were forced to sell Edgehill, their home, to pay off their debt. However, their oldest son, Thomas, bought Edgehill, and the property remained in the family. It was also the estate where my grandmother Eva was living as a "servant" in 1900.

Martha must have been disappointed with the way her life, which had begun with such promise, turned out. The sharpest blow came in 1826 when her father died. Jefferson was so deeply in debt that Monticello had to be sold. As disheartening as this may have been for Martha and her children, the potential sale was far worse for the enslaved. In January 1827, six months after Jefferson's death on July 4, one hundred men, women, and children were auctioned on the West Lawn, where more than a century later tourists would pose for pictures in front of the mansion's famous dome.

Thomas Mann Randolph died in 1828, followed by Martha in 1836 at the age of sixty-four. She spent the last years of her life moving from one child's house to another, including a daughter's home in Washington City, what we know today as Washington, DC.

That's where an event described in Kierner's book happened in 1833, an event that captivated and sickened me all at once. According to a letter between two of Martha Jefferson Randolph's daughters, an enslaved girl identified only by her first name—Sally—was sent to the constable for a "whipping." In the eyes of her owners, Sally's behavior was so grave that it required a "correction" from the authorities. A typical flogging at the hands of an official meant being tied to a post and stripped to the waist, the back exposed to the sting of a whip. There's no way to know the severity of Sally's punishment, just that her owners thought it was "far too moderate."

When Sally's behavior again met the disapproval of her mistresses, she was again punished. However, the second time, the person who administered the stripes was Martha Jefferson Randolph herself. The book excerpted just a few of the letter's passages from the letter, but Cinder sent me a more complete electronic copy:

> You will laugh to hear what disciplinarians we have turned out to be. Not a week after Sally was put in the hands of the constable who gave her by far too moderate a correction, she stole a pr of stockings & gave them to Melinda's Ann. . . . We held a council about what was to be done, Mama, Melinda & myself. I thought we had better send for the constable again without any delay but Melinda said no it would give us a bad reputation, that she would whip her if we chose, whereupon we decided, took her down into the basement, Melinda & myself held her & mama inflicted the flagelation [*sic*] pretty severely but Melinda said it was not enough . . .

The book's passage about the whipping did not include the entire letter, just a few words from it. I would not see the letter for several months. However, the four paragraphs I read in Kierner's book about the incident were chilling—and haunting. I read the section over and over again, so often that I practically memorized it. "A slave girl named Sally," and "Martha whipped Sally," and "the unfortunate

Sally," Kierner had written. Every time I read her name—Sally—I was moved. I felt that I knew her. Sally, after all, was the name of Rachel Robinson's mother, my great-great-grandmother whose married name was Sally Robinson.

I shared my gut feeling with Cinder that the enslaved girl Martha Jefferson whipped, the "unfortunate Sally," and my great-great grandmother were the same the person.

Months later, a cache of notes landed in my email—excerpts from Jefferson/Randolph family letters. The most intriguing was from March 1865, from Jefferson's great-granddaughter Mary B. Randolph to her sister Jane Nicholas Randolph Kean. It was written when Union commander Philip Sheridan and his troops occupied Charlottesville one month before the end of the Civil War, destroying buildings, bridges, and railroads, but, more than anything else, horrifying residents.

The letter was several pages long and included references to "Yankees" and "staunch southern women." It was like reading a chapter from *Gone with the Wind*. Mary mentioned several characters, including white family members, the enslaved, Union soldiers, and Confederates. The names of the enslaved attracted me above all others, names like Henry and Rachel with which I had become familiar, and especially "Sally." What follows is a transcribed excerpt from Mary Randolph's letter that was written one month before Confederate general Robert E. Lee's surrender at Appomattox Court House:

I had put on the watch I took out of your trunk and I was so uneasy at having it and at Carry's having her's we called to Sally and she came and took them from us, we had put on our cloaks after the first arrival [of soldiers] to prevent their being stolen. Carry and I went to the parlor window to see if we could'nt see some officer whose protection we could claim but all we saw was these horrible wretches riding as hard as they could through the garden gate strait up the hill and dashing round to the back door. All of them we saw were as drunk as they could be and no officer amongst them.

My courage was all gone now I was terrified to death and clung to Carry's arm standing in the dining room door she says as if my arms were made of iron. Aunt Sidney, Peg and the children were in the dining room. The storm soon burst. A drunken wretch rushed into the back door cursed Mama shook his pistol over her and told her to give him her gold and silver or he would burn the house down—'I have no gold or silver' she said. he went in to her room cursing and making a noise followed by a stream of others. the house was filled with them coming in and going upstairs we could hear them pulling the things about in the garret and going about. This drunken man rushed up to Carry & I. 'Give me your watches give me your watches'—'We have no watches.' 'let me see let me see' I threw back my cloak but Carry could not get hers open as soon and he clutched hold of it Mama flew at him as if she had been a wild tiger Carry got the cloak open or I think he would have torn it open. Haven't you a mother & sisters Ma said ringing her hands in his face. 'what.' 'have not you a mother & sisters.' 'yes I have a mother & sisters.' just then he caught sight of the three rings on my fingers—I had quite forgotten. 'Rings on your fingers,' 'give me those rings' and I thought he would have torn them off my finger so I gave them to him.

His pistol was flourishing over us all the while but I did not care any more for it than if it had been a stick he turned to Carry for her rings and then to Aunt Margaret. you want this, she said, quite coolly and pulled off her little black ring she has been wearing for forty years Just then a young man rushed down the stairs his pistol in his hand 'what's this about taking rings from women'? 'give them back [sir?] give them back- -take men's property as much as you please but when it comes to taking rings from women you shant do it, give them back, give them back. three others joined him and they had it as [loud?] as they could talk threatening this horrid wretch until at last he gave the man two of our rings.

Mary lamented the loss of the family's valuables, including "12 negroes." Then, reflectively, she seemed to recognize the humanity of the people she owned:

whatever happens and whatever they may do here after I shall always feel an affection for them for their sympathy & kindness—particularly Sally she was as good as she could be and showed so much sense

As I read the letter, the same rush I had felt when I heard my grandmother's voice say "Tell my story" coursed through my veins, the same tingling sensation I had when I read about "Sally" in Kierner's book, and the same sensation I would feel time and again in the future as I walked the grounds of Monticello.

Cinder and I started calculating. We knew from the census records that Rachel and Henry were two of Sally Robinson's children, so it made sense that their mother also would have been at the Edgehill property during Sheridan's raid. We also knew from the census that in 1880 Sally Robinson was fifty-eight years old. (It is possible that Sally was unsure of the exact year of her birth.) That would have made her forty-three as the Civil War closed and eleven when the girl Sally was whipped in the basement of the Washington City house. Children younger than the age of ten were generally put to work caring for other children. The 1833 letter from Washington, from Martha Jefferson Randolph's daughter describing the beating of an enslaved girl name Sally said, "She is kind to the animals & fond of Ellen's child." Given the paucity of legal documentation for enslaved people, it is impossible to say exactly when Sally was born, but Cinder and I estimated around 1820, give or take a year or two.

Compiling all the data, we were convinced that we had found my great-great-grandmother, Sally Robinson. Throughout her life, she was apparently intimately connected to the family that owned her. The question then became, Who were *her* ancestors?

20

THE PLOT THICKENS

April–August 2013

Publishers Weekly, April 19, 2013:

I began to know that I would need to write a version of this book in the late '90s, when DNA tests confirmed that chromosomal patterns on the descendants of Sally Hemings matched the patterns on the chromosomes of descendants of Thomas Jefferson. . . . It was a fierce wake-up call, because I am a white descendant of Thomas Jefferson.

The acknowledgment in the April 2013 online edition of *Publishers Weekly* was in a review of *The Forage House*, a book of poetry. I came upon the review as part of my routine internet search for Jefferson descendants. The poet was a woman named Tess Taylor. The article had an excerpt from one of her poems. I found her reflections on race and her famous ancestor enlightened. She wrote that she longed for ancestors to "explain their America, their prodigal." Race was not to be spoken of, not a topic discussed among family:

"The record's scratched. I don't recall. I never knew.
Anyone who'd tell you's dead. And: No one would
tell you."

Since Tess's last name was Taylor, the same name my grandmother Eva sometimes claimed, I calculated that we might be descended from the same line. I also thought she might be receptive to an overture from me. I decided it was worth trying to connect with her, so I posted in the magazine's comment section:

I am an African-American Jefferson descendant. My grandmother was a Taylor (although her mother didn't exactly marry into the family!), a direct descendant of J.C. Randolph Taylor and Martha Jefferson Randolph. Tess Taylor—I wonder if we share great great-grandparents? The plot thickens.

My thought was that the proposition would spur the poet's curiosity. An email from her days later proved I was right. "Interesting comment on PW site. I'd love to learn your story," she wrote. Thus, began a relationship with my white Jefferson and Randolph cousins. Contacting Tess, it turned out, was pivotal.

She lived in El Cerrito right outside of Berkeley, California, a three-hour time difference, so scheduling a conversation required some coordinating. After some negotiating, we agreed to chat on the last Saturday in April. She would call me.

My cell rang right at the agreed time, 10:30 a.m. for me, 7:30 for her—an early riser, I assumed. The voice on the phone sounded high-pitched, lilting, and a little excited. I am not sure how I sounded to her, but my intent was to convey a relaxed assuredness. I did not want my voice to allow a smidgen of doubt in my story's veracity.

Tess was thirty-six, twenty years younger than I, married, and the mother of a little boy. I too, was married and the mother of a son. Already we were finding things in common. We were both writers, had master's degrees in journalism—hers from New York University, mine from Northwestern's Medill School—and we both loved history.

Her great-great-grandfather was named Bennett and was the older brother of Moncure, my presumed great-grandfather. If Cinder's and my assumptions were correct, then I was one generation closer to Jefferson than my presumed white cousin. Yet she and her family had what many people considered a privilege, one that Jefferson's Black descendants were denied: access to the family cemetery at Monticello.

Whether Black descendants wanted their final resting place to be among white kin who would not have wanted them there was not the point. It was that the right, "property rights" some called it, should have been theirs as much as any of Jefferson's white descendants. My family's oral history and the documents Cinder and I had uncovered offered strong support that I was a direct descendant of Martha and Thomas Jefferson. The so-called privilege of being buried at the family cemetery should have belonged to my family as well.

Tess had witnessed the racial acrimony that followed an attempt to comingle the Black and white cousins at a 1999 meeting orchestrated by one of the more progressive white descendants. The event followed one year after a DNA study indicated that Jefferson was the likely forebear of a Hemings descendant and the father of Sally Hemings's children. Tess told me the incident was an emotional source for some of her poetry.

Our conversation was expansive, covering topics from that doomed 1999 meeting to her liberal West Coast upbringing. For my part, I talked about my Washington, DC, roots and the long pursuit of my family's Jefferson lineage. She had relatives in Richmond, she said, a grandmother, an aunt and uncle, and cousins, whom she visited as often as time permitted. Perhaps during her next trip, we could meet. The conversation ended upbeat and with a commitment to speak again soon.

Meanwhile, Jack and I were preparing for our *own* guest—my sister Jan. After her husband's death, Janice had been content living alone for ten years. But at age seventy-four, she acknowledged that for her safety, it was time to surrender some of her independence. While she considered her future—moving to a senior apartment or in with her daughter in DC or son in New York—I invited her to stay with us.

I spruced up the guest room with fresh paint and new bedding. I even bought dishware, hoping to impress my meticulous older sister, who never saw framed art on a wall that did not need adjusting. When she arrived in May 2013, everything was perfectly positioned, even the bars of French milled soap.

Of course, I was thrilled. Jan was good company, volunteering wardrobe advice for me and swapping *TIME* magazine war stories with Jack. While Wally's tenure at *TIME* preceded Jack's by a decade, they had known and worked with many of the same people. Sometimes I felt left out of the conversation but was delighted that two of my favorite people found so much joy regaling one another about old times.

Naturally, I wanted Jan to meet Cinder, so we arranged to have lunch at the same restaurant where she and I had met several months earlier. It was late spring, and as Jan and I strolled along the Downtown Mall, she recognized shops she had seen in the 1980s when her daughter had been a UVA student. Approaching a bookstore to window shop, she commented on the value of some things remaining the same. At the moment, we couldn't have predicted the radical changes that challenged our family's stability as nothing had since our parents' deaths, that she would be moving out of the country, or that we would lose more loved ones. Our focus that day was on the past, not what might await us in the future.

We arrived at the restaurant before Cinder. Jan, as she did for all occasions, insisted on arriving early. After introductions that bore more formality than usual—because of my sister's regal air—we ordered lunch. Little time was wasted with polite "how are you enjoying the weather" conversation. We were all eager to dig into Jan's reminiscences. Because she was almost twenty years older than I, she was a generation closer to our most important informant, Aunt Peachie. And even though Cinder had heard it all before from me, Jan was another source.

Jan painted a vivid picture of growing up in Washington, DC, in the 1930s and 1940s, how people used to "dress up," how close-knit the neighbors were, and how, as an eight-year-old, she walked unaccompanied and safely to school. She recalled throwing little brother Dickie's diapers down the stairs after Aunt Peachie had carefully folded them and charming Dad's father, "Papa," while bouncing on his knee. She remembered going with Mom's sister to the National Gallery of Art and hearing her brother sing opera.

And now that *she* was the family elder, she knew more of our history than anyone else alive. Affirming in greater detail what I had already told Cinder, Janice described Aunt Peachie, that she was "completely illiterate" and childlike. "She was quiet and spent most of the day in a dining room chair, looking out the window," said Jan. But Aunt Peachie was confident in her conviction of the family's lineage. "'You're descended from Thomas Jefferson,' she would say, 'I'm not but you are.'"

Cinder listened intently, taking notes as she had when she and I had met for lunch back in January. She wondered whether Jan knew when Aunt Peachie was born or whether she had talked about her childhood. "She had a stroke, you see," explained my sister. "There's no telling what damage was done to her memory." But Jan guessed she was about eighty years old when she died in the early 1960s. She never talked about her parents or her upbringing. What seemed most important to her was that her half-sister's children were Jefferson descendants.

The first time Cinder and I had lunch, I brought old black-and-white family pictures with me. This time, I had what we had begun calling "the Taylor Bible," my inheritance from Uncle Eugene.

The black, leather-bound book was about the size of my hand. Its yellow and stained pages lacked the dog-ears that distinguished frequently read books. I knew from the census record that my great-grandmother Rachel from whom the book might have been passed down could not read. Although my grandmother Eva was literate and a religious woman, she apparently did not read from the Taylor Bible either. Like so much about my ancestors, their habits would remain a mystery. However, the significance of the Bible to us was incalculable, like finding a rare blue diamond. With the inscriptions "1821" and "D:T" inside the front cover, it was the oldest tactile link to our family's past—so valuable to me that I kept it in a bank safety deposit box.

Cinder carefully examined the heirloom, her eyes bright with interest. She gently opened the cover, turning to the first page. She was looking for the printer and the printing date, she explained, which might help us track down the book's original owner. We found what we were looking for in the first pages: "Edinburg, Printed by Sir D. Hunter Blair and J Bruce, Printers to the King's Most Excellent Majesty, 1819." That was seven years before Thomas Jefferson's death, and he had not been to Europe since 1789, so the book was certainly not his. Nor did we know of any Taylors with the initial "D."

The original owner of the Taylor Bible, like so much else, would remain unknown; however, the book meant enough to my uncle, his mother, and his grandmother for them to treasure it. As Cinder handed it back to me, I wrapped it in tissue, placed it in a plastic bag, and returned it to my purse. The next day, it would be back in the safety deposit box.

"What did you think of Cinder?" I asked Jan as we drove the seventy miles back to Richmond.

"She's really smart and I'm so happy that you found her," my sister cooed, her voice warm with affection. And then, as gracious as always, she thanked me for what I had accomplished. In fewer than three years, thanks to Cinder, we knew—or at least strongly suspected—our Jefferson link. However, until we had more proof, Moncure Robinson Taylor and Rachel Robinson would remain our "presumed" great-grandparents. And that proof could only come from more documentation, which was unlikely, or science. If DNA could prove that Hemings descendants were related to Jefferson, then it could show that we were as well. But we needed a white descendant to provide a sample. I already had a candidate mind.

Janice stayed with us about five months before deciding to move to Harlem to be with her son and daughter-in-law. New York was her favorite city, so she had a lot to look forward to. And so did I, as I would soon be meeting Tess Taylor.

21

THE RANDOLPHS

Colonial Virginia, 1650

In Virginia's social pecking order FFVs—First Families of Virginia—the Randolphs are at the top of the heap. Their ancestors were the wealthy British colonists who settled in Virginia, many of whom accumulated land, traded enslaved humans, and amassed fortunes. The Carys, Carters, Taylors, and Randolphs—all my white relatives—were among Virginia's most prominent families. However, the Randolphs were first among equals. The dynasty's founders, Mary Isham and William Randolph, had so many children marry into other FFVs that they are known as the "Adam and Eve of Virginia." They produced America's first US attorney general, a Supreme Court justice, governors, congressmen, and the third president of the United States—being Thomas Jefferson's great-grandparents. Confederate general Robert E. Lee was a Randolph. A descendant of the only child of Pocahontas, the daughter of the Powhatan chief and wife of Englishman John Rolphe, married into the Randolph family. Decades later, one of their descendants, Ann Cary, married her second cousin, Thomas Mann Randolph Sr. They were my five-times-great-grandparents, making me a lineal descendant, albeit a distant one, of the world's most celebrated American indigenous woman.

Cousins married cousins, allowing families to consolidate their wealth, political power, and social standing. Thomas Jefferson's mother, Jane, was a Randolph. Martha and Thomas Jefferson's younger daughter, Mary, married a cousin, John Wayles Eppes. Jefferson's eldest daughter with Martha and my four-times-great-grandmother, Martha, married a third cousin, Thomas Mann Randolph Jr., Jefferson's great-granddaughter, my great-great-grandmother, also named Martha, married a cousin, John Charles Randolph Taylor. It was all perfectly legal then, as it is now. In Virginia and in half of the United States, cousins can—and do—marry.

Tess Taylor, a documented descendant of the Jefferson, Randolph, and Taylor clans, was a verifiable FFV. According to a nineteenth-century practice, however, descendants of a "natural union," that is, one between a white man and an enslaved woman, were not considered FFVs. But in the twenty-first century, I felt that my FFV status, and that of thousands of others from "natural unions," was as legitimate as any white person's.

This was one of the genealogical lessons I shared with a Richmond newspaper columnist as he, Jack, and I drove to Charlottesville to meet Tess Taylor in mid-September 2013. Michael Paul Williams was also a friend who had long been interested in my family's lore.

Tess was in Charlottesville promoting her book, whose online *Publishers Weekly* review had brought us together. We had exchanged countless emails and had several conversations since our first one in April. She was chatty and talked a lot about her upbringing in the Berkeley area, about attending public school and having Black friends. Her mother, who did missionary work, and Jack had both attended Swarthmore College at around the same time. They both had been student civil rights activists but did not know each other.

Now that Tess and I were about to meet, I would get an up-close impression of her. We planned to rendezvous at what had become my usual spot, Hamiltons' on the Downtown Mall. At Tess's suggestion, we invited Cinder, who knew Tess from her stint as an International Center for Jefferson Studies (ICJS) fellow at Monticello. I thought it was a gracious gesture. I also wondered if Tess felt having Cinder present would ease any anxiety we might have, or more pointedly, that *Tess* might have. Meeting a cousin from across the racial divide could be awkward. When the shared ancestor is Thomas Jefferson, it could also be momentous, which is why I invited Michael to witness the event.

Lunch was set for 11:30, but Tess was late. Five, ten, fifteen minutes went by before she arrived, breathless, her forehead dotted with light beads of sweat. She apologized for running behind, a little jet-lag, she said. No problem, we told her, as she slid into a seat beside Cinder. She was wearing a blue dress and carrying a heavy-looking bag. Her hair was blond, her jaw square, and her nose perky. She was not tall, maybe five feet two or five feet three, and of medium build. It was odd for me, looking at this pretty white girl and thinking, "She's my cousin."

The first few minutes of the conversation were indeed awkward, with Tess directing most of the conversation toward Cinder, almost as if she were too timid to engage with me. But I pushed myself into the conversation. "Did you bring pictures?" I asked, wondering if her father, the Jefferson descendant, looked anything like mine. She had not. In fact, as she described her dad's short height and mixed grey hair, he sounded just the opposite of mine, who was six feet two and had red hair before he lost most of it. "Did he," like my dad, "have the Jefferson nose with the raised bridge?" I asked. No, said Tess. I thought to myself that my Black father had more physical character-istics in common with Jefferson than her white one.

Allowing us some privacy, Jack and our columnist friend sat at another table as Tess and I got acquainted. By the time coffee and dessert were served, we were seated together and engaged in a robust conversation about politics, history, and the importance of family. Tess had a book signing at Monticello later that afternoon and in-vited us to join her. The signing was hours away, so we decided to walk up to the family cemetery while we waited.

Aside from grounds caretakers, only Monticello Association members, a group made up of white Jefferson descendants and their immediate families, are allowed behind the cemetery's gate. Guests are welcome to accompany family members on special occasions, such as the gathering for the annual holiday wreath laying. To get access, members have to request the key from guest services at the Visitor Center. I watched Tess walk confidently into the ticket office and ask for the key. No one asked her for proof of her Jefferson/Randolph bona fides. Again, thoughts of who had access to Jefferson's legacy crossed my mind. I believed that I had the same rights as Tess to the key and to the cemetery where our ancestors were buried.

Two days later the story "Confronting Jefferson's Legacy Unites Two Women" was promoted on the front page of the *Richmond Times-Dispatch*, along with a picture of Tess and me. Michael had taken the shot of the two of us standing in front of Jefferson's tomb in the cemetery where I and other Black Jefferson descendants were not welcome. Examining the photo, the two of us staring into the camera lens of a cell phone, I searched for physical resemblance that would be evidence that we shared DNA, and found none. I won-dered whether I could find common ground with this white woman who was 20 years younger than I and whose white privilege gave her access to places that I was denied, including our family's cemetery.

I felt resentful that her color—her whiteness—gave her entrée that I did not have, that she could document her family—our family—back to Great Britain, that her claims to the Jefferson mantle were not disputed, that she was an unchallenged FFV. While I didn't doubt my family's lineage, I knew others questioned it. After meeting Tess, who breezily collected the key to the family cemetery, I became more determined than ever to get proof that my family's legacy was as credible as my white cousin's.

22

COUSINS

After our meeting, Tess and I became regular chit-chatters, both of us wanting to learn as much as we could about the other. We were so in sync, it seemed, that I suggested we write a piece about discovering a cousin on the other side of the racial divide. Not this time, she said, but maybe we could collaborate later. Right now, she was writing her own piece for the *New York Times*.

I was admittedly taken aback, wondering what kind of story she could write without my input. Was she going to make *our* experience all about *her*? A piece by the two of us—Black and white cousins—I felt had great potential to add to the country's conversation about race—and not what separates, but what brings us together. Although disappointed, I agreed to go along with her plan, proposing that perhaps the *Times* might accept a companion piece from me. Tess had given me her editor's name and contact information.

The *Times*'s electronic version of Tess's essay was published on January 22, 2014. At first, I was excited to see my name in the preeminent *New York Times*, an experience I had not had since my byline appeared decades earlier. But after reading the piece several times, I began to feel—well, cheated. My voice was missing. More convinced than ever that my perspective deserved attention, I spent a day at my computer writing my own piece. I sent it to Tess's editor at the

Times in hopes that it would run in the paper's hardcopy edition. She turned me down in follow-up email. "This is really interesting, but unfortunately we don't do opinion essays in response to other essays we've published," she wrote, while suggesting that the Letters to the Editor section might be interested in a scaled down version. She offered to send the piece to the letters editor. I felt insulted but agreed to the submission. I never heard from him.

Jack suggested that I pitch the piece to *The Root*, an online publication in the spirit of great Black newspapers of an earlier era, like the *Amsterdam News* or the *Chicago Defender*. It was not the *New York Times*, but it had a following among young African Americans. At least I would get my side of the story out there.

Tess's piece, "Cousins, Across the Color Line," ran in the hardcopy of the *Times* Sunday Review section on January 26, 2014. My piece for *The Root*, "Ties to Thomas Jefferson Unravel Family Mystery," also ran on January 26.

To compare the stories would be unfair. They were both well-crafted essays that swelled with emotion. Typing at my home office desk, I fought through tears as I wrote, reliving the heart-wrenching conversations with Dad. I don't know how Tess felt as she composed her piece, but I know how her article made me feel—like a supporting player in my own production.

From the very first line, I felt that my humanity was compromised. "I learned about her through the comments section of an article in Publisher's Weekly," Tess wrote. What followed felt worse. She introduced me as "the woman, Gayle Jessup White." Something about that phrase, "the woman," was off-putting to me. It reminded me of the crime stories I had written as a young reporter—"The woman" was arrested for shoplifting, "the woman" was accused of drug dealing, "the woman" was charged with whatever. Maybe I was being hypersensitive, but two paragraphs into the essay and I was already feeling violated.

Much of the piece was extracted from the conversation we had the first time we met at lunch with Cinder. She consigned to me feelings that I did not have, suggesting "frustration," or watching me "stiffen" when she seemed to doubt my family's lineage. She went so far as to quote my response after she questioned whether I was looking for proof.

"You know," Gayle said firmly. "This is my story. This is my family's story. I don't really need any more proof."

I did not like reading quotes from our private conversation in the newspaper. And I did not like being called "the woman." In my view, what Tess did was tantamount to cultural appropriation. She was using my Black experience to tell her white story.

The Root gave me a platform to present my own narrative, one that I controlled. I was grateful. The essay condensed forty years of searching for Dad's family into a thousand words. Some of the same players were mentioned—Tess and Cinder—but the piece was about my family and my journey. The photo of my grandmother in her blue-striped "Gibson Girl" shirt was featured above the first paragraph:

More than 40 years ago, I learned of my family's ancestral ties to Thomas Jefferson. It was a blood connection impossible to prove, and one seldom discussed, as my father was ashamed of his mother's out-of-wedlock birth. Still, he acknowledged that he'd heard from an older generation that Jefferson was his lineal ancestor. The tie was a mystery because the only black descendants we knew of were from Jefferson's relationship with Sally Hemings, and we couldn't find the link.

Dad also painfully confessed that his mother's life was a mystery—she and his five older sisters died of tuberculosis in 1920 when he was 5 years old, leaving him and his older

brother to be raised by a taciturn father and a cold step-
mother. He remembered little about his mother and seemed
to know even less. He did offer these tidbits: She was born
in Charlottesville, Va., home of Jefferson's Monticello, and
she sometimes called herself Eva Robinson, other times
Eva Taylor. No one knew why.

Like most African Americans, oral history is my primary source for deep family roots. There are no birth certificates, marriage licenses or census records. Our great-great
grandmothers, great-great grandfathers, aunts, uncles and
cousins were items on manifests, bills of sale and plantation ledgers. Sometimes, our forefathers or their families
owned our foremothers. This was apparently the case in my
family. But I wasn't to learn that for decades.

No, 40 years ago, I was accepting of what scant evidence
I had, and for me, there was little doubt of my father's
Jefferson family bona fides. Dad was tall—6 feet 2 inches—
freckle-faced and, in his youth, redheaded. He even had, I
would learn years later, the Jefferson family nose, one that
sloped gently. It was evident that there were whites in the
woodpile, as folks used to say.

So when after years of collecting what little tangible proof
was available, including a Bible engraved with the initials
D.T. and the date 1821, which belonged to my grandmother
and which I inherited from my uncle, and a baptismal certificate signed Eva Taylor Jessup, I was thrilled to find more
circumstantial evidence. With the help of Thomas Jefferson
scholar Lucia (Cinder) Stanton, I saw a 1900 census record
listing my grandmother. She was a domestic servant living in
the home of Jefferson's great-granddaughter. I almost wept
when I read Cinder's words: "Could this Eva Robinson be

your grandmother?" Cinder, who had built a highly regarded career studying Jefferson and his Monticello slaves and is the author of *"Those Who Labor for My Happiness": Slavery at Thomas Jefferson's Monticello*, seemed very confident.

It wasn't long before she found my great-grandmother, one Rachael Robinson, in the 1870 census records, unmarried and with two children described as "mulattos." Living as a bachelor and just one household away was Moncure Robinson Taylor, my probable great-grandfather and Jefferson's great-great grandson, and the man who most likely fathered her children. Additionally, in 1901, my grandmother, Eva Robinson Taylor, left Charlottesville for Washington, DC, where she was married. Around the same time, Moncure Robinson Taylor, then 40 years old, married for the first time. An interesting coincidence, or had Rachael, my great-grandmother, died, leaving Eva free to move to the city and Moncure free to marry? There's no written evidence of that, no death certificate, but it's possible. Cinder said the discoveries made her tingle. To say I felt the same would be an understatement.

So I've learned my family is probably descended from the Taylor line, explaining why my grandmother sometimes used that surname. I started attending lectures about Jefferson, taking my friends to Monticello, Googling Thomas Jefferson and African-American descendants. It was the Googling that delivered. I read about Tess Taylor, a poet and a white Jefferson descendant. She'd written a book of poems, *The Forage House*, about her conflicting feelings of being descended from the country's most enigmatic slave-holder. I sensed a connection, I reached out and she reached back. I would learn later that Tess's great-great-grandfather was

Moncure's brother, and my great uncle. That would make Tess my third cousin, once removed.

So began a series of conversations that led to a lunch meeting in Charlottesville last September. Tess, who's from California, was visiting Virginia, where I live, promoting her book. I found Tess a little reserved at first, directing most of her interest toward Cinder, who was dining with us. I wouldn't allow that to last, pulling the conversation toward me, toward us. Eventually we were engaged in a conversation about our families. I wondered if she'd heard stories (she hadn't), if our dads looked alike (they don't).

Here's the thing, I wasn't looking for validation or proof from Tess, who wrote of our meeting in the *New York Times*. It's interesting that Jefferson is in the genealogical chart, and I always knew I had white cousins whom I'd probably never know, so it's nice to have connected with Tess. I'm also pleased that historians may have yet another intriguing tale to pursue in the Jefferson family saga.

But I was looking for something more meaningful, more personal. I was looking to solve the enigma of Eva Robinson Taylor, whose death at an early age had left a void in my father's life, one that was with him until he died at almost 90 years old. A death that caused so much pain for a family Eva would never know, and for me, who started this journey as a young girl and just wanted a happy father.

I haven't learned from Tess more about Eva Robinson Taylor, but I have learned something about my white Taylor family ancestors. And I've discovered an interest from people, Black and white, who see their family's history in my own, people wanting to connect across racial, cultural and ethnic boundaries. I'm still searching for more about Eva

Robinson Taylor, for more cousins—black, white, brown. And I wish my father had lived long enough to know all this. For me, at least, some healing has begun.

I had a couple of small details wrong, the spelling of Rachel's name and Moncure's age when he married (he was fifty, not forty), but aside from that, I felt that the essay hit its mark. The essay's last line carried weight for me, and writing the piece helped assuage the antipathy I was feeling toward Tess and her *New York Times* story. At the time, I didn't tell her how I felt. In fact, I wrote to her that I was "thrilled." But the more I absorbed her words, the more unsettling they became. Still, I said nothing. It was part of the Jessup culture not to criticize. "If you can't say something nice . . . ," Mom always said. Besides, I didn't think she would understand how I felt. I believed that her white privilege was would stand in the way.

Whatever my agitation, all was forgiven by a fortuitous outcome. Tess concluded that "it's not unreasonable to assume that Gayle and I are cousins. But it's unlikely that we'll see a DNA test that proves this." She had apparently forgotten one of the principal rules of journalism: never make assumptions.

•   •   •

Millions of people were familiar with Harvard professor Henry Louis "Skip" Gates Jr. from years of watching him on PBS. Not only did he host *Finding Your Roots*, a program that exhaustively researched the genealogy of celebrities, but he also produced critically acclaimed programs about Black history and culture, including the award-winning 2013 series *The African Americans: Many Rivers to Cross*. Viewers appreciated his accessible approach to complicated and often painful historical material. But Jack and I knew Skip on a more personal level.

Ever since Jack had written a story about Skip for *TIME* magazine in the 1980s, the two had been friends. It was through Skip, who co-published *The Root* with *The Washington Post*, that I connected with the online magazine. We dined with him during summer vacations on Martha's Vineyard where he regaled celebrity-struck restaurant patrons with his robust storytelling.

However, it was Tess's *New York Times* piece that attracted the attention of *Finding Your Roots*. When the program's geneticist reached out to Tess to ask whether she and I would be interested in taking a DNA test, it was apparent that Skip had not noticed my name in her piece. The oversight further confirmed my assessment of Tess's work—that I had become a bit player in my own story. I had to keep seeking ways to wrestle it back. Of course, I was willing to take a DNA test.

However, because there was always a chance that the test would produce unwelcome results, that we were not Jefferson descendants, I couldn't accept the offer without consultation. With so much at stake, including whether Aunt Peachie was a fabulist, I checked with Jan before committing.

She was at one of her favorite Harlem hangouts—the International House of Pancakes—when I called her. Jan at an IHOP was as incongruous to me as an elegant swan in a rubber tub, but she loved their famous stacks, bathed in butter and syrup. We were on the phone at least an hour, weighing the pros and cons of DNA testing.

The plus side was self-evident. If my DNA matched Tess's, we would finally be able to put to rest any doubts about our Jefferson lineage. Additionally, it might help us find other members of Dad's family, perhaps descendants of his mother's siblings. We knew her sister, the one we called Lucy, had not had children. She might have thought it too risky for a Black person passing for white. Her children might have "thrown back" to a brown ancestor. But Dad said there were brothers who also crossed the color line. If they had children and grandchildren, they would be our second and third cousins—and unbeknownst to them, Black. If we found them, that would be an interesting conversation!

On the other hand, if there was not a match, everything we believed, everything Aunt Peachie had told Jan, everything Cinder and I had uncovered, would have to be challenged. Our claim would forever have a cloud of doubt. It had already happened to one family whose oral history attached them to Jefferson and Monticello. Now, every time the family's name was mentioned in genealogical circles, it was with an asterisk.

The science was precise but not perfect. For instance, it was possible for one sibling to inherit DNA that another sibling did not, or to have no traces of DNA from a distant ancestor. In other words, it was possible for us to be related to the Jefferson/Randolph/Taylor clan and not have a DNA match. Commercial companies like AncestryDNA and 23andMe process millions of samples from around the world (although not as many from Africa as from Europe). Results were persuasive. However, they were based on DNA samples, individuals' family trees, and computer algorithms. Inaccurate input could mean inaccurate outcomes. My sister and I didn't pretend to understand the process but nonetheless agonized over possible mistakes. Despite our anxiety, some of it feigned, for we both enjoyed the drama of it all, we always knew what our decision would be. Of course, I would take the test. Besides, Jan said from her IHOP booth, "No matter the results, it's our story and we're sticking to it."

The kits arrived from AncestryDNA and 23andMe, courtesy of *Finding Your Roots*, in colorful, plastic-wrapped packaging. I let them sit on the dining room table for a full day before opening them, wanting to stretch out the magnitude of what I was about to do. The instructions were simple: spit in a vial, click it shut, shake it, seal it in an envelope, and return to sender.

We waited for the test results, like expectant parents. Days and then weeks went by without a word. Meanwhile, Tess's *Times* piece—and tangentially, mine for *The Root*—continued to attract attention. A producer from a public radio program called the "The Takeaway" invited us to New York for an interview. The show aired on 230 stations nationwide and had 1.5 million listeners. It seemed that Tess and I had a story with legs. We scheduled the interview for February 5, 2014.

I arrived in the city the day before the taping. It was clear and cold—in the high 20s—and too icy for Jan to meet me. But I was so excited that I barely noticed the chill as I made my way to the hotel. However, by later in the day, sitting in a restaurant across from a snow-covered, midtown park, I felt very alone and very nervous.

As a journalist, I had interviewed celebrities from Oprah Winfrey to Janet Jackson. I had posed questions to scores of mayors, governors, and members of Congress. I had met US presidents, including George H. W. Bush and Barack Obama, and two First Ladies, Barbara Bush and Hillary Clinton. However, with few exceptions, I had been on the side with control of the microphone. I was wary of being on the other end of the questions. Unfortunately, a glass of white wine with dinner didn't help to soothe my frayed nerves. Only the comforting words of a dear friend, also a journalist, gave me the confidence I needed. "You know how this works," she said. "Get your talking points together and you'll be fine."

It was good advice. I arrived at the studio early, unflustered, with my talking points in order. WNYC studios where the show was taped was bright with a minimalist décor, an environment where I felt at home. I sat near a door and waited for Tess.

It would be our third time together. After Charlottesville, she had a poetry reading at a suburban Maryland church. I and a couple of my friends made the two-hour drive from Richmond to meet her.

Afterward, we had dinner and martinis. Tess had left her wallet at the hotel, so we ended up covering her meal.

I was truly pleased to see Tess. It felt like we were building something, that we could actually become family. As we walked into the studio for the interview, we chatted as if we had known each other for years.

Wearing a headphone and seated on a stool in front of a mic that looked like a large gourd, I was the first to speak: "I was really excited to meet Tess. I wanted to know if her family looked like mine, if her father looked like my father, for example . . . I wanted her to help me unravel the secrets of my family."

During the sixteen-minute interview, we chatted about how we met, about our shared history, about how we "seemed to like each other," as Tess put it. It was a good conversation. But the most poignant moment for me was when the interviewer asked what it would be like to trade places. That gave me the chance to talk about race, about being fearful of losing my middle-class status, and most frightening, about worrying for my son's well-being:

> I have an extraordinary son—a senior at MIT. He's about to graduate. He's a nice kid. He's smart. He's thoughtful. He holds the door open for people. He loves his mother . . . Every day, I worry that something horrible is going to happen to my son because some wicked person will stereotype him . . . No mother should have to endure that. But African American mothers do every day.

The interview did not run until April 10, scheduled to correspond with Jefferson's April 13th birthday. If we had waited to record the interview around airtime, there would have been much more to add, for soon after the February taping, the DNA results arrived.

23

DNA DOES NOT LIE

March–August 2014

"Great News," exclaimed the subject line in the March 10 email from the geneticist mining our AncestryDNA matches. She could see that I was a match with several Jefferson descendants, including a relative of Martha Jefferson's daughter, which was described as "very strong." But there were no AncestryDNA matches with Tess. Plus, 23andMe results offered a weak match. Tess shared 17 centimorgans, or 0.22 percent, of my DNA. While that was not enough to support my family's oral history, the AncestryDNA matches were. When Tess's father and his cousin agreed to participate, the results were more conclusive. Their DNA indicated that I was their third cousin, a genetic profile that fit perfectly with the circumstantial evidence Cinder and I had collected.

It was enough for me to approach *The Root* about writing another story, this one an homage to the woman who had started it all. The editor agreed, and on April 4, the story ran: "DNA Does Not Lie, and Neither Did Aunt Peachy [*sic*]."

She couldn't read or write and didn't know her own age. By 1942 she was old and without a job. For decades, she'd been a domestic for a wealthy white family, the McKnews, in Washington, DC, until she suffered a crippling stroke. The McKnew family put her out and ours took her in. For 20 years she was part of the Jessup family. Her name was Virginia, but everyone called her Aunt Peachy.

According to my older siblings, Aunt Peachy helped around the house, gave them pennies to purchase candy, and shared their secrets. I never knew her—she died in the early '60s when I was a toddler. But her life had an everlasting impact on mine because it was Aunt Peachy, her nuclear family's sole survivor, who carried tales from past generations to ours.

Her most remarkable and often repeated commentary would begin like this: "You're descendants of Thomas Jefferson," she would say. "I'm not related, but you are." It's that story, which could easily have died with Aunt Peachy, that put me on the path of discovering my family's mysterious and tragic history.

Aunt Peachy, born Virginia Robinson in about 1870, was the half-sister of my grandmother Eva Robinson Taylor, who died when my dad was 5 years old. Dad, almost 90 when he passed away in 2005, didn't remember his mother and recalled very little about his five older sisters, all struck down within two years of each other by tuberculosis. Three girls died in their teens, and two were toddlers. Of the children who survived—two boys—Dad became Aunt Peachy's favorite, and she became his only link to his mother's past.

Eva and Virginia, the two half-sisters, seemed a study in contrasts, according to the few who knew them. They didn't look alike—one tall, the other short; one light, the other brown. While Eva was remembered as soft-spoken and cheerful, educated and refined, Virginia was described as illiterate and superstitious, kindly and childlike.

One of Aunt Peachy's favorite stories, according to my oldest sister, Janice, was an explanation for pigs squealing during thunderstorms: They saw blood in the clouds, she said, and a man had extracted fluid from their eyes to prove it. No one believed that, but everyone believed her when she said Jefferson was our ancestor. Everyone took the word of an old woman who couldn't read, write or do math, a woman who believed that pigs saw blood in clouds.

Now, more than 50 years after Aunt Peachy's death, DNA evidence supports her claim. According to AncestryDNA, I share a connection with white descendants of Thomas Jefferson and his wife, Martha. The sturdiest link goes back to Jefferson's daughter Martha. "There's a very strong match," says genealogist CeCe Moore, who is a genetic genealogical consultant for the PBS program *Finding Your Roots* (produced by *The Root* Editor-in-Chief Henry Louis Gates Jr.). Moore conducted the test and interpreted the results at Gates' request. "This provides fairly strong evidence" for the oral history, says Moore.

Gates had seen a story in the *New York Times* written by a woman with whom I'd recently connected, Tess Taylor, a white Jefferson descendant, who turned out to be my cousin. I'd reached out to her after reading an online review of *The Forage House*, her poetry collection largely about the burden of being the descendant of a slaveholder who happened to write the Declaration of Independence. Taylor wrote about meeting me for the first time last year in Charlottesville, Va.

Tess and I are probably from the same family line, whose patriarch, J.C.R. Taylor, married Jefferson's great-granddaughter Martha Jefferson Randolph. It was their son, Moncure Robinson Taylor, who likely had a relationship with the woman who is believed to be my great-grandmother Rachael Robinson.

The evidence of family ties is circumstantial: Rachael worked for the Taylor family. She and Moncure were about the same age, and she lived alone with her children near the Taylors. She never married. My grandmother sometimes used the name Taylor on official documents, such as baptismal and death certificates. She named one of her daughters "Cary," a name shared among the Jefferson-Randolph-Taylor clan and the Robinsons.

There aren't enough official documents to definitively make the case, but according to Jefferson scholar Lucia "Cinder" Stanton, what's available is convincing. "The records are still fragmented, but the ones that have been found seem to leap together to confirm the oral history," says Stanton, pre-eminent expert on Jefferson's private life, author of two books on Monticello's slaves and founder of the Thomas Jefferson Foundation's Getting Word oral history of Monticello's slave descendants.

My presumptive great-grandparents, Rachel Robinson and Moncure Robinson Taylor, had several children, most of whom crossed the color line, as did Jefferson and Sally Hemings'. My grandmother did not. She moved to Washington and married Arthur Jessup on Dec. 1, 1901. They had seven children and lived comfortably and happily for many years, until tragedy destroyed their family. I've often thought that it was the senselessness and pain of that loss that compelled me to learn more about my grandmother, that discovering Eva's mysterious past would mitigate my dad's pain.

Or maybe I was simply intrigued to learn that we are Jefferson descendants and wanted to know the truth.

These discoveries have some historical value. According to Stanton, "It bears on the sexual exploitation of servants and women of color that didn't end when slavery ended, it speaks to the division in families because of the color line, and it's relevant to how history is transmitted in families and what is valuable enough to remember."

There's still more DNA discovery ahead. Moore is looking for more scientific evidence that Moncure Robinson Taylor was indeed my grandmother's father. That means reaching out to his white descendants for their DNA samples. Tess Taylor's DNA has already been sampled. Meanwhile, my siblings and I are satisfied that the DNA results we have support what Aunt Peachy always said: that we are Thomas Jefferson's descendants. Not that we ever had any doubts.

It was a good piece that led to a few invitations for public speaking. In the following months, I was a panelist at a college symposium on slavery, a speaker at a Richmond church, and a guest at Poplar Forest, Jefferson's retreat thirty miles from Charlottesville.

I also met Tess's family—her parents, an aunt and uncle, her sister, and her four-year-old son. There were friendly pictures of me with Tess's dad, who as she said, looked nothing like mine. Yet in spite of my earlier hopes and our attempts to act and feel like kin, we never became family. That we were "cousins across the color line," and not simply "cousins," was one of the barriers that kept us apart. Tess and I never bonded. And while we would make a few presentations together and see each other again at Monticello, eventually the emails and calls became less frequent, like the slowing beat of a heart monitor.

●   ●   ●

I had a part-time job as an "educator" with The Valentine, a Richmond museum of the city's history, and I was also working as a Realtor. Additionally, I had recently applied for a fellowship at Monticello's academic arm, the International Center for Jefferson Studies, to research my family's history and felt confident that I would be accepted as an ICJS fellow. Jack and I were enjoying our lives in Richmond, and Charles was set to graduate from MIT. Everything was looking up for me, until a phone call I received on Monday, June 2, 2014.

It was my son, and his voice was stricken with fear. He was just one week away from graduation, but instead of celebrating completion of four intense years of studies, he was at a suburban Washington hospital. "It's Dad," he said. "I think you should come up right away."

I knew my ex-husband was sick with multiple myeloma, a form of cancer. A year earlier, comforting me through my torrent of tears, he assured me that he had years to live. By that time, Chuck and I were well beyond the differences that had destroyed our marriage. We were friends and the parents of a fine young man. We enjoyed occasional phone conversations and even managed to laugh over memories that had mellowed over the years. I expected us to have more time.

When Charles called, I at first thought his father was having a setback from which he would bounce back, certainly in time for our son's graduation. But the urgency in my son's voice said otherwise. He needed me. I cancelled the day's plans, grabbed an overnight bag, and was at the hospital in less than two hours.

I raced from the garage and up the sidewalk leading to the emergency room entrance. Charles rushed out the door, ran over to me, and fell into my arms. We both cried. He did not have to say what I already knew. His father was dead. It was the most painful day of my life—even worse than my own parents' deaths—for there is nothing more heart wrenching than watching your child suffer.

After a couple of days, Charles was composed enough to go

back to Cambridge. Commencement was that Friday, June 6. I took him to the airport, but before I got on I-95 to head back to Richmond, I stopped at Arlington National Cemetery. My grandfather, Arthur Eugene Jessup, a Spanish-American War veteran, was buried there in sight of the USS *Maine* Mast Memorial. I had never been. I am not sure why it was imperative for me to see his grave that day, but like so many mystical experiences, I felt called to do so. It was not unlike the moment on the back porch when I heard my grandmother's voice imploring me, *Tell my story.*

When I found my grandfather's marker, I fell on my knees in gratitude. There lay the remains of the man who knew, loved, and lost my grandmother—the man who taught my father strong values and morals, the man who never finished school, but whose great-grandson would soon graduate from one of the world's top universities. Arthur Eugene Jessup was an American hero. Like my other ancestors, his strength and fortitude were in my DNA, and in Charles's DNA too. Whatever we had to do to get through that week, we would.

It was in our blood.

● ● ●

I spent much of the summer in Cambridge with Charles, who decided to make the city his home. He was resilient and would soon be working as a software engineer. He would be fine. When I got back to Richmond, good news was waiting for me. I had been accepted as a Monticello ICJS fellow. My month-long stint would begin in August. Not only would I receive a stipend, but I would get on-site housing. And best of all, I would have access to the world's greatest Jeffersonian libraries, scholarship, and scholars. After a heartbreaking summer, a month at Monticello was a much-needed balm.

24

WHAT'S IN A NAME?

August 2014

My first few days at Monticello, I didn't know where to begin. The Jefferson Library has more than twenty thousand books, journals, newspapers, audiovisual recordings, and ephemera. It was dizzying. At first, I wandered around the property and through the offices and library, just trying to get my bearings. Before my fellowship, I had seen only the house, nearby grounds, and Visitor Center. The Monticello estate covers twenty-five hundred acres, half of the five thousand acres it once was, but still substantial.

There are several dwellings—many used for offices, others for housing—a farm and nursery, archeological offices and sites, the state-of-the art Visitor Center and museum, and a research complex, including the Robert H. Smith International Center for Jefferson Studies. And of course, there was "the mountain," where Jefferson had his enslaved workers build his architectural masterpiece. Gazing at the horizon from the top of the mountain is like looking into a distant world filled with possibilities. However, in Jefferson's time, a ten-foot fence around a vegetable garden that fed the white household would have blocked workers from seeing the view. Besides, the seductive vista might have been a source of ecstasy for the free and agony for the enslaved. For me, it was a mixture of both. It was impossible not to marvel at such beauty, marred only by imagining the enslaved, whose dawn-to-dusk labor would not have permitted time for indulgences like admiring the scenery and dreaming of the future.

Truth is, I didn't have time to waste either. I had one month to try to uncover the identity of my family, the Robinsons. Once again thanks to Cinder, I had recently found Sally Robinson, Rachel Robinson's mother and my great-great-grandmother, in the 1880 Census, living with her children and grandchildren in Goochland County, Virginia. She was listed as head of household, either widowed or divorced. A son, thirty-five-year-old James, who was not on the 1870 Census, was living with her, as were two younger sons, Peter and Henry. Their names would become very important in tracing the Robinson family. Rachel, my great-grandmother, was not living with them. She was living in Albemarle County with her two children near Moncure's home.

Even with this limited data, I was beginning to sketch a profile of my Robinson ancestors. They were extremely mobile and willing to leave the only home they knew for something different. And they were close. Three of Sally's adult children lived with her, as did several of her grandchildren. And they were light-skinned. Of the ten people living in the 1880 household, seven were described as "Mu" for mulatto. Three of the grandchildren were "b" for Black.

I learned a lot about the people enslaved at Monticello by studying a massive two-volume book called *The Slave Families of Thomas Jefferson* by B. Bernetiae Reed, who had also been a fellow. Reed had meticulously collected the names and occupations of the hundreds of people Jefferson and his family owned, from Shadwell, his childhood home, to Poplar Forest, his Bedford County retreat. I learned a lot about my relatives by reading Reed's book.

For example, there was the practice among my family of passing names from one generation to another. My great-grandmother Rachel

Robinson was apparently named after her paternal grandmother, enslaved at Poplar Forest. Rachel's father was unnamed in the records, but her mother was Cate, a skilled spinner and weaver. Marriages among the enslaved weren't legally recognized but nonetheless were commonly practiced. When Cate married James Hubbard, an enslaved headman over enslaved laborers at Poplar Forest, she became Cate Hubbard. Rachel took his name as well.

Cate and James had several children and extended family enslaved at Poplar Forest. Many of them held positions of authority. Not only was James a headman but so was one of his sons. Cate's sister Hannah was a cook and was literate. A letter she wrote to Jefferson is one of a few preserved from the people he owned. In the letter, written on November 15, 1818, she assures Jefferson that his home is well cared for and asks about his health:

> Master I write you a few lines to let you know that your house and furniture are all safe as I expect you would be glad to know I heard that you did not expect to come up this fall I was sorry to hear that you was so unwell you could not come. It greive [*sic*] me many time but I hope as you have been so blessed in this that you considered it was god that done it and no other one we all ought
>
> to be thankful for what he has done for us we ought to serve and obey his commandments that you may set to win the prize and after glory run
>
> Master I donot [*sic*] my ignorant letter will be much encouragement to you as know I am a poor ignorant creature, this leaves us all well adieu, I am your humble servant Hannah

Hannah clearly had a special relationship with Jefferson, but that did not stop him from selling her son, Billy, after Billy had fought with a white overseer.

While researching the Hubbard family, I discovered that two of Cate and James's sons were so-called runaways. Today we would call them escapees. One son, Phil Hubbard, "ran away" from Poplar Forest to Monticello, where he sought Jefferson's intervention in a disagreement he was having with an overseer. And indeed, Jefferson did intervene on his behalf. His brother James tried to unsuccessfully escape—twice. A "runaway" notice offers a rare description of what one of my distant relatives looked like: "about six feet high, stout limbs and strong made, of daring demeanor, bold and harsh features, dark complexion." James was captured and brought back to Monticello where Jefferson had him "severely flogged in the presence of his old companions, and committed to jail." He further wrote that "all circumstances convince me he will never again serve any man as a slave. The moment he is out of jail and his irons off he will be off himself." With that as a conviction, Jefferson, who had sold James in absentia, recommended that his new owner sell him out of Virginia. I was sickened by Jefferson's cruelty but proud of James's attempts to gain his freedom and inspired by his courage.

CATE, MY FOUR-TIMES-GREAT-GRANDMOTHER, WAS BORN AT SHADWELL, Jefferson's childhood home. From what I gleaned from Reed's book, her mother was a woman named Old Sall, an enslaved nursemaid. It is likely that Old Sall, my enslaved five-times-great-grandmother, nursed the child Jefferson, who would become my five-times-great-grandfather. It is also notable that Jefferson, as he came into his manhood, also came into possession of his father's property, including his old nursemaid. Generations of comingling between the enslaved and the enslaver demonstrates the complexity and bizarre nature of their relationships.

Monticello's scholars and staff were very helpful, and after a few days, I was beginning to feel like an amateur historian. Up to that point, I had leaned on secondary sources—books and the research of others. But as my confidence grew, I wanted to examine primary sources. That meant venturing away from Monticello to the University of Virginia, where many Jefferson family letters and memorabilia are stored and catalogued. There is even a lock of his hair, apparently clipped when he was older, as it is a mixture of grey and a pale chestnut.

I plied through boxes filled with letters folded into small rectangles, ledgers of daily expenditures, old photographs, and handwritten family trees. There were moments when I could not believe I was holding two-hundred-year-old letters in my hand.

There were photographs and drawings of my white forebears— my great-great-great-grandparents and great-great-grandmother. I studied the images, in much the same manner that I had studied Tess Taylor's visage, looking for shared features. My ancestors' stern faces looked nothing like mine—not their narrow mouths, dark eyes, or broad foreheads. They didn't feel like family, not the way Sally and Edmund Robinson did, or Cate and James Hubbard, or Old Sall.

I read through scores of letters hoping to find a passing mention of my enslaved ancestors but was disappointed. However, I did find comments about my white great-grandfather Moncure. They were snapshots of a man who seemed to be struggling. There was a letter from West Virginia in 1890 in which a nephew had written to his sister that "Uncle Cure is going to work a force on Mr. Pages Road . . . which will be a very good job." The reference was likely to William Nelson Page, cofounder of the Virginian Railway. Another from 1895 between his sisters Cornelia and Patty was less hopeful: "Cure has just been [illegible] he looks really badly and thin and each time he hates more and more to go back. He has only $300 more to pay on the place and I hope will be able to settle down in another year."

The last letter I found was dated June 19, 1896, from sister Margaret Taylor to a niece: "I hope Cure's hand is not serious he has had that place on his skin for some years. When he came in Willie thought it had a growth in it and that it would be best to burn it out which he did, but very slightly." This letter was written four years before the 1900 Census that showed my grandmother Eva living as a servant in the same household as Jefferson's great-granddaughter and sixteen years after the 1880 Census that listed Moncure as the unmarried head of household living a few doors away from my great-grandmother Rachel.

I appreciated having some insight into the life of my great-grandfather. But what I really wanted to find was anything at all about my Black ancestors, especially Rachel Robinson. I went to the Albemarle County Courthouse in Charlottesville looking for deeds, hoping to find her name attached to property, but found nothing. I visited the town's segregated graveyard and walked among the tombstones. Again, nothing.

I headed to the Albemarle Charlottesville Historical Society, where I was told that a little old lady had worked there practically since the place was founded in 1940. Folks said she held in her head almost all there was to know about Charlottesville. Of course, they were exaggerating—but only a little. The breadth of her knowledge was encyclopedic.

She found pictures of Lego, the Taylor family plantation that had once been Jefferson's property. She also had an image of Edgehill, the plantation Jefferson's grandson Thomas Jefferson Randolph left to his unmarried daughters. It was also where the 1900 Census listed Eva, my grandmother, living and working as a servant.

Most interesting was an 1861 Roll of Book of the Charlottesville Baptist Church that included the names of their congregants, among them three people whose names I recognized and who were owned by Thomas Jefferson Randolph, Jefferson's grandson and my three-times-great-grandfather. Henry, James, and Sally were baptized on

September 8, 1861; I knew from the 1870 and 1880 Censuses that my great-great-grandmother Sally Robinson had sons named James and Henry. I was confident I had finally found some of my Black family. On the eve of the Civil War, they were attending church.

At the end of my fellowship, I made a presentation to about thirty people, among them Jeffersonian scholars and Monticello's staff. My lecture included what I had discovered about my white ancestors, about their pain and disappointments, including the deaths of family members. A letter from my three-times-great-grandmother Jane Hollins Nicholas Randolph lamented the loss of her adult children. "And they are such good children," she wrote. The heart-wrenching letter made her real for me. I sympathized with her suffering, as any mother would have, even though she was mistress to my enslaved ancestors.

While I didn't uncover as much as I had hoped about my Black ancestors, I did learn their names, and that was important. It was the names—Sally, Peter, Cary Ann, James, Lucy—that established a pattern. They were names held by the Hemings and Randolph families, and by mine. "What's in a name?" I asked during the presentation. I didn't have the answer yet, but I knew I was onto something because I was tingling.

25

THE ROBINSONS

May 2015

Since returning to Richmond from DC, I had wanted a career change, and real estate was not it. History, and not just my own family's, was my passion. I loved reading biographies and watching TV programs about the founders and the nation's origins. American presidents held a particular fascination. Rather than counting sheep at night, I counted the people who have held the office. I was usually out by the time I got to eight—Martin Van Buren.

As I contrived paths to a career at Monticello, I thought, *Why not become a historian?* I had the job as The Valentine Museum educator and a few history classes under my belt. Cinder was founder and facilitator of a group of amateur historians, which I joined. I even started the application process for a certificate in public history.

Since my fellowship, I had become a regular at Monticello, getting to know the staff and attending lectures and other special events. I was there when Mulberry Row, the plantation's "Main Street," was commemorated on May 2, 2015. When descendants were asked to stand, I was proud to oblige, even though I felt a bit like an impostor. At the time, I wasn't sure my ancestors actually had been enslaved at Monticello. Thanks to my work with Cinder and DNA testing with Tess, I knew I was related to the man who had owned Monticello. However, my legacy felt incomplete, like a book I never got around to finishing.

That summer, I joined descendants who spent the night in extant and reconstructed slave dwellings. It was part of an initiative called the Slave Dwelling Project that seeks to raise awareness about the people who once slept in the cabins, kitchens, and hallways of their owners. I felt a fellowship with the group of about twenty people, even though I wasn't sure how my heritage related to theirs, aside from my white ancestor having owned their forebears.

I spent a hot and humid August night on the floor of the early nineteenth-century kitchen located in an underground wing attached to the main house that Jefferson called a "dependency." Throughout that sleepless night I waited to feel the presence of my ancestors but felt only the hard floor against my back. It wasn't until the next morning when we rose at dawn, as our ancestors had, that I experienced the emotion that had eluded me the night before. At the African American Burial Ground, the descendants gathered around the stones that were the only markers of the souls laid to rest there. As we prayed and sang, I remained unmoved—until it was my turn to say out loud, as the others had, the names of our ancestors. I heard my own voice rise, heavy and mournful, "Cedric, Billye, Eva, Arthur, Rachel, Edmund." And when the tears finally flowed, they were as much for them as they were for those whose names we would never know.

• • •

As I wrote in *The Root*, much of what motivated my determination to find my family's connection to Jefferson was the search for my dad's lost family. The line was almost completely severed when his mother and sisters died. I thought it might bring my father, if not happiness, at least a little peace if I found his family. I couldn't make that happen for him; however, some ten years after Dad's death, it did happen for me.

In the fall of 2015, I *finally* found a Robinson descendant. My DNA had been banked with Ancestry.com for two years when I connected with a fourth cousin, Kevin Nelson. He lived in a DC suburb not far from where I grew up, and we were about the same age. However, the fact that we had never crossed paths was not surprising in a metropolitan area of some six million people.

Nonetheless, I was more than intrigued when I learned that his ninety-plus-year-old mother, the Robinson descendant, was named Louise. Perhaps it was a coincidence, but my father's oldest sister was called Louise, and it was also my middle name. "*Gayle Louise!*" Mom would scold when I needed a reprimand, contributing to a disdain I had for the mere sound of the name. But as I began to understand the significance of caring for my family's legacy (the name Louise also belonged to a maternal aunt), I embraced the name.

My DNA match with Kevin seemed to indicate that Edmund, the man I presumed was my great-great-grandfather, and Kevin's great-great-grandfather were brothers. Rachel, the woman I presumed was my great-grandmother, was the cousin of his great-grandfather. That meant that our shared ancestor was third-great-grandmother Rachel Hubbard, the woman my presumed great-grandmother was named after.

I had very little documentation that Rachel Robinson was indeed my great-grandmother, only hunches. What we knew, thanks to a death record, was that as early as 1868, she was working in the Taylor household. According to the records, she had a two-year-old child, Kate, who died from "croup." Rachel would have been fifteen or sixteen years old when she had little Kate, and if Moncure was the father, he would have been fourteen or fifteen.

I also had documentation with my grandmother's use of the Taylor surname, and of course, the family's oral history. Now, with DNA matches to Robinson descendants, it was confirmed that I was indeed a Robinson, just as DNA had demonstrated that I was related to the Jefferson/Randolph clan.

Kevin told me he remembered childhood visits to the Goochland farms where Sally Robinson's son and grandson lived. He knew tales about the family's history, including how the wife of one of the Robinson men died. After an accident, she was denied admission to a white hospital. The practice was common during the Jim Crow era of institutional racism. Many hospitals were "white only" or had a limited number of "Negro beds." The number of Blacks who died or suffered as a result is impossible to determine.

Kevin also knew the identity of the mysterious cousin, sixteen-year-old May Robinson, who according to the 1910 Census was living with the Jessups. She was the grandmother of one of the only cousins Dad knew. Kevin also knew the names of her descendants. It would take several months, but I eventually tracked them down living in the DC area. They were excited to learn that they were descended from Monticello's enslaved community.

Ancestry.com proved an invaluable tool in finding Robinson cousins. I traced Cary Ann, one of my great-grandmother's sisters, to Washington, DC, where her husband drove a cab. Her grandson would graduate from Harvard in the 1950s. Cary Ann was undoubtedly among the mourners at my grandmother Eva's funeral.

Kevin told me there was another man on Ancestry, Andrew Davenport, who likely was also a Robinson cousin. I sent Andrew a note through Ancestry's message board. Days later, we were on our cell phones chatting. He was my son's age—mid-twenties—and we hit it off immediately. He lived in Connecticut and taught high school history. His passion for uncovering his family's genealogy matched mine. Andrew would become the pivotal link to the people in Dad's past and many of his lost cousins. I would eventually become an important link to Andrew's future.

It was exhilarating to find Robinson cousins. As I reached out to a half dozen newly discovered family members, I found them smart, engaging, affable, and judging from the pictures they emailed, good looking. They looked like family to me. Still, after hours spent with them over the phone and the internet, I was no closer to knowing who Sally Robinson was. My cousins knew less about our family's ancestors than I did, and no one had information about the Monticello link. However, that was about to change. Cinder and I would soon uncover a century-old document that for my family was as transformative as the Rosetta Stone had been for antiquarians.

While I was busy getting to know my Robinson cousins, Cinder was making discoveries of her own. Although she was retired, she still enjoyed the detective work that is part of genealogical research. The email she sent me in October 2015 said she was looking at Virginia death records that Ancestry.com recently had made available. She was looking for another family when, she wrote, "I found myself entering 'Robinson' in the search box."

Two relevant documents emerged: the deaths of Peyton Robinson at the age of fifty-four in 1921 and Peter Robinson at age fifty-nine in 1924. They were nephew and uncle, but matriarch Sally Robinson raised them as brothers. They were so close that they married sisters and had farms next to each other, the ones my newfound cousin Kevin had visited when he was a boy. Reading the death certificates, as I had my own grandmother's, I was impressed by how much can be extrapolated by a small amount of information. Peyton, for example, died from liver cancer, often caused by excessive alcohol consumption. His father was "not known," but his mother was a Robinson. He was a farmer and a husband who was born in Albemarle County and died in Goochland.

It was a small snapshot of his life, but interesting. However, it was the information in Peter's death certificate that was the most enthralling. He died of heart disease, and like his nephew, he was a farmer. His father, the record said, was Edmund Robinson—we knew that from 1870 and 1880 Censuses. However, it was his mother's name that made our heads spin: Sallie Hemmans.

Said out loud, "Hemings" could very well sound like "Hemmans," and the death certificate's inscriber could have spelled it phonetically. Also different from other documents, such as the census, was the spelling of "Sallie" rather than "Sally." As no documents exist bearing my great-great-grandmother's signature, I have no way of knowing which she preferred. However, in Randolph family letters, her name is spelled "Sally." That was a small adaptation. It was the name "Hemmans" that captivated Cinder and me.

Once again, we had a hunch. The famous Sally Hemings had a brother named Peter. Could "Sallie Hemmans," my great-great-grandmother, be his daughter? Was my great-great-grandmother named after her aunt? Was she another Sally Hemings?

The prospect was so exciting that I couldn't sleep that night. I spent the evening reading over Annette Gordon-Reed's *The Hemingses of Monticello* and Cinder's *"Those Who Labor for My Happiness."* The next day, Cinder and I were again exchanging emails. The Hemingses were known to pass down names to family members—Peter, Sally, Lucy, James, and Anderson were Robinsons with Hemings first names. Again, it was circumstantial evidence, but still, the clues were demonstrative. Although the names were not spelled the same on Peter's death certificate, it appeared that Sally Robinson, my great-great-grandmother, was named after her aunt, Sally Hemings. Further, "my" Sally apparently named her son Peter after her father, Sally Hemings's brother.

Two years earlier when I had been an ICJS fellow presenting what I knew of the Robinsons, I had asked, "What's in a name?"

Now, with the information from Peter Robinson's death certificate, I knew. The Robinsons were related to the country's best-documented enslaved family, the Hemingses.

It had been decades since Jan and I had speculated that we were descended from Sally Hemings, and I had been disappointed to learn that we were not. We felt it was an honor to be a Hemings. However, armed with Peter Robinson's death certificate and excerpts from Randolph family letters that mentioned Sally—"my" Sally—Peter, and his wife, Betsy, I discovered that I was a Hemings after all.

Sally Hemings, it turned out, was my four-times-great-aunt. The records and documents that Cinder and I had assembled and Robinson family DNA indicated that her brother Peter was my three-times-great-grandfather. Enslaved at Monticello, he was a cook and respected brewer who trained others how to brew malt. Jefferson described him as possessing "great intelligence and diligence." He was also a tailor. However, those qualities didn't save him from being sold after Jefferson died.

Studying the historical documents and pondering what I was learning about my family, I recalled the Monticello kitchen where I had spent a miserable August night. I didn't know that I was sleeping where my great-great-great-grandfather had served as head cook.

Learning that Sally Robinson was the niece of Sally Hemings also exposed another corrupt aspect of enslavement. Martha Jefferson Randolph's mother, Thomas Jefferson's wife, was Sally Hemings's half-sister. That meant that Sally was Martha's aunt. The two were close in age. That also meant that in 1833 in Washington when Martha beat the restrained Sally—"my" Sally—she was torturing her own cousin. The blood that might have spilled on the basement floor was the same that ran through Martha's veins, as it is the same running through mine.

• • •

"Every generation was supposed to have a Sally after Sally Hemings," my ninety-year-old cousin explained the first time we met. Ruth Johnson lived in Richmond with her eighty-eight-year-old baby brother. They lived about twenty miles across town in a predominantly Black, middle-class neighborhood. Their tidy ranch was decorated in the tradition of their social standing in the Black community: plush, upholstered living room furniture; a formal dining room set, including sideboard and China cabinet displaying porcelain and crystal finery. Family photographs were strategically displayed on an end table, a shelf, and a storage cabinet. The décor was not unlike that of my childhood home, the neighborhood not unlike Eastland Gardens where I grew up. The moment I stepped through Ruth's door, I felt as if I belonged.

Looking at Ruth, no one ever would have guessed that she was ninety. With her stylish, asymmetrically styled blond hair and flawless, honey-colored complexion, she appeared twenty years younger. Her grandfather Anderson and my great-grandmother Rachel were siblings, the children of Sally and Edmund Robinson.

She was born in Goochland where her family owned a popular night club called Cooke's. Some of the biggest names in 1960s R&B performed there, including Ike and Tina Turner and Roy Charles Hammond, better known as Roy C. "That was the place," said Ruth. "People came from miles around." Like me, she earned her undergraduate degree at an HBCU, Virginia State University, and her master's at a predominantly white institution, the University of Virginia. She taught school for years but also dallied in a few businesses, including an upscale clothing shop in Goochland.

Even though Ruth and I lived in the same area, it is doubtful that we would have met. It was Andrew Davenport, the young cousin I had connected with through Ancestry.com, who facilitated our introduction. Even he hadn't met her. In fact, Andrew knew very few of his Robinson cousins because they were Black, and his family was "passing" as white. Throughout his youth, Andrew did not know he was Black.

The first time we spoke in January 2016 he was eager to share his story with me. He grew up in Fairfield County, Connecticut, with his mother and grandmother. Like my family, they were devout Catholics. His father was white, as was his grandmother's late husband. And for the first eight or nine years of his life, Andrew also believed he was white.

It was not until he overheard a conversation during which his grandmother confided that she had been called a "nigger" at her class reunion that he started wondering about his racial identity. He never got the full story from his grandmother, but one of her sisters told him the truth shortly before she died.

She put him in touch with a cousin, an attorney, who traversed the color line, passing for white when it was convenient. She gave him Ruth's contact information, which he shared with me. I called her, and a few weeks later, I was sitting in her living room.

The beautiful woman offering me cookies and tea was Daddy's second cousin, as were many of the relatives I would soon meet. Sitting at Ruth's dining room table, I was filled with contentment and gratitude. After a forty-five-year search, I finally had found my father's family.

PART THREE

26

WHITEWASHING HISTORY

August 2015

Leslie Greene Bowman, president of the Thomas Jefferson Foundation, sat in her office overlooking the grounds that had once been
home to Thomas Jefferson, his family, and one hundred fifty or so
enslaved men, women, and children who lived there at any given
them. Jefferson owned more than six hundred people during his lifetime. A copy of a *Washington Post* story rested on her desk.

She was not pleased.

The thirty-three-room mansion whose construction had been
Jefferson's lifelong hobby could be seen from her office window. So
could Mulberry Row, the half-mile industrial stretch where many
of the people Jefferson owned had lived and worked. Four miles of
road separated the twenty-five-hundred-acre remains of the original
five-thousand-acre plantation and the city of Charlottesville. At the
time, the college town of fifty thousand was known as the "happiest
city in America." Two years later, the world would see a horrifyingly
bleaker place.

But in August 2015, the executives who managed the city's most
influential institutions—the University of Virginia, City Hall, and
Monticello—were dealing with the usual issues: student registration,

zoning changes, and visitor satisfaction. It was the last that rattled Leslie as she studied the story written by a dissatisfied guest.

A museum careerist in her fifties, Leslie's petite stature belied a fierce ambition. Since joining the Thomas Jefferson Foundation, she and her team had raised millions of dollars to support the nonprofit's mission: to preserve Monticello and to educate the community. Millions of dollars would be devoted to restoring Monticello's physical landscape to the way it had been during Jefferson's lifetime, with a focus on how the enslaved lived.

There were restored workhouses, a historically reconstructed slave cabin, an exhibition about enslaved domestic servants, and panels describing the work performed by enslaved people. But for one disgruntled guest, Desiree Melton, a Notre Dame of Maryland University philosophy professor, that was not enough. On August 14, she went public with her criticisms in a scathing *Washington Post* op-ed titled "Monticello's Whitewashed Version of History," which was reprinted in papers around the United States.

Melton's essay described how she had to "steady" herself to "stomach" a visit to a former planation. She didn't take the guided tour, she wrote, because she did not want to "share the experience with strangers." However, she could not avoid what she described as the "utter lack of reverence and solemnity" that other guests, all of them white, displayed while touring Mulberry Row.

"One preteen white boy bounded into one of the cabins and exclaimed to his father, 'This isn't so bad!' The father looked around and agreed. I was stunned. But I should not have been," she wrote. Melton went on to criticize Monticello for not providing a complete and honest narrative, of dodging the truth of slavery's brutality, as well as Jefferson's. She wrote, "How does Monticello reconcile its claim that Jefferson was 'kind' to his slaves with the fact that his favorite overseer was the most brutal? How can 'kind' ever be an adjective used to describe a slave owner?"

Melton concluded that a closer examination of the history of America's enslavement of millions of Black people might not solve today's racial tension, "But at the very least, it would be one small step on the way toward facing the truth."

Her words were stinging, and in some ways, prescient. The racial unrest that the country experienced in 2020 was seeded in enslavement and the unrelenting oppression of Black people since 1619. However, Monticello's gatekeepers felt that some aspects of Melton's criticism were unfair. There was the "Slavery at Monticello Tour," which she declined to take, and expanded exhibitions about enslavement at Monticello. Additionally, there was the traveling exhibition, "Slavery at Jefferson's Monticello: Paradox of Liberty," that opened in partnership with the Smithsonian Museum of African American History and Culture and had been on the road since 2012. Leslie and her team did not feel they were "whitewashing history." However, they also knew that perception could become reality, especially when it comes from a Black college professor writing in a newspaper with one million subscribers.

The fact that Jefferson owned 607 people during his lifetime was as unfamiliar to many Americans as his crushing debt. Few knew that when he died, he owed his creditors $100,000, the equivalent of $4 million in 2020. To pay off his debt, most everything he owned was sold, including his home, furnishing, livestock—and people.

On a cold day in January 1827, bidding began on 100 humans who, over five days, were auctioned on Monticello's West Lawn, which had a view of the house familiar to many today as the image on the back of the "Jefferson nickel." Two years later, more people were sold, for a total of 130 men, women, and children. Parents from children, siblings from each other, families from their roots. My ancestors, including Peter Hemings, were among the bereaved. For some, it would be as if their loved ones had died.

Peter eventually obtained his freedom, but his wife, Betsy, and their children, including my great-great-grandmother Sally, remained enslaved. They were the property of Jefferson's son-in-law, Thomas Mann Randolph Jr. Aside from my great-great-grandfather Edmund, the fate of the Hubbards, my ancestors at Poplar Forest, remained unknown. Jefferson's grandson and estate executor, Thomas Jefferson Randolph, purchased Edmund; his mother, Rachel; and as many other enslaved people as he could afford. But it was not enough to keep families together.

The stories told about Monticello's enslaved people were as much a part of the plantation's history as Jefferson and his white family. But if that was not getting across to a woman as steeped in knowledge about history and culture as Melton, then the foundation had more work to do. However, there was a problem, and a big one. Of the five hundred full- and part-time staff members at Monticello, only a handful were Black, and there were no Black or brown people on the leadership team. Even the Getting Word African American Oral History Project lacked leadership diversity. The foundation's two Black historians had left for reasons that were theirs. There was one Black person on the Board of Trustees and there was an African American Advisory Board. But they played no role in day-to-day activities and had an arguably limited influence in policy-making. Melton's piece had actually just scratched the surface.

27

A COFFEE SHOP CHAT

January–May 2016

I started lobbying for a job at Monticello almost immediately after my 2014 fellowship. I applied for a position as Marketing and Communications Manager but did not get a call back. I considered becoming a guide, but the salary would barely cover the cost of the 140-mile round-trip daily commute from Richmond. However, I was unwilling to give up. When I was encouraged by one of my Monticello contacts to apply for a new position, Public Historian of Slavery and African American Life, I thought my moment might finally have arrived. In January 2016, I confidently submitted an application letter:

> *It's rare that a job opportunity fulfills the applicant's passions, aspirations, and professional experience. The Thomas Jefferson Foundation's new position of Public Historian of Slavery and African-American Life offers all those qualities to this candidate. As a former Robert H. Smith International Center for Jefferson Studies Fellow and direct descendant of the Jefferson/Randolph family, I am thrilled to submit my qualifications for what I consider a dream job.*
>
> *I believe that my experience as a reporter, researcher, and*

*teacher—I am currently a Valentine History Museum instructor—
has equipped me with all of the skills required for the "Public
Historian" position. But more than that, it's my deep appreciation
for the Thomas Jefferson Foundation and my personal ties to your
work that best support my candidacy.*

*For the past several years, I have cultivated a life-long love
of history, especially exploring the lives of Thomas Jefferson, his
family, and Monticello's enslaved people, some of them my own
ancestors. More recently, I have joined my cousin, another Jefferson
descendant, in delivering a series of lectures seeking to make that
history relevant and meaningful to today's audiences, especially
among the young, African-Americans, and other minorities. It is
this base of knowledge, along with my 20 years of experience as a
broadcaster, public speaker, and outreach coordinator that I would
bring to the position.*

*My love of history and all things Jefferson have taken me
to places I had never imagined, including, as part of the "Slave
Dwelling Project," a night sleeping on Monticello's kitchen floor.
But the most gratifying experience was as an ICJS Fellow in
August 2014. My research took me closer to the heart of Jefferson's
plantations and to the enslaved people who worked there. My
research continues, and the "Public Historian" position would offer
an extraordinary opportunity to dig deeper and share more.*

The email that soon followed from the human resources office
caused me to spring from the chair like a church lady "feeling the
spirit." The HR officer wanted to know when I would be available for
a phone interview. It was a filter, a first official step toward my dream.
I was measured and deliberate during the interview, enough for her to
pass me to the next level, a series of panel interviews. But if I was eager

to move forward, the folks at Monticello were taking their time. I applied in January but did not get a face-to-face interview until March.

I chose a print jersey green dress to meet the group of historians and administrators who would be deciding my fate. Sitting at a conference table in a paneled room at the Jefferson Library, I tried to follow Dad's maxim: *Never let people know what you're thinking.* Grilled by three senior staffers at the opposite end of the table, I did my earnest best to conceal how much I wanted the job. There were the obvious questions about my background and ones about the kinds of programs I might develop. But the answer that seemed to garner everyone's approval was when I responded to a question about fund-raising. "Everyone works for development at a nonprofit," I said. "No matter what your title is, everyone is a fund-raiser." There were nods all around. When the interview ended almost two hours later, I was sure that all that was left was the offer.

Two weeks later, I got an email from Monticello's new HR director, a woman named Charise, inviting me for coffee. We both lived in the Richmond area, so we agreed to meet at Panera Bread near one of the malls. "Extremely casual," she wrote, punctuating her sentence with a smiley face. I hoped that Charise wanted to meet with me to discuss the terms of my employment, but something told me that was not the purpose of her invitation.

I was delighted and only mildly surprised when the woman who walked briskly toward my café booth was Black. There was a familiarity in her emails, one impossible to define, that told me I was communicating with a sister.

Brimming with energy, Charise, a pretty, chestnut-brown woman with a pixie haircut and bright smile, slid into the seat across from me. Without missing a beat, we started gabbing as if we were old friends. Within a few minutes, I knew that she was the mother of four young children, that her mother was a frequent houseguest, where she liked to shop, and what she liked to drink. It wasn't long before she revealed the reason she wanted to meet, and as I suspected, it was not about the job. In fact, it was a warning.

Monticello was a very difficult place to work, she said, a domain of "haves and have-nots" where many people weren't paid equitably. She was the only Black person in management and one of a few on staff. Most days, she confided, she felt powerless and voiceless. Her advice was, "You might want to think twice about working there."

I listened with as much empathy as possible. It was clear that Charise and Monticello were a bad fit. Indeed, many Black people would have been daunted by the prospect of working at a former plantation with the constant reminders of slavery's exploitation and abuse. And at Monticello the lack of Black staff didn't help. However, I was confident that I could overcome those issues. Throughout my adult life, I was often one of few African Americans in the room—whether in a classroom or a newsroom, on a stage set or at a social setting. Like many Black people from a similar socioeconomic background, it was a reality I had learned to deal with. So I decided to ignore Charise's warning. Working at Monticello was my dream, and I wasn't going to let one person's negative experience ruin that for me.

As it turned out, the concern was for nothing. The Public Historian position went to someone else, a Black UVA grad with a background and experience in public and architectural history named Niya Bates. I was crushed, having been so sure that the job was mine. My disappointment didn't last very long, however. I soon found out there was a new job that appeared to have been created with me mind.

Another email from HR arrived in April, four months after I had applied for the Public Historian position:

Dear Gayle,

We all think so highly of you and your many talents and we
would love to explore some options with you beyond the Public
Historian role. Please see the position description attached and
let me know if this might be something of interest to you.

I felt like the high school senior who has been accepted to the
college of her choice, with a full scholarship. The new job description for Community Engagement Officer read as if my resume had
been next to it when it was composed: "excellent communications
skills . . . strong interpersonal skills . . . working knowledge of historical content related to Jefferson and Monticello."

It appeared as if my dream of working at Monticello was about
to come true.

28

MY ANCESTORS' FOOTSTEPS

June 2016–July 2017

There were no negotiations. The offer came and I accepted it. I wasn't happy with the salary, which was half of what I had once earned. But the truth was I was so excited about the job that I would have agreed to less. I started as Monticello's first Community Engagement Officer on June 6, 2016. And as I would later enjoy telling audiences, I was also the first descendant of the enslaved and the enslaver to work at Monticello and be paid for it.

My office was in the same building as the offices of Leslie and most of the executive team, on Mulberry Row with a clear view of the mansion. She greeted me on my first day with a blinding smile and a hug. "There she is," she beamed, making me feel welcome. Again, I dismissed Charise's forewarning. If Leslie's reception was an indication of what it was like to work at the Thomas Jefferson Foundation, I would be fine. Unfortunately, Charise wasn't around long to share my excitement. After a disagreement with her manager, she quit one month after my first day.

As I settled into my windowed office, looking at the redbrick mansion once occupied by my ancestors—Black and white—I wondered what they would have thought of me. Thomas Jefferson, who chose in his only book to describe Black people as "inferior," posited in *Notes on the State of Virginia:*

> Deep rooted prejudices entertained by the whites; ten thousand recollections, by the blacks, of the injuries they have sustained; new provocations; the real distinctions which nature has made . . . will divide us into parties, and produce convulsions which will probably never end but in the extermination of the one or the other race. To these objections, which are political, may be added others, which are physical and moral. The first difference which strikes us is that of colour. . . . They have less hair on the face and body. They secrete less by the kidnies, and more by the glands of the skin, which gives them a very strong and disagreeable odour. This greater degree of transpiration renders them more tolerant of heat, and less so of cold, than the whites. Comparing them by their faculties of memory, reason, and imagination, it appears to me that in memory they are equal to the whites; in reason much inferior, as I think one could scarcely be found capable of tracing and comprehending the investigations of Euclid: and that in imagination they are dull, tasteless, and anomalous.

Would my five-times-great-grandfather have thought that I had a "disagreeable odour"? Did he think, as he lay with my four-times-great-aunt Sally, that she was "dull, tasteless, and anomalous"? And what of my Black forebears? What would they have thought? My lineal ancestors, as well as aunts, uncles, and cousins, labored their entire lives at the same place that now employed me. Some worked in the very building, the plantation's textile and weaving workshop, that housed my office.

I imagined that they, like the ancestors of my Black brothers and sisters who overcame decades of bigotry and institutionalized racism, would have been amazed and proud. Jefferson, on the other hand, might have been shocked.

Niya, the woman who got the Public Historian's position, and I came on board the same week—hires that made the local papers. I had been taught that an event which "goes against the status quo" is newsworthy. It spoke volumes that our new jobs were considered "news." My colleague and I, as one headline stated, would "Look to Better Tell Story of African-American Life at Monticello."

However, the quote that set the tone for my expectations as a new employee was in a piece written by my friend Michael Paul Williams, the Richmond columnist who had written the story about Tess and me. The last lines of his column captured my sentiments perfectly:

> On her first day on what amounts to a dream job, she was asked whether she planned to make the commute from the Richmond area to Monticello every day.
>
> "Oh yeah," she replied. "Because every day, I have an opportunity to walk in the footsteps of my ancestors."

At fifty-eight years old, my new life was about to begin.

•   •   •

Journalist Harry Smith was a network veteran, spending much of his career as one of CBS's stars, including on *Face the Nation*, *Sunday Morning*, and *The CBS Evening News with Dan Rather*. However, after twenty-five years with CBS, Smith moved to NBC to become a senior correspondent on the *Today Show*, the morning show juggernaut. In August 2016 he was at Monticello covering a story on the Slave Dwelling Project. It was the second year at Monticello for the program that invited people to spend the night in housing that had once been for the enslaved, and it was also my second year participating. This time, however, not only did I know the identities of my Robinson ancestors, I was joined by Robinson descendants—my son, Charles, and my cousin Andrew. It was also my first time on the national stage as a Monticello representative. I was nervous.

My previous experience as a TV reporter, anchor, and actor should have helped, but it didn't. My discomfort was obvious enough for Smith to notice. "You're editing your comments," he remarked. He was right. I was so concerned that I would say something wrong that I struggled to say something right. My twenty-minute-long interview was cut to about four seconds. I would see Smith again four years later, resulting in a very different outcome.

Meanwhile, I was getting ready for another public appearance, this one in real time. For months, Monticello's team and its advisors had been planning a summit on race. Titled "Memory, Mourning, Mobilization: Legacies of Slavery and Freedom in America," the event featured panels with cultural and scholarly luminaries, among them authors Annette Gordon-Reed and Jon Meacham, children's rights activist Marian Wright Edelman, artist-activist Bree Newsome, and journalist Jamelle Bouie. Henry Louis Gates was one of the moderators.

However, it was I, the girl from Northeast DC, "Little Gayle," who would set the stage. Leslie and her team asked me, along with Cinder, to make the opening remarks. Cinder and I planned for weeks—what to say, what to wear, how to project. When Leslie convened a rehearsal in her office a few days before the summit, I felt well prepared. Maybe even a little overconfident.

One of the first lessons I learned when I started at Monticello was how to work with Leslie. She had a reputation for having a tough management style, demanding perfection of herself and of her staff. She could be ice-cold brusque one minute and butter-melting charm the next.

Apparently, the pressure was paying off. Since her tenure as foundation president began in 2008, Leslie and her team had raised lots of money. Many of the funds were allocated for restoring Mulberry Row and other representations of what it was like to be enslaved at Monticello. However, Leslie's management approach could be off-putting.

At the rehearsal, I found out first-hand what was required to meet her expectations. I sensed some tension in the room where about eight staff members—all white—were seated at a conference table. My guess was that a summit about the legacies of slavery at the home of Thomas Jefferson was causing the team a bit of anxiety. Placing the blame for some of the country's racial discord at the feet of the author of the Declaration of Independence was a risk. Many Jefferson admirers might not be inclined to donate to Monticello if they thought the foundation was knocking their hero off his pedestal.

As I took a seat beside Cinder, I spotted a podium a few feet from the table and wondered what it was doing there. Leslie didn't waste any time getting down to business. Peeking above the rim of her glasses, she shot a question to Cinder and me. "What are you going to say?" she asked with the bluntness I'd been hearing about. Cinder and I took turns reading, beginning with our introductions. Leslie wasn't impressed, especially with mine. "No, no, no, that's all wrong!" she said when I began with the necessary, if prosaic, exercise of introducing myself. "You need more drama," she insisted. "Rewrite it—now."

I bristled at her sharp tone, which felt more like an assault than a critique. I felt that she was talking down to me. And the silence that followed suggested that others in the room were taken aback as well. I could feel my cheeks heating up as humiliation displaced my usual confidence. And all the while I was thinking to myself that this could go south fast. But I was not going to let that happen. "Rise to the occasion," my parents always said. Feeling flustered, I took a breath, quietly composing myself. *I can do this*, I thought, *I have to do this.* The reframed introduction came to me like a spiritual inspiration and my confidence was restored during the few minutes it took to make the revisions. The podium, I realized was there to help set the stage. I stood, walked toward it, took my place behind it, and began to read:

"My ancestors were enslaved here at Monticello—generations of people bound to the earth by blood and by law. I'm Gayle Jessup White."

Everyone applauded, including Leslie.

• • •

I delivered the remarks, excerpted here, five days later on an overcast Saturday morning before a racially mixed crowd of fifteen hundred people:

Why a summit about race at Monticello? Jefferson, who wrote in the Declaration of Independence that "all men are created equal," owned six hundred men, women, and children in his lifetime. When he died fifty years later, families he owned were auctioned right here on these very grounds—many were my relatives, including my three-times-great-grandfather, Peter Hemings.

It's that family story, and hundreds of others, that would've been lost had it not been for Monticello's years-long commitment to unearthing the complete history of the enslaved people who lived at Monticello. In spite of their bondage, this is where they created the best lives they could under circumstances that most of us find impossible to imagine. This is where they considered home.

Thanks to the remarkable work of Cinder Stanton and her colleagues, we know more about the lives of the enslaved and their descendants than most other historic sites.

Had it not been for Cinder, I wouldn't be standing here today—a witness to a story similar to that of so many African Americans whose own ancestry has been lost.

Our hope is that you leave here with a greater understanding of how slavery shaped much of our country's history. And that you'll walk away feeling hope for the future knowing that the American dream belongs to all of us.

I was surprisingly self-possessed, energized by the crowd rather than intimidated by it. At several points as Cinder and I made our remarks together, the audience rewarded us with applause, and when we finished, they gave us a standing ovation. As I walked off the stage, Jack overheard the Board of Trustees' chairman say, "She knocked it out of the park."

In spite of the day's success, I struggled to fit in at an organization that was overwhelmingly white. It wasn't just the racial imbalance, although that played a part, such as at my first foundation Christmas party. I wore a black suit, high heels, and a little more makeup than usual to the annual event at a Charlottesville hotel. It was evening after all. Maybe that's why one of my colleagues assumed I was on the hotel staff. "Where's the coat check?" she rudely snapped at me. I didn't bother to explain that I was also a guest. "Over there," I said pointing her in the wrong direction.

What I found most disconcerting was feeling on display, that I was there because I was Black, not because I had a strong and valued voice. One executive team member once told me I spoke up too much at meetings, adding that I didn't know enough about Monticello, Jefferson, or the enslaved community. I didn't agree but knew not to challenge the assertion, not if I wanted to keep my job. I was suspended from all engagements with the public and the media until management thought I was ready. I couldn't even talk in public about my own family's history. "Say what you want at your cocktail parties," I was warned, "but not when you're representing Monticello."

I had been at Monticello for less than a year when the colleagues closest to me started asking if I planned to resign. I had no intention of quitting or of being let go, not after I had come so far. Perhaps it wasn't the dream job I had long imagined, but I was on a mission. The voices of the ancestors needed to be heard, and I believed mine was the best to speak on their behalf.

I was intent on addressing any issues my managers had with my performance. Whether I agreed or not, the perception was that I needed to be more knowledgeable, so I immersed myself in Jeffersonian history, reading some two dozen biographies and related histories, including Cinder's book, *"Those Who Labor for my Happiness,"* for the third time.

I had a new manager, and to his credit, he supported my campaign of self-education, recommending what to study and allowing me time to do so. I also had the support of the few Blacks who were on staff, with whom I had formed an informal group. We called ourselves the Monticello African American Committee, or MAAC. There were only four of us, and we met regularly for lunch, always off site for privacy.

Within weeks, I was ready but remained sidelined. It wasn't until that summer when I was the only staffer available to meet with a visiting freelance reporter that the situation changed.

The story that was published July 3, 2017, on NBC.com about the excavation of the room historians and archeologists believed was Sally Hemings's was a turning point for me and for Monticello. The piece generated so many hits that Monticello's website traffic that day increased fourfold.

"I am appreciative of the work that my colleagues are doing at Monticello because this is an American story, an important story," the story quoted me saying. "But for too long our history has been ignored. Some people still don't want to admit that the Civil War was fought over slavery. We need to face history head-on and face the blemish of slavery and that's what we're doing at Monticello."

With that NBC.com feature, I felt I had won the executive office's confidence and was back online.

29

VELMA & RUTH

1920 and 1926

California resident Velma Williams was born on July 4, 1920, the year my grandmother Eva died. She was ninety-six years old when she boarded a train alone in the fall of 2016 for the cross-country journey east. She had cousins she wanted to see in New York and Virginia. And since recently learning that she was descended from a Hemings—she is the great-great-granddaughter of Peter—she wanted to see Monticello.

Velma was staying with Ruth, my newly acquainted Robinson cousin. The two were first cousins and lifelong friends. Given their ages, ninety-six and ninety, respectively, there was no telling when—or if—they would see each other again, so they were making the most of their time together. I had been working at Monticello for a few months when I picked them up on a crisp October day for the ride to our ancestral home, where they would be interviewed for the Getting Word African American Oral History Project.

We made easy conversation during the hour-and-a-half-long ride to Monticello as if we had known each other forever. Even though I had known Ruth but a short time and had just met Velma, they felt like family. They *were* family, part of a large one.

Their mothers were from a family of eleven—six girls and five boys, most of whom had children. "There were so many Robinsons," Ruth told me, "I thought we would always be around." But their numbers were shrinking. Many in their generation had died, and others were in their eighties and nineties. They had never met one of their first cousins—Andrew's grandmother—because she was passing for white. They knew about *her*, but she did not know about them—not yet anyway.

By the time we arrived in Kenwood, the interview site, which was also where my office recently had been relocated, I was well caught up on the family's history.

Both women were excited as they entered the building, a stately 1930s brick home where capacious former bedrooms now served as office space. They were both sprightly and independent, turning down the hand I offered as they crossed the threshold.

Kenwood had a history of its own. During World War II, the estate was a retreat for President Franklin D. Roosevelt. The office that was now mine had once been his bedroom. Explaining this to my cousins conjured up memories of their own. Velma remembered being a Hampton biology student when the war broke out. Ruth was a high school student planning on a career in education.

"This is unbelievable," said Velma, a petite woman with light brown skin who, like Ruth, looked decades younger than her ninety-six years. Her brown eyes widened beneath a tan, brimmed hat as we walked toward the parlor, where cameras were awaiting us. "It's wonderful," gushed a smiling Ruth. They were so joyful, so delightful, and such a pleasure to be with.

During the interview Velma recounted her years living in Ghana as the wife of an American diplomat. It was in the 1960s as many African nations were shedding European colonialism. The night she left for Ghana, she said, many in her family were boarding a bus from New York for the landmark 1963 March on Washington.

Ruth talked about her efforts to maintain what was left of the Goochland farm that had been in the family since the end of the Civil War. The property included a family graveyard where her grandparents, parents, aunts, and uncles were buried.

I was captivated by their stories, especially hearing about the graveyard. I had spent so little time at cemeteries and had only two years ago seen my grandfather Jessup's grave at Arlington National Cemetery. But with a new purpose—reclaiming the lost legacy of my ancestors—I also wanted to visit their graves.

After the interview, driving back to Ruth's house, I asked if she would take me to the family graveyard in Goochland. "Of course," she said, and the next day she, Velma, and I were paying respects to their dead loved ones.

The burial ground was a small plot on 30 acres of what had been a 125-acre farm. Thanks to a caretaker Ruth had hired, it was as verdant and manicured as a well-loved suburban lawn. There were sixteen headstones, most bearing the last name Robinson. I spotted the tombstones of people I knew from census records and death certificates—among them Anderson, Lucy, and Andrew Robinson. Marveling at the commitment and tenacity of Ruth and Velma, I wondered if those traits were passed down from "our" Sally. She had endured beatings, enslavement, and war. As a middle-age woman, she apparently divorced or separated from her husband and bought acres of farmland that more than a century later were still in her family. Sally Hemings Robinson must have been a formidable woman.

The following spring, April 2017, more of her descendants met for the first time, including Andrew Davenport, who had spent his youth not knowing his family had Black roots three generations before he was born. His Black great-grandmother had shuttled her children from the South when they were young, leaving their Black identities behind. But by the time Andrew reached puberty, he had learned the truth, that his family was passing. While to many he looked white, Andrew embraced his African American roots. The truth mattered to him.

That his grandmother's family made a choice to live as "Americans," as they put it, was a consequence of the brutality of racism. Being "white" meant having a better life. It also meant breaking up families. My grandmother Eva's sister Aunt "Lucy" made that choice, which left her alone and longing for family when she was old and dying in New York while an acquaintance desperately called a long-abandoned relative—my father—looking for help.

However, Andrew's grandmother was lucky. She had her family—children and grandchildren, nieces and nephews—all of whom, aside from Andrew, identified as white. But at eighty-eight years old, she felt the longing to connect with her family's history and was being drawn back to her roots. She had never met Ruth, Velma, and the Black Robinson cousins; had never been to the family's gravesite; had never seen her father's tombstone. Yet her grandson had been named after him, and she kept a framed photograph of her father at her bedside. In April 2017, she thought it was time to go home.

On a day draped in sky blue and sunshine yellow, Andrew's grandmother and Ruth, who were first cousins, met for the first time. They greeted each other as family. "I remember when I opened the door," recalled Ruth three years later about her cousin's visit. "She just came in and we hugged, and we've been close ever since." Sally Robinson's descendants were coming home.

30

CHARLOTTESVILLE

May–August 2017

Any notion I had about Monticello being a sleepy historical museum where scholars and staff were as reverent as medieval monks was disabused after a year of working there. On the contrary, Monticello was a bustling multimillion-dollar operation with international influence, employing hundreds of people. Anyone who did not live up to the Thomas Jefferson Foundation's rigid professional standards or who could not tolerate the hierarchical management practices didn't last long.

As I passed my one-year anniversary, I was pleased that after a bumpy start, I hadn't only survived but had begun to thrive. I was back on the media and public speaking circuit and getting really good at it. Gone was the self-editing that had crippled my *Sunday Today* interview with Harry Smith. I had a new manager, and we got on well. Occasionally, I was invited to leadership team meetings to introduce my projects, a clear indication that Leslie's trust in me was growing, as was mine in her. It's not that we always agreed. And when we didn't, the exchanges could get intense but nothing like that first face-off in her office. There was growing mutual respect between me and many of my colleagues and true friendship with others. Those relationships and the support they provided would be tested in the months ahead when events brought the attention of the world to Charlottesville.

The concept I shared with many about the town as an idyllic university enclave was shattered on May 13, 2017. That evening, a group of extreme right-wing protesters with lit tiki torches descended upon a city park that had become the focus of heated controversy. For almost a hundred years, an equestrian statue of Robert E. Lee and the park named after him had been a source of pride for some city residents, and of intimidation for others.

In the fall of 2016, the town's city council voted to chip away at the white supremacy the Lee statue represented by removing it and renaming the grounds Emancipation Park. The decision raised the ire of a University of Virginia graduate named Richard Spencer, a white nationalist, neo-Nazi activist of the so-called alt-right. It was Spencer who organized the chilling tiki torch rally in May.

Chanting anti-Semitic and racist slogans, such as "You will not replace us" and "Blood and soil," the scores of white men dressed in button-down collared shirts and preppy khakis looked like college students, not the menacing terrorist threats they actually were.

The statue of Lee on his horse was like hundreds of Confederate monuments that had been erected across the country, primarily in the South, during the Jim Crow era. They were a grim reminder that even though the North had won the war, Black Americans were still not free.

Statues of Lee, Thomas "Stonewall" Jackson, Jefferson Davis, "Johnny Reb," and even the first grand wizard of the Ku Klux Klan Nathan Bedford Forrest rose like towers on city landscapes, similar to the ones I regularly drove by on Richmond's Monument Avenue. They were symbols of white supremacy with the intent of reminding Black people to stay in their place. At least seven hundred dotted the country, including eight in the US Capitol. Scores would come tumbling down in the summer of 2020, but few would have predicted that in 2017.

By the time the white terrorists brought their own intimidation tactics to Charlottesville, I had established relationships with many of the town's influential community members. I joined a group of clerics called the Charlottesville Clergy Collective, ironic since I hadn't set foot in a church in longer than I could remember, and the local NAACP. I also got to know many of the people who would become the area's nexus of Black Lives Matter. I felt like an insider, a part of the community, even though I lived seventy miles away in Richmond.

After the May protest, rumors began circulating that a bigger, more alarming event was planned for July. At the time, I couldn't imagine what could be more disturbing than white men with torches shouting Nazi-inspired venom. I couldn't imagine in 2017 a Ku Klux Klan rally. But that was what happened in Charlottesville when the hooded from North Carolina decided to make "America's happiest city" their target.

My family and friends pleaded with me not to attend. "It's not safe," cautioned one of my white buddies who, while visiting the remnants of a slave jail, had been assaulted by young white men. But I wasn't dissuaded. Having attended a half dozen community meetings about the city's preparedness, I felt confident that local authorities would maintain control. Besides, there was no way I was going to miss a chance to see grown people parade around in pointy caps and white sheets. The idea of such a display seemed so absurd that it was almost humorous.

Jack insisted on going with me, and we arrived at the recently renamed Justice Park, where the Jackson statue stood, around midday where a large crowd of counterprotesters that eventually swelled to a thousand was beginning to form. We pushed our way to the front where police had set up steel barriers to hold back the crowd. In front of us was a partitioned area, almost like a circus ring, reserved for the KKK marchers. The atmosphere was almost festive among the diverse crowd waiting for the robed protesters to arrive. Friends hugged and posed for cell phone pictures. Some carried signs, others waved flags.

When the fifty or so ragtag men and women paraded into view wearing white robes and clownish head gear, waving Confederate flags and brandishing the Nazi salute, the crowd began chanting "go home." As they paced inside their circus ring shouting "white power," the counterprotesters, Black and white, blasted back with "Black lives matter."

In less than an hour, the KKK demonstrators, acknowledging defeat, abandoned their campaign. They got in their vehicles and went home. Social and racial justice had won the day. However, the fight was just beginning. The Klan and their demon offspring began making plans to return to Charlottesville the next month on August 12.

The Charlottesville Clergy Collective, the group that had embraced me as their own, began organizing a counterprotest, putting out a call to faith leaders across the country to come to Charlottesville for the rally. Many answered, including social activist Cornel West, United Church of Christ Associate General Minister Traci Blackmon, and scores of others. Other local groups started organizing as well. Hundreds, perhaps thousands, were expected in Charlottesville on August 12, and the city wanted to be prepared. But who could have been ready for what happened?

I wasn't there to witness the horror that unfolded that Saturday. I was on a plane headed east from a conference in New Orleans. Like people around the world, I watched the violence explode on a TV screen. Shocked by what I saw on the small monitor embedded in the back of the seat in front of me, I couldn't hold back the tears.

It started with hundreds of people, some carrying clubs, sticks, and chemical sprays, congregating in downtown Charlottesville. White nationalists of all stripes—neo-Nazis, the KKK, Skinheads—waved Confederate flags above the heads of the crowd and headed toward Emancipation Park. They were met by an equal number of counterprotesters, linked arm in arm, set on defending the city. Counterprotesters had been training in the techniques of peaceful resistance; however, with the emotional temperature broiling, violence was inevitable.

Exchanges of angry words, racial epithets, and ethnic slurs exploded into pushing, shoving, punching, and then chaos. Quaint streets that were usually the domain of university professors, parents with strollers, and tourists turned into battle zones. Men and women were pelted with clubs, sprayed with chemical weapons, struck with water bottles, and kicked as they lay on the ground. And for about an hour, the police did nothing.

Finally, the governor declared a state of emergency, and police dressed in riot gear shut down the rally. But it wasn't over.

As hundreds of peaceful demonstrators walked toward the Downtown Mall, a car deliberately plowed into them, tossing people into the air like ragdolls. A thirty-two-year-old woman, Heather Heyer, was killed, and scores were seriously injured, including children of my colleagues and friends.

People around the world saw images of the day's combat. Charlottesville soon became synonymous with America's racial strife and inequities. The president of the United States added to the division that was pushing the country to a breaking point with incendiary remarks. "You also had people that were very fine people, on both sides," said the leader of the free world.

I found out later that a group of people, among them my friends in the Clergy Collective, were forced to take shelter inside a "sanctuary" church when a white nationalist mob threatened them.

Monticello was not a target of the protesters, but the staff was shaken by what happened. The few Black staff members felt especially vulnerable. Our discomfort was exacerbated when several weeks later, what appeared to be a noose was found near one of the exhibitions.

My white colleagues were more solicitous than usual, concerned that I was emotionally bruised by the racially ignited violence. And I was. All decent people were. But like my ancestors, I was tough, resilient, and determined. They had survived much worse than "the summer of hate." Meanwhile, the media adopted a new shorthand to describe racial hatred and unrest in a single word—"Charlottesville."

31

SALLY HEMINGS ROBINSON

October–January 2017

The University of Virginia, often called Mr. Jefferson's University after its founder, was approaching a significant milestone, its two-hundredth birthday. To celebrate, the bicentennial planning committee wanted a spectacle. Flush with resources, they hired a Hollywood producer to help plan an extravaganza. His name was Mitch Levine, and when he got in touch with me to discuss my participation, I was ready for my next close-up.

The planning committee tasked me with organizing a group of Monticello family descendants—Black and white—to take part in the extravaganza. Like Monticello, the US Capitol, and the White House, UVA was largely built by enslaved laborers. The university wanted to give voice to their suffering and contributions through their descendants. After the horror of August 12, the committee thought a show of racial unity among descendants was a worthy message. I invited Jan's daughter, Lisa, an attorney and UVA grad, and her children; my cousin Ruth, also a UVA alum; and other Robinson, Hemings, Randolph, and Eppes cousins to be part of the program.

The celebration kicked off on October 6, 2017, marking the date in 1817 when Jefferson laid the university's cornerstone. Inspired by his appreciation of Palladian and neoclassical architecture, he designed the main campus, called the Academical Village. Surrounding the lush stretch of lawn at the village's center were pavilions for student and faculty housing. At one end was the Rotunda, a domed, brick building with sandstone steps leading to its columned entrance. It sat at the top of the "Grounds" the way the head of the household might sit at the dinner table or a CEO at a conference room desk. Jefferson used the Pantheon of Rome as his architectural inspiration. On the evening of the opening session, the Rotunda served as a backdrop for a full-scale, Hollywood-style production.

The fall weather was pleasantly mild for the party's twenty thousand guests—students, faculty, alumni (including Katie Couric in person and Tina Fey on camera), dignitaries, and politicians. Because the show included light projection technology, it had to start after sunset. Images conveying the university's two-hundred-year history were blasted onto the Rotunda's façade, including a dramatic interpretation of a nineteenth-century fire that had gutted the original building. Andra Day sang her Grammy-nominated song "Rise Up." Former US Poet Laureate and UVA professor Rita Dove read a poem, and the Martha Graham Dance Company performed.

However, it was Tony award-winner Leslie Odom Jr., most famous for his role as Aaron Burr in the Broadway sensation *Hamilton*, who most excited an already ginned-up crowd. He sang six songs, including two of my favorites from the show—"The Room Where It Happened" and "Wait for It." I was there but didn't hear a single note. I was behind stage preparing for my own entrance.

From behind the stage, I nervously peeked through the heavy curtain. The stage looked massive, worthy of Beyoncé and Jay-Z, whom I almost expected to emerge from a cloud of smoke. But moments later, I and descendants of the enslaved and their enslavers, including presidents Madison and Monroe, were the ones walking onto the stage. Wearing a ruby-red dress and black patent leather heels, I led our contingent from behind the curtain. Head high and mind focused, I walked straight up to the mic at the front of the stage as if I owned it. I was stunned to see the audience on their feet and thunderously applauding. I turned slightly to look at the family standing behind me. They appeared just as dumbstruck as I. The applause lasted a full minute.

When the clapping died down, I began:

I'm Gayle Jessup White and I work at Monticello, where my ancestor Thomas Jefferson enslaved four hundred men, women, and children, including generations of my family.

When my great-great-grandmother Sally Robinson was thirteen years old, her mistress had two women hold her down while she beat her. The person who beat her was Martha Jefferson Randolph, Thomas Jefferson's beloved daughter. Sally and Martha were first cousins. Both are my ancestors.

Years later, Sally Robinson showed her courage by protecting her white owners' valuables when Union troops invaded their home. But after the Civil War, Sally and her children left this place, moving fifty miles away to Goochland, where they bought hundreds of acres of farmland. A well-cared-for family graveyard is on land the family still owns.

By the twentieth century, Sally Robinson's grandchildren had moved north to Washington, DC, Philadelphia, and New York where they became doctors, lawyers, educators, husbands and wives, fathers and mothers.

Her descendants are graduates of the country's great

universities—Harvard, Brown, Penn, MIT, Howard, Hampton, William and Mary—and yes, the University of Virginia.

Tonight, my family and I proudly stand on the shoulders of Sally Robinson.

With those words and with thousands of people watching, I gave my long-forgotten great-great-grandmother Sally Hemings Robinson the recognition she deserved. I wanted people to see her as I did, as a symbol of the millions of Black women who toiled under near intolerable circumstances. Women who came home to take care of their own children after caring for someone else's all day. Women who worked in tobacco, cotton, and indigo fields from dawn to dusk and then came home to tend their own gardens. Women who were sexually assaulted and raped and then forced to raise the offspring of their attackers. They were women who against so many obstacles provided a path to a better life for their children and grandchildren. They were the women whose descendants would one day protest at lunch counters, sit in board rooms, walk the halls of Congress, and live in the White House. My goal that evening, as it continues to be, was to humanize Sally, to humanize Black women, to humanize my people.

The next day, I heard from Mitch, the Hollywood producer. "You were magnificent on stage," he wrote. "Thank you for sharing your ancestors' stories and so much of yourself." But I didn't think the triumph was mine. It belonged to Sally Hemings Robinson.

The following month—November—two more of her relatives visited Monticello for the first time: Kevin, the first Robinson cousin I had met through AncestryDNA, and his ninety-year-old mother, Louise. The five-times-great-granddaughter of Old Sall, the enslaved woman who had likely been Jefferson's nursemaid, was an elegant figure. Her silver hair perfectly coifed and her slender frame wrapped in a warm wool coat, she nodded approvingly as she and Kevin toured the mansion. I nodded too, proud that I was bringing more of my dad's family home.

● ● ●

Yes, my first year at Monticello had been difficult. I often felt like a token, like window-dressing, and powerless. However, by the time I walked onto the UVA stage, I felt in charge. My manager and I had a good rapport, I had my colleagues' respect, and Leslie and the executive team often considered and acted upon my advice.

I was also back as a foundation spokesperson. My UVA presentation cemented my ability to tell a stellar and compelling story that could captivate an audience. Adding to my sense of well-being was the camaraderie of my officemates. Because our building once had been a private residence, we used a key to enter the front door. The lock and key were similar to the one at my parents' house. Sometimes when I unlocked the door and walked into the building, I announced "I'm home," just as I had when I was a kid. The Kenwood office felt like family.

By the end of 2017, I had a firm grip on the job. But most important, I was giving voice to the ancestors. *"Tell my story. It's all I have. Tell my story."*

In the months ahead, my grandmother's command was answered when her family's story became part of an exhibition that attracted international attention. "The Life of Sally Hemings" was born from the foundation's acknowledgment that she was indeed the mother of six of Jefferson's children, that she had negotiated for the freedom of their four surviving children, and that she was an American icon.

When Sally Hemings died in 1835 at age sixty-one, she was unique among enslaved people. She had traveled to Europe and as a lady's maid had attended lavish events with her charges, Jefferson's daughters Martha and Mary. By the time she was sixteen, she had witnessed the burgeoning French Revolution and negotiated with a powerful man privileges for herself and her unborn children. Unlike most enslaved women, her children were allowed to stay with her and not put to work at the age of eight or nine, or "in the ground," as Jefferson would describe fieldwork. However, they did learn a skill. The sons were trained in carpentry and woodworking, and the daughter, in spinning and weaving. Upon her owner's death, Sally was given "her time," or unofficial freedom. She spent the last years of her life living with her sons in Charlottesville. The site of her grave is unknown. Thanks to her, all of her children gained their freedom two generations before the Civil War freed all enslaved people. Hers was a very powerful American story.

As a Hemings family descendant and Community Engagement Officer, I sat in on early discussions about the exhibition at Monticello. A major concern was how Sally Hemings should be portrayed. There were no pictures of her, just two contemporaneous descriptions of her physical appearance. From the memoir of Isaac Granger Jefferson, a formerly enslaved tinsmith and blacksmith at Monticello: "Sally Hemings' mother Betty was a bright mulatto woman, and Sally mighty near white . . . very handsome, long straight hair down her back." And from Jefferson's grandson and my three-times-great-grandfather, Thomas Jefferson Randolph: "light colored and decidedly goodlooking."

Because her father was white and her mother was racially mixed, she might have been light enough to pass as white. She might have even resembled her half-sister, Jefferson's wife. If she had magically appeared in the 1998 DNA test that indicated at least one of her children was Jefferson's, her results would have shown that she had far more European than African DNA. However, in America in 1773, the year Hemings was born, one-hundred-year-old slave codes were baked into the law. A child took on the condition of the mother, not the father. Thus, children born to enslaved women were enslaved, even when their father was president of the United States.

Since the Monticello team had no way of knowing what Hemings looked like, we decided on no images at all. Instead, she would be symbolized by clothing, the kind an enslaved woman would have worn—an ankle-length shift of cotton and linen and a short jacket that tied at the neck. The outfit would be draped over a frame shaped like a woman. Images meant to represent periods of Sally Hemings's life would be projected onto the cloaked frame. It sounded compelling, but I had my doubts. I was not convinced that a headless Sally Hemings would win public approval. As Community Engagement Officer, it would become my job to collect the impressions of Charlottesville's Black influencers.

WHILE CURATORS WERE CREATING "THE LIFE OF SALLY HEMINGS" AND other exhibitions focusing on the enslaved community and their descendants, archeologists were also at work. They began unearthing a room where historians believed Sally Hemings had lived. According to one of Jefferson's nineteenth-century biographers, her room was in the South Wing, an underground passage connected to the main house. The room, he wrote to a friend, was "smoke blackened and sooty"—in other words, not a place you would expect to find Jefferson's "concubine." For years, the Randolph family denied that their patriarch and his enslaved woman had any sort of relationship, claiming that one of his nephews was the father of her children.

But Hemings's son Madison testified in an 1873 newspaper memoir that he was Jefferson's son. He stated that "it was her duty, all her life which I can remember, up to the time of father's death, to take care of his chamber and wardrobe, look after us children and do such light work as sewing." Kind of sounds like a "housewife."

Further, the 1998 DNA research project supported Madison's claim. Additionally, every time Jefferson returned to Monticello for a break during his presidency, Hemings would have a child nine months later. It was implausible to deny that the two had a relationship or at the very least "relations," as my mother used to say. Some people have romanticized whatever they had, believing they were in love. Others have condemned Jefferson, who was in his forties when relations began with fourteen-year-old Hemings, as a rapist and a pedophile. Then there are those who believe, as I do, that Hemings briefly exercised her own agency by enthralling an older man, thus providing a better life for herself and for her children. Whatever existed between Jefferson and Hemings, it will likely always be a mystery.

The room where Hemings and her children lived was not seen for decades. In 1940 and 1960 restorations, the foundation covered it and other South Wing rooms with men's and women's bathrooms. In another iteration, the area was used as a mechanical room and storage space. There is no indication that the decision to cover up any extant evidence of Sally Hemings's lodgings was intentionally designed to quite literally bury her memory, but it had that effect. The image of a men's bathroom over the space that was Hemings's was vulgar and disgusting.

Archeologists started chipping away the twentieth-century concrete and tile bathrooms in 2017. What they found underneath were several rooms—including the one believed to be Hemings's and Monticello's original kitchen. Their findings were based on Jefferson's sketches of the South Wing. All the rooms—the kitchen, a dairy, a smokehouse and Sally Hemings's room—would be part of the new exhibition. There would also be an exhibition about the Getting Word Oral History Project and descendants of Monticello's enslaved community. I provided the voiceover for the exhibition's video that played in a continuous loop.

The kitchen was an especially emotional space for me. It was where Ursula Granger, the plantation's first cook and the woman who had nursed back to health Jefferson's first baby and my four-times-great-grandmother, Martha, had made her beloved pastries. It is also where James Hemings taught his brother Peter, my three-times-great-grandfather, the art of French cookery. When the cooking lessons ended, James, who had trained in Paris and negotiated his manumission with Thomas was freed while Peter remained enslaved most of his life. If only the kitchen's secrets had been unearthed the way archeologists uncovered its artifacts.

In 1808, Jefferson wanted a new state-of-the-art kitchen. He had enslaved workers bury the old one in several feet of dirt and built a laundry after a new kitchen was constructed on the opposite end of the outdoor corridor. The original kitchen remained under mounds of red clay, concrete, and ceramic tile for around two hundred years until Monticello's archeologists started digging.

When enough tile and dirt had been removed for me to safely survey their work, they invited me to see the results. The room I entered easily could have hosted a half dozen busy kitchen workers. But without artificial lighting it would have been dark even though there was one window. The walls were made of exposed brick and plaster, and I could see the outline on one where there had once been a staircase. The steps that used to be there led to a one-room brick dwelling where Thomas and his wife, Martha, lived before construction of the manor house. Facing the back wall, I could see a drop into the section below. I gingerly walked toward the edge and looked over the side. That was where the original eighteenth-century cooking appliances had been. There were remnants of a stew stove and a dresser that was used for preparing food. Archeologists even found ashes from the last meal prepared on the stove—a meal possibly cooked by my great-great-great-grandfather Peter Hemings.

I jumped into the pit to stand on the ground where he once had stood, allowing my emotions to stir. Stooping to the ground, I rubbed my hands in the red clay and up my arms toward the sleeves of my yellow jacket, seeking an intimacy with the earth that my enslaved ancestors had once touched. Closing my eyes, I sensed their struggle, their pride, their love, and their losses. In the bowels of an ancient kitchen where the enslaved began their work before the sun rose, where children labored alongside their parents, where one brother taught the other how to cook so he could be free while the other remained enslaved, I heard a chorus. *"Tell our story."*

32

HOMECOMING

The months leading up to the premier of the exhibitions were a blur. Moving from one meeting to the next felt like riding the subway and getting off at every stop. Most of the sessions included representatives of the people who were enslaved at Monticello, which made for long and lively discussions. Everything was given detailed attention, for example what language to use for the Hemings exhibition panels. Especially stressful was whether to describe Sally Hemings's sexual connection with Jefferson as rape. The team decided to post it as a question—"Was it rape?" Another was how to describe her. We decided on a kind of word bubble: "mother," "daughter," "world traveler," "seamstress," "emancipator." We reviewed the images that would be projected onto the dress and the wall behind it. There was a ship's porthole window representing her voyage to Europe, a flower motif indicating the kind of garment she would have worn as a servant in France, a spinning wheel for her work as a seamstress, and a silhouette of her braiding her daughter's hair. There were sound effects—harbor bells clanging, looms whooshing, and a violin playing, a skill acquired by at least two of Hemings's children.

Not everything worked. For example, there was a heartbeat, which

I thought evoked images of a horror film. It reminded me of Edgar Allan Poe's story "The Tell-Tale Heart," in which a murderer believes he hears the sound of his dismembered victim's heart through the floorboards. My visceral reaction wasn't lost on my fellow planning committee members, at least one of whom had the same reaction. The sound effect was nixed. So were projections of looms that looked as if they were cutting into the dress-cloaked frame, thus into Sally Hemings. In the end, the exhibition appeared graceful and effortless, belying the arduous and complex process that went into creating it.

Finally, the exhibition was ready for the Monticello team to view. Only a few people could enter the small room at one time—fifteen maximum. But there were only a handful at the staff debut—Leslie, Niya, the curators, a few others, and me. As the lights dimmed and the sound effects rose—a foreboding hum followed the hubbub of an eighteenth-century harbor, a spinning wheel at work, and a violin playing—images were projected onto the dress and the wall; there was no narrator, just images and sound effects. The words of Sally Hemings's son Madison also streamed across the wall, telling his mother's life story. How she traveled to France to care for one of Jefferson's daughters and became, as Madison described, his "concubine." How she was beginning to learn French and how she "demurred" when it was time to return to America because she knew that in France, she was free. How she negotiated "extraordinary privileges" for herself and freedom for her unborn children in exchange for returning to Virginia with her enslaver. How she agreed to go back to America where she was reunited with her family. And finally, how based on the terms of that negotiation made when she was only sixteen, all of her children lived free and she was given "her time" to live the few years she had left as a free woman. The presentation ended with a stark reminder of the inhumanity with which the enslaved were treated, for Sally Hemings's gravesite, like those of millions of other enslaved people, is unknown. When the presentation was finished, I don't think there was a dry eye in the room.

A few days before the exhibition opened, I invited influential community members to see it. "Powerful," "honest," "moving" were among their comments. One person said somewhat ruefully, "It's about time." Any doubts I had previously held about the public's acceptance of a disembodied figure were put to rest.

The opening was planned for summer 2018, on June 19—Juneteenth or Freedom Day, marking the date in June 1865 when enslaved Texans learned they were emancipated a month after the Civil War ended.

Monticello's Juneteenth commemoration and exhibition debut would be no ordinary event. We planned to host a weekend of activities, including a gathering to celebrate the twenty-fifth anniversary of the Getting Word Oral History Project, the Board of Trustees biannual meeting, a cocktail party and banquet for about five hundred people, and a tented public event for hundreds more. And, of course, media from across the country and potentially from around the world would attend as well. We had only a few months to put together what could easily have taken a year to plan. However, Monticello's team of dedicated professionals from marketing and communications, to event planning, to development, to maintenance responded as if they had heard from their parents what I constantly heard from mine. They "rose to the occasion."

I did my part keeping local community members informed, helping plan activities, collaborating with my colleagues in the communication department, and working with the media. I arranged a staging for StoryCorps, an oral history initiative that has for years recorded conversations representing the complex relationships Americans have with each other. Over the weekend, the team recorded interviews with descendants and staff, Black and white, including one with me and a Randolph cousin. Our interview, like thousands of other StoryCorps segments, is stored at the American Folklife Center at the Library of Congress.

People began arriving Thursday and throughout the weekend, including some twenty-five descendants of Peter Hemings. My son was there, my nieces, and the biggest surprise of all, my brother Bruce. He usually eschewed my near obsession with finding our family's connection to Jefferson. Our grandparents were as far back as he needed to go, he said. But that weekend he showed up for me.

Ruth came, and so did Velma, once again traveling from California on a train by herself. Andrew was there with his grandmother, as were cousins from DC, Maryland, Virginia, New York, Georgia, and Utah, many of us meeting for the first time. My sisters didn't make it. In California, Pat no longer enjoyed flying, and Jan, living overseas in Berlin by then, was too far away. I missed them, especially Jan because in many ways she had been responsible for my journey. If she had not listened to Aunt Peachie or had not believed what seemed an improbable tale—*"You're descended from Thomas Jefferson"*—we would not have been at Monticello that evening. We would never have known our family's legacy.

The weather for Friday's cocktail party and banquet was perfect—mild and sunny. Descendants of the enslaved mingled on the West Lawn with wealthy donors, sipping wine and enjoying hors d'oeuvres, smoked tomato gazpacho, cheddar grits cake with grilled shrimp remoulade, and toast rounds with smoked bacon and tomato jam.

Wearing a yellow dress and a lemon quartz necklace and earring set Janice had given me, I worked the crowd, as any good host would. Because so many of my family and friends were there, it felt like *my* party. At the banquet, after guests dined on the most succulent fried chicken, lusciously rich whipped potatoes, and tender cabbage and kale, I took the stage to make the evening's only toast.

That Leslie agreed that I should be the one to honor the occasion spoke to the progress we had made since that first meeting in her office early in my tenure. We had worked hard to build each other's trust and respect. Furthermore, she and Monticello's leadership recognized what a powerful symbol I had become. Not only was I a staff member who was descended from Monticello's enslaved community, but I was also an unapologetic Jefferson descendant. I acknowledged that to his legacy's eternal damnation, he was a slaveholder and a racist. Those were valid reasons to feel contempt for the man, and sometimes I do. But he also wrote the nation's foundational document that inspired millions of people of all colors in the United States and around the world to claim their human rights. We raised our glasses that evening to an enslaver, but we gave equal honor to the enslaved and their descendants, who, as heralded in the toast, "fought to make Jefferson's words a reality."

Unlike my first public event at Monticello two years earlier when I opened the summit on the legacies of race and racism, on the night of the banquet I was a seasoned pro. Speaking before a receptive crowd, many of them my family and colleagues, was as easy as flipping a light switch. Still, I couldn't help but feel proud at the "hear, hear!" that followed the toast.

The next day, Monticello hosted a public event called "Look Closer," the second gathering of its kind in as many years. Once again, hundreds of people collected under massive tents as scholars and thought leaders explored issues of race and racism. This time, the descendants were part of the panel.

Although I wasn't onstage, my imprimatur was. I collaborated with the executive team, event planners, and marketing and communications people on the program's theme and character. Two jumbo screens showed an interview with me shot earlier inside one of the South Wing rooms while it was still under construction. I appeared to be inside a lit cave, which made the interview feel all the more

compelling. With a modulated tone, I explained the complex emotions that I and many other Black people have for our country, one
that we love but that doesn't love us. I spoke of a nation paradoxically
and hypocritically built on the ideals of freedom while enslaving millions on the basis of the color of their skin.

"There are complicated feelings I have when I'm in this space," I
said into the camera. "But there are also feelings of comfort because it
feels like home . . . The people who come into these spaces are thinking about it when they walk in. They know enslaved people worked
here. They know the mark that's left on America. That it's America's
greatest contradiction. So, I think when people come here, they are
seeking some sort of solace, peace, answers to the great dilemma of
how America was founded."

Sitting in the audience watching the video, Charles, Jack, and
Jan's daughter and granddaughter at my side, it was hard for me to
believe that I was the woman on the screen. The woman I saw on
the jumbo screen with a voice many described as mellifluous was
thoughtful, insightful, and fearless. She was not the girl abandoned
in a Las Vegas pool by her new white friend, or the unsure, if com-
bative, young reporter protecting her career, or the unhappy doctor's
wife fulfilling her mother's ambitions. She was a woman of gravitas,
who against the odds found professional fulfillment late in life. A
woman whose voice was used as an instrument, not for herself, but
for those written out of history. A woman who after a lifelong journey found her family, her home, her purpose.

• • •

I should have been exhausted after the Getting Word family reunion.
Instead, I was exhilarated. Thank goodness! I needed the energy because Monday, one day after the weekend's whirlwind events, I was
on a plane to Dallas to make plans for the opening of Monticello's

traveling exhibition, "Slavery at Jefferson's Monticello: Paradox of Liberty."

The first time I saw "Paradox" at the Smithsonian in Washington in 2012, I was an outsider and not at all sure how I was related to the enslaved people whose names were part of the display panel. In 2018, I was the ultimate insider, the exhibition's principal promoter and spokesperson. I could point to scores of names on the panel and say exactly how we were related.

Aside from showing in DC at the Smithsonian, the exhibition's first tour traveled to museums in Philadelphia, Atlanta, and St. Louis, none of them historically African American museums. For the second go-round, Monticello wanted to target Black museums. It became my job to find which ones. The task was more difficult than it sounded because while 150 Black history museums populated the country (some days it felt like I called all of them), many operated on the fiscal margins. Exhibitions were expensive, costing tens of thousands of dollars to lease, curate, and promote. Many Black museums didn't have the resources or the space for a show that included three hundred artifacts crafted or owned by the enslaved, from china fragments found along Mulberry Row, to furniture made by Monticello joiner John Hemmings, to a French pharmaceutical jar that belonged to Sally Hemings. My favorite items were two toothbrushes. Nothing was more humanizing, I thought, than an everyday tool that looked like an item found in our own bathrooms.

I was lucky to find our first venue as a result of a relationship I had been cultivating for almost two years with the founding director and CEO of the African American Museum of Dallas. Dr. Harry Robinson Jr. was a trailblazer. In the 1970s, not only had he developed a career in the then-fledgling field of African American museums, he also was a founding member and past president of the Association of African American Museums. My June visit would be one of many to Texas as we prepared to make the African American Museum of Dallas the first historically Black institution to host "Paradox," a milestone for both of our organizations.

Opening night in September 2018 was a gala event attended by the city's crème de la crème. International evangelical preacher, author, and filmmaker T. D. Jakes was the honorary chair. Guests filled the museum's top two levels to hear welcoming remarks from Bishop Jakes, public officials, and a few of us from Monticello. "Paradox" was in Dallas through January 2019, and in spite of the heavy rains in the city that fall, it brought in more visitors than any exhibition in the museum's history.

Much of the exhibition's success was attributed to saturating the media with stories, with me as a central figure. I was given the star treatment, traveling by limousine to radio and TV stations for interviews. Newspaper and magazine reporters treated me like a celebrity. People recognized and pointed at me as I walked through my hotel lobby. I was invited to T. D. Jakes's mega-church, seated in a front pew, and introduced to his congregation. It was a heady experience that I hoped to duplicate at our next stop, the Charles H. Wright Museum in Detroit.

Monticello's team pulled into the Motor City in the winter of 2019. As had been the case in Dallas, we were invited to Detroit as a result of a relationship that I had cultivated, this one with a Wright Museum board member who happened to be white. The friendship became a contributing factor to a tense situation that unfolded while we were in Detroit.

"Paradox" was set to break records at the highly respected Wright Museum, just as it had in Dallas. However, a group of protesters, frustrated by the gentrification of their city, used the exhibition as a proxy in their fight to hold on to their city. I understood their grievances, as I shared the same sentiment about what was happening in my own hometown. In 2011 I had bitterly witnessed historically Black DC communities losing their identity. Even a Black-owned funeral home was sold and turned into condos. What the folks in Detroit missed was an opportunity to use a show about white exploitation of enslaved families to illustrate threats to their own Black community. Instead, they used a public forum to attack the exhibition and to confront me.

The Wright's team thought the protesters would be convinced of the exhibition's Black "authenticity" if they heard my story. "Who could object to hearing from a real descendant?" a staffer asked. It made sense to me, so I agreed to do a presentation at the museum's auditorium, to be followed by questions.

If we had just stuck with the presentation, it would have been fine. It was the questions that left me feeling pummeled. Why don't you talk about slavery, someone asked, after lecturing me about Monticello's failures to present the history of Monticello's enslaved people.

"We do," I explained, "in fact that's what this exhibit is about."

What about Sally Hemings? Why don't you talk about her, came another hostile accusation posed as a question.

"We have an entire exhibition about Sally Hemings," I said, struggling to remain poised. But it was no use; the crowd continued to heat up. Unaccompanied onstage, I felt under assault, as if I were fencing with five people at once. I didn't want to turn on my heels and walk away, but I didn't want to fight either. Finally, someone from the Wright ended the exchange. Some in the crowd were so visibly angry that at least one person thought I needed protection. A woman, touching her waistband as if she had a gun, offered to escort me to my car. I turned her down, but I was shaken and used the backdoor to slip away.

I refused to let one disagreeable experience taint how I felt about Detroit, a great city with a proud history. I returned many times after that night, including for the opening reception and for private gatherings. But in order to avoid the potential for negative publicity, I did less than a handful of interviews, as opposed to the scores I had done in Dallas. There were no live TV appearances, no gushing reporters, no limo rides. It was back to being mortal. In spite of the lack of publicity, thousands of people saw the exhibition. It was a success.

From June 2018 through 2019, I covered some forty-eight thousand miles—crisscrossing the country for conferences, speaking engagements, and promoting Monticello and "Paradox." And when I was in Virginia, I was still making the 140-mile daily commute from Richmond to Charlottesville and back.

A heart-wrenching trip during that period was a civil rights pilgrimage that took us to landmarks of the movement. I walked across the Edmund Pettus Bridge in Selma Alabama, visited the Sixteenth Street Baptist Church in Birmingham, and saw the National Memorial for Peace and Justice, also known as the Lynching Memorial, in Montgomery. Attacks on peaceful protesters, the murders of innocent young girls, and the massacres of Black families were the kinds of horrors my parents had hid from me when I was a child.

I stared unblinkingly at the atrocities inflicted upon Black Americans, grateful that my parents had spared me, thankful that as an adult, I had a platform to speak the truth.

In June 2019, Leslie invited me to attend the Aspen Ideas Festival with her. The annual event in Colorado invites just about everyone who is anyone—too many politicians, journalists, writers, civil leaders, thought leaders, dignitaries, celebrities, and billionaires to name. Among the headliners that year were rapper/actor/activist Lonnie Corant Jaman Shuka Rashid Lynn, better known as Common, and Facebook founder Mark Zuckerberg. I didn't meet them, but it was fun breathing Aspen's rarefied air.

However, the best part of the trip was getting to know Leslie.

Not only did she pick me up at Aspen's boutique airport—"Everyone wants to be met at the airport," she said—we shared accommodations at the resort home of one of her friends. We stayed up late some nights drinking wine, laughing, and exchanging stories. Ah, the distance we had traveled in three years! I had grown to admire her efforts to present an honest history of Monticello and the enslaved community. Her campaign giving Black families parity with Jefferson and his white family was not easy, as there was always the threat of pushback from Jefferson stalwarts. But to her credit, she prevailed. Rarely did I hear her give a speech without addressing the paradox of the author of the Declaration of Independence owning human beings.

October 2019 was the last big trip I would make for Monticello that year and throughout 2020. I was a panelist at a conference on the international slave trade at the University of Liverpool. I traveled with colleagues and family, including Leslie, Jack, Niya, and Cousin Andrew, who was also a panelist.

Reminiscent of what had happened in Detroit, an audience member challenged what she apparently interpreted as my pride in being a Jefferson descendant. Her tone was accusatory, as if I had somehow offended her personally. I took just a few beats to consider how to respond. After all, I had been to this show before. Then I answered with the kind of composure that only comes with experience. I was not proud or ashamed of my ancestry, I told a room of international scholars. That I was related to Thomas Jefferson was simply a fact.

Just as Aunt Peachie had said.

EPILOGUE

I was busy when the hospital called. It was March 30, 2020, almost three weeks into a shutdown caused by the COVID-19 pandemic. Like millions of Americans, I was working from home. When the cell phone rang, Monticello's tech team and I were moments away from the foundation's first Zoom event, an interview with artist Robert Shetterly. I would be interviewing him about his collection "Americans Who Tell the Truth," portraits of social and civil rights activists. Several of his paintings were on display at Monticello and at other venues in Charlottesville.

Using unfamiliar technology and my laptop as a TV studio was enough to make me nervous. Sitting at the dining room table and staring into the screen perched on a stack of books, I was also scared. My brother Dickie had been hospitalized for several days with flulike symptoms. The call confirmed that he had the virus. By then, thousands of Americans had already died from COVID-19. No one could have imagined that one year later, the number of deaths would exceed half a million.

My brother had survived MRSA, a deadly bacterial infection, a few years earlier. "He's strong," his caregiver assured us. "He can beat this." But I wasn't confident. Dickie was eighty years old and in declining health, with diabetes and high blood pressure. I tried to push aside my worry as we prepared to begin the program. No one watching had a clue of what I was going through, or what we would all be going through in the months ahead.

My brother died on April 11, 2020. I had his body cremated and his remains delivered to my home to rest on the fireplace mantel with Mom and Dad's. I wept when he died, as much for the pain my parents had felt when they sent him away as for him. His death was sad, but it was his unrealized life that had been a tragedy.

My siblings and I, separated by thousands of miles, mourned our brother together. Pat consoled herself by creating art and by being the matriarch of her growing family. Just before the lockdown, she had become a great-grandmother. The family's youngest member, Mirah Jade, is an American bouquet—Black, white, and Latina. Bruce, the only one of us who followed Dad's advice and took a "good government job," continued spending his days much as Daddy had in retirement—reading the paper, watching television, and tending his garden. And Janice was living in Berlin with her son and daughter-in-law, her health failing.

We soldiered on, all of us, through a global pandemic, social and political upheaval, and personal loss. During protests that followed the murder of George Floyd by Minneapolis policemen, demonstrators tore down or mutilated Monument Avenue's monstrous statues. Only Robert E. Lee's remains, temporarily protected by a state statute. However, the monument is covered with bright paint and messages commemorating Black lives and losses. Similar protests, most of them non-violent, brought down statues across the country and around the world. In Charlottesville, the Lee and Jackson statues that ignited that city's 2017 "Summer of Hate" remained in place another year. But finally, they too came tumbling down, removed by the city after years of legal wrangling.

During 2020 I continued working, mostly remotely but on site when necessary. Such was the case as July Fourth approached and

Harry Smith was back for another feature. This time my interview with him, aside from the masks we both wore, was unfiltered.

It was a tough year, but by the beginning of 2021 I felt there were reasons to feel hopeful. On January 20, a Howard University graduate was sworn in as the country's first Black, Asian, and female vice president. Dad would have been overjoyed and so would have Mom. I had never met Vice President Kamala Harris but had followed her career for years. She was HU through and through, a true sister.

Janice and I talked for hours the Sunday after the inauguration, as we have every Sunday since she gave me her bad news. It had been one year since she had been diagnosed with untreatable bone cancer. My eighty-two-year-old sister approached what lay ahead with grace and good humor. "I've had a life full of adventure," she said. "Who could ask for more than that?"

Inevitably during our three-hour-long Sunday conversations, we drift back to old times, the Sundays at Mom and Dad's, the old neighborhood, and growing up in DC. There's a generation between us, so Jan had twenty more years with the family than I. She knew them all—Grandma, Papa, Aunt Peachie, the aunts, the uncles, even the great-grandmother Mom said had been a "child slave" in Upper Marlborough.

We also discuss the family legacy and what it has meant to finally know our heritage. It was always my goal to uncover my roots, to understand my family's place in American history, and to restore them to the nation's narrative. It is my right and the right of every descendant of enslaved people to claim their stake in America.

The family tree is firmly planted at Monticello and continues to grow. My son, Charles, is a member of the Thomas Jefferson Foundation's Young Advisors, and my cousin Andrew, who with my encouragement had been an ICJS fellow, has joined the staff full time. He replaced Niya, who is pursuing her doctorate at Princeton University, as Public Historian and Manager of the Getting Word Oral History

Project. I have visions of a descendant becoming Monticello's president some day. In 2021, a Black woman, Melody Barnes, became the chair of the foundation's Board of Trustees.

Several miles from Monticello at the former home of Jefferson's friend, President James Madison, descendants of the people owned by the fourth president and the father of the US Constitution were making history. After years of collaboration, the Montpelier Board of Trustees granted descendants "equal co-stewardship," which means that descendants will have considerable influence over the narrative of their enslaved ancestors.

The Monticello Association, the organization that for so long resisted accepting the descendants of Sally Hemings and Thomas Jefferson, is going through its own reckoning. Whether that means Jefferson's Black descendants will one day be buried on the mountain is for other descendants to decide. My ambition was never to be buried there, but to gain recognition for the contributions of my family and those of the millions of people whom the United States enslaved.

The gravesite where some of my ancestors are possibly buried is also undergoing a transformation. The foundation has approved a renovation at the cost of hundreds of thousands on the site that will include a buffer of trees, flowering vegetation, copper fencing, new signage, and benches reserved for descendants, who will also have a separate entrance and reserved parking. I was on the committee of staff members that helped plan the renovation and on the committee of descendants that renamed the cemetery. It will be called "Burial Ground for Enslaved People."

After fifty years of searching and an abundance of evidence, I feel gratified that I have found my father's lost family, identified in our lineage at least two of the families that Jefferson enslaved, and confirmed our relationship to him and to America's founding. Every time I step onto the site that is now my place of employment, I am reminded that it was once my ancestors' home—my home—Monticello.

ACKNOWLEDGMENTS

This story would not exist were it not for the inspiration of my ancestors, so I first thank them: the Jessups, the Greens, the Hunts, the Diggses, the Howards, the Robinsons, the Hemingses, and the Hubbards. Nor would it have life were it not for Virginia Robinson, "Aunt Peachie," as our family called her, the only member of her generation left to pass down the Jefferson family legacy. And then there is my sister Janice, who absorbed everything she heard, including Aunt Peachie's many ruminations. For fifty years, Janice has shared this adventure with me, for which I am grateful beyond words. I thank my parents, Cedric and Theresa Jessup. Like all humans, they were flawed, but their love for me was not. In spite of the tension that sometimes gripped our home, I always felt their love and support, which sustains me to this day.

My husband Jack and my son, Charles, have spent incalculable hours with me, listening, reading, suggesting, and encouraging. Jack, a retired *TIME* magazine correspondent and columnist, has been a partner, a cheerleader, and a critic. I am a better writer because of him. Charles is a mother's gift—smart, sensitive, and thoughtful. His insights helped me navigate through difficult memories, some involving him.

I am so thankful to my sister Patricia for her boundless energy, creativity, and joy. Her art, inspired by our family history, fills my home. And I am grateful to my brother Bruce, who always makes me laugh and reminds me not to take myself too seriously. I am in awe of Mary Lewis, who cared for my brother Dickie with love and kindness. I will always be grateful for the lessons learned from my late brother-in-law Wallace Terry.

My gratitude extends to the extraordinary people who helped shape this story, including my friend, mentor, and Monticello Descendant Community patron saint, Lucia "Cinder" Stanton; my agent, the indomitable Jennifer Herrera; and my editor, the Amistad editor, the visionary Patrik Bass. Much appreciation to HarperOne Group president Judith Curr and Amistad vice president Tracy Sherrod, all of whom believed this was a story that needed telling. Endless appreciation belongs to photographer Ryan Kelly and HarperCollins art director Stephen Brayda for their stunning cover art. Among the many from HarperCollins I would also like to thank are Brieana Garcia, Maya Lewis, Courtney Nobile, Tara Parsons, and Francesca Walker. The team's copy editors were extraordinary.

I am grateful to my cousins Carol Restifo and Terry Plater, for preserving the Green family legacy, including official White House artifacts, and to Eugenia Carter and Neil Jessup, for sharing their childhood memories. Affection and appreciation go to my nieces and nephews Lisa and Tai Terry, Noah and Sophia Marcus, and Peter Jolley for listening to endless history lessons on Thanksgiving and Christmas. Thanks also to David and Serda Terry, Dante Woodlin, Renior Woodlin, Dawn Jessup, and Saundria Jessup. Heartfelt appreciation goes to Robinson and Hemings cousins Maurice Brewington, Bill Collins, John Collins, Andrew Davenport, Pamela Duffy, Richard Hackett, Calvin Jefferson, Julius Jefferson, Ruth Johnson, Alice Mitchell, Amy Mitchell, Kevin Nelson, Louise Nelson, Bill Webb, Carol Williams, and Velma Williams, and to Jefferson cousins Prinny Anderson, Linda Carr-Kraft, Rob Eppes, Charles Taylor, Jack Taylor, Tess Taylor, Debbie Truscott, Lucian Truscott IV, David Works, and the dozens of family members I have met over the past five years.

Thank you to my mother-in-law, Sara White, for sharing her home with me, and to her children, Diane, Loraine, and Marilyn, for sharing their mother, and to my stepchildren, Kyle, George, James, and Kristen, for sharing their grandmother.

There are so many friends and colleagues who have supported me through the years to whom I am indebted. Many thanks to my dearest and oldest friends Lisa Bass Cooper and Miriam Rudder for their long memories and hours of conversation. They are my sisters. Thanks to Jason Wood and his mother Arminta, Anna Anderson, Richard Block, Anita and Paul Delaney, Kwame Holman, and Clarence and Lisa Page for remembering the old days. Thank you to my St. Francis de Sales classmates who visited Monticello and to my Notre Dame alum sisters for the monthly Zoom calls.

Much love and appreciation to Ralph and Judy Anderson, Sherman and Jacqueline Curl, Janet Daniels, John and Karen Franklin, Richard and Eucharia Jackson, and Tred and Janine Collins Spratley for creating new memories. Gratitude and affection also belong to Diane Bechamps, Rita McClenney, James and Eva Cunningham, Melani Douglass, Ron and Betty Crutcher, Lauranett Lee, First Lady Pamela Northam, Justin Reid, and Tim and Daphne Maxwell Reid.

Many thanks and affection to my Kenwood "family" for long lunch conversations and Zoom gatherings, especially Niya Bates, Aurelia Crawford, Andrew O'Shaughnessy, Whitney Pippin, Laura Sandy, Mary Scott Flemming, and Gaye Wilson. Much appreciation to Gaye and Whitney for reasons they know.

I am deeply grateful to the Reverend Lehman Bates for his friendship and spiritual uplift, to the Reverend Alvin Edwards for his support, Henry Louis Gates Jr. for his friendship, to Annette Gordon-Reed for her research about the Hemings family, to Michael Cottman and Michael Paul Williams for their journalism, to Rita

Dove for her inspirational poetry, and to CeCe Moore and Shannon Christmas for their genealogical expertise. Special thanks to the Honorable John Charles Thomas.

Among the many colleagues and community members I wish to thank are first and foremost Thomas Jefferson Foundation President Leslie Greene Bowman and Vice President of Strategy & Chief Content Officer Gary Sandling. Thank you to Valentine Museum Executive Director William Martin who gave me my first museum job. Monticello's Board of Trustees, including former chairs Don King and Jon Meacham and chair Melody Barnes, deserve recognition for their support of Monticello's shift toward diversity and inclusion.

I also appreciate the support of Neil Barclay, Charise Beckett, Anna Berkes, Michael Cheuk, Frank Cogliano, Christa Dierksheide, Carolyn Dillard, Brandon Dillard, Will Dillon, Andrea Douglas, Michelle and Joshua DuBois, Robin Farmer, Nicholas Fitzgerald, Wayne Gannaway, Don Gathers, Emily Greenfield, Beverly Grey, Linnea Grim, Gardiner Hallock, Jobie Hill, Iris Holliday, Megan Howerton, Petrina Jackson, Adele Johnson, Emilie Johnson, Stephen Light, Ann Lucas, Jenn Lyon, Lucy Macon, Mia Magruder, Mary Massie, Sharon McElroy, John McKee, Shelly Murphy, Stephen Ninneman, Margaret Martin O'Bryant, Eric Proebsting, Crystal Ptacek, Harry Robinson Jr., John Ragosta, Regina Rush, Leni Sorensen, Maya Smart, Susan Stein, Ann Taylor, Emily Tenhundfeld, Melissa Thompson, Sam Towler, Chad Wollerton, Monique Woodson, Dianne Swann-Wright and Mary Blair Zakaib. I have been buoyed by the many friends and family members who have visited Monticello since my tenure there began. Thank you.

I appreciate the research and institutional support of the Albemarle Charlottesville Historical Society, Central Virginia History Researchers, the Commonwealth of Virginia Chapter of the Links,

Incorporated, the Jefferson Library at the Robert H. Smith International Center for Jefferson Studies, the Mooreland-Spingarn Research Center at Howard University, the Albert & Shirley Small Special Collections Library at the University of Virginia, Thomas Jefferson's Poplar Forest, and the Virginia Museum of History & Culture. I also appreciate the assistance of St. Francis de Sales Catholic Church, Church of the Incarnation, and St. Margaret of Scotland Catholic Church. Thank you, All.

ABOUT THE AUTHOR

Gayle Jessup White is a third generation Washingtonian whose lineage extends as far back as the indigenous people who inhabited the Chesapeake area before the arrival of Europeans. Her American roots are in Virginia going back to the Jamestown settlement, and also in Maryland. Her international lineage is principally Nigerian and British. She attended the city's private and public schools and graduated from Howard University, where she earned a bachelor of arts in communications. Although she lives in Richmond, Virginia, she still considers herself a "DC girl."

A former award-winning TV reporter and anchor, Gayle began her career in journalism at the *New York Times*, where she interned in the Washington Bureau. She left the *Times* for Northwestern University's Medill School of Journalism, earning a master of science in journalism. Gayle spent several years as a TV news reporter and anchor before becoming a public television producer and on-air host at Howard University.

After a twenty-five-year career in communications, Gayle seized the opportunity to pursue her passion for history, beginning as an educator at Richmond's Valentine Museum, and ultimately with her landing a position at the Thomas Jefferson Foundation, the nonprofit organization that owns and operates Monticello, her ancestral home.

In 2014 she first joined the foundation as a Robert H. Smith International Center for Jefferson Studies fellow, combing through old letters, documents, and records for clues to her family's past. Two years later, she joined the staff as community engagement officer, becoming a principal spokesperson and making history as the first descendant of Jefferson and the families he enslaved to work for the foundation. She is currently the foundation's public relations and community engagement officer.

Gayle serves on Virginia's Citizens Advisory Council on Furnishing and Interpreting the Executive Mansion, where she is founding chair of the Descendant Committee. She is also a member of the Council of Historic Richmond, and the Albemarle Charlottesville Historical Society. She is on the board of the Poplar Forest African American Advisory Group, and a member of the Commonwealth Chapter of the Links, Incorporated.

She and her husband, retired *TIME* columnist Jack White Jr., have a blended family of four sons, one daughter, and seven grand-daughters. Gayle's son, Charles, lives in Cambridge, Massachusetts, where he attended college.